WITHDRAWN

Regis College Library
100 Wellesley Street West
Toronto, Ontario
Canada
M5S 2Z5

PRAISE FOR *O LORD, I SEEK YOUR COUNTENANCE*

"Cardinal Joachim Meisner famously described Joseph Ratzinger as the Mozart of theology. This book is likely to establish Fr. de Gaál as the Liszt of Ratzinger interpreters. This presentation of Ratzinger/Benedict's many insights into the theological crises of our times is a virtuoso performance. It includes reference to some of the lesser known of Ratzinger's interventions at the time of the Second Vatican Council, hitherto unpublished lectures from his period as a university professor, and highly penetrating expositions of Ratzinger's better known 'high points of European Intellectuality.' One can read this collection of essays and feel proud to be a Catholic. Intellectual rigor is matched with love for the subject and with an elegance in expression which can only be the fruit of the high culture of the Incarnation in its middle-European embodiment."

Tracey Rowland
University of Notre Dame (Australia)

"Fr. Emery de Gaál's *O Lord, I Seek Your Countenance* will surely be indispensable reading for those wishing to understand both the shape and impact of Joseph Ratzinger's thought. Not only does it survey an impressive range of Ratzinger's published writings, both before and after his election as Benedict XVI, but it supplements these with heretofore unseen archival materials and the recollections of close collaborators. The author argues convincingly that Ratzinger's theology centers on the concrete person of Christ, whose 'face' the theologian must seek. I learned much in reading it!"

Aaron Pidel, SJ
Marquette University

"This is an impressive work. It blends compelling biographical detail with sustained theological insight and displays meticulous and exacting scholarship. Reading *O Lord, I Seek Your Countenance* will enable those with little knowledge of Benedict XVI to appreciate the big-picture significance of his work, but will also enlighten enthusiasts with a sophisticated interpretation of the Pope Emeritus's contributions to fundamental theology. De Gaál draws lavishly on a remarkable number of hitherto neglected or underappreciated texts and discloses startlingly new aspects by entering into the depth of Benedict XVI's engagement with perennial questions in theological epistemology."

Jacob Phillips
St. Mary's University (UK)

RENEWAL WITHIN TRADITION

Series editor: Matthew Levering

Matthew Levering is the James N. and Mary D. Perry Jr. Chair of Theology at Mundelein Seminary. Levering is the author or editor of over thirty books. He serves as coeditor of the journals *Nova et Vetera* and the *International Journal of Systematic Theology.*

About the series

Catholic theology reflects upon the content of divine revelation as interpreted and handed down in the Church, but today Catholic theologians often find the scriptural and dogmatic past to be alien territory. The Renewal within Tradition Series undertakes to reform and reinvigorate contemporary theology from within the tradition, with St. Thomas Aquinas as a central exemplar. As part of its purpose, the Series reunites the streams of Catholic theology that, prior to the Council, separated into neo-scholastic and *nouvelle theologie* modes. The biblical, historical-critical, patristic, liturgical, and ecumenical emphases of the Ressourcement movement need the dogmatic, philosophical, scientific, and traditioned enquiries of Thomism, and vice versa. Renewal within Tradition challenges the regnant forms of theological liberalism that, by dissolving the cognitive content of the gospel, impede believers from knowing the love of Christ.

Published or Forthcoming

Reading the Sermons of Thomas Aquinas: A Beginner's Guide
Randall B. Smith

Self Gift: Essays on Humanae Vitae *and the Thought of John Paul II*
Janet E. Smith

Aquinas on Beatific Charity and the Problem of Love
Christopher J. Malloy

Christ the Logos of Creation: Essays in Analogical Metaphysics
John R. Betz

On Love and Virtue: Theological Essays
Michael Sherwin, O.P.

The Culture of the Incarnation: Essays in Catholic Theology
Tracey Rowland

The Church of Christ: According to Vatican II
Stephen A. Hipp

The Trinitarian Wisdom of God:
Louis Bouyer on the God-world Relationship
Keith Lemna

The Love of God Poured Out:
Grace and the Gifts of the Holy Spirit in St. Thomas Aquinas
John M. Meinert

Newman & Us: A Guide for Our Time
Reinhard Hütter

One of the Trinity Has Suffered
Joshua R. Brotherton

O Lord, I Seek Your Countenance

O Lord, I Seek Your Countenance

Explorations and Discoveries in Pope Benedict XVI's Theology

EMERY DE GAÁL

Steubenville, Ohio
www.emmausacademic.com

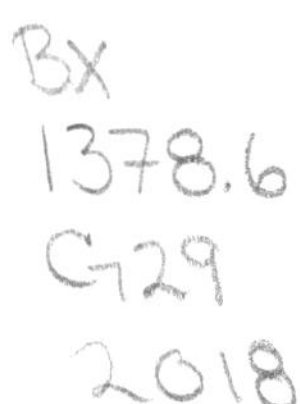

EMMAUS
ACADEMIC

Steubenville, Ohio
www.emmausacademic.com
A Division of The St. Paul Center for Biblical Theology
Editor-in-Chief: Scott Hahn
1468 Parkview Circle
Steubenville, Ohio 43952

© 2018 Emery de Gaál
All rights reserved. Published 2018
Printed in the United States of America

Library of Congress Cataloging-in-Publication Data
Names: Gaál Gyulai, Emery de, author.
Title: O Lord, I seek your countenance : explorations and discoveries in Pope Benedict XVI's theology / Emery de Gaál.
Description: Steubenville : Emmaus Academic, 2018. | Series: Renewal within tradition
Identifiers: LCCN 2018017243 (print) | LCCN 2018023313 (ebook) | ISBN 9781947792852 (ebook) | ISBN 9781947792838 (hardcover) | ISBN 9781947792845 (pbk.)
Subjects: LCSH: Benedict XVI, Pope, 1927-
Classification: LCC BX1378.6 (ebook) | LCC BX1378.6 .G29 2018 (print) | DDC 230/.2092--dc23
LC record available at https://lccn.loc.gov/2018017243

Unless otherwise noted, Scripture quotations are taken from the New Revised Standard Version Second Catholic Edition, copyright © 1989, 1993 National Council of the Churches of Christ in the United States of America. Used by permission. All rights reserved worldwide.

Excerpts from the Catechism of the Catholic Church, second edition, copyright © 2000, Libreria Editrice Vaticana—United States Conference of Catholic Bishops, Washington, D.C. Noted as "CCC" in the text.

Cover image: *Christ Blessing* (1512–15) by Andrea Previtali, The National Gallery, London, UK

Cover design and layout by Margaret Ryland

To Pope Benedict XVI
in gratitude for his erudite and lasting faith witness

TABLE OF CONTENTS

CHAPTER 1

The Christocentric Shift

An Appreciation of the Theological Achievements of Pope Benedict XVI's Pontificate[1]

However the winds blow
You should stand against them
When the world falls apart
Your brave heart may not despair.
Without the heart's bravery which
Has the courage to withstand unshakably
The spirits of the time and the masses,
We cannot find the way to God.
And the true way of Our Lord.[2]

THE YOUNG PRIEST Joseph Ratzinger wrote these lines on May 24, 1952, in the poetry album (*Poesiealbum*) of a pupil of his during his time as parochial vicar at Precious Blood Parish in Munich-Bogenhausen. He did not seek nonconformity as an end in itself in the sense of the American philosopher Ralph Waldo Emerson's (1803–1882) *dictum* that "to be a

[1] This essay was originally published in *Chrystus Paschy*, edited by Bogdan Ferdek and Wojciech Szukalski, *Colloquia Disputationes* 28 (Adam Mickiewicz University: Poznań, 2014), 57–78. Used by permission.

[2] "Wie auch die Winde wehen:/ sollt ihnen zum Trotze stehen;/ Wenn auch die Welt zerbricht—Dein tapferes Herz verzage(t) nicht. Ohne die Tapferkeit des Herzens, die den Mut / hat, unerschütterlich den Geistern der Zeit und / der Masse zu trotzen, können wir den Weg zu Gott und den wahren Weg unseres Herrn nicht finden" (Joseph Ratzinger, as cited in Emery de Gaál, *The Theology of Pope Benedict XVI: The Christocentric Shift* [New York: Palgrave Macmillan, 2010], 306).

non-conformist means to be great." The triune God is the only source of true life. It is the dogma of a triune God that grants humankind dignity and is the ultimate standard of a meaningful and fulfilled life. Such a discernment of spirit is based on the figure of Our Savior. Ratzinger inherited such a disposition from the ambience of his family. Ultimately it is in this mindset that one must localize the lasting contributions of this great theologian-pope, Benedict XVI (r. 2005–2013). As the current Russian patriarch, Kirill I, underlines: "With great sense of responsibility he bears witness to Jesus Christ in the modern world."[3] The words of the founder of the Benedictine Order, St. Benedict, were programmatic for Pope Benedict XVI: "Nihil amori Christi praeponere"—"Prefer nothing to the love of Christ" (*Regula Benedicti* 4.2).

In retrospect, Pope Benedict's theological legacy comes vividly and vitally into focus. Under the heading "une œuvre immense," *La Documentation Catholique* lists the accomplishments of Benedict XVI's papacy.[4] In fact, it is hard to imagine that a *Summus Pontifex* will again author such a great number of philosophical, spiritual, and theological texts that are so essential and profound for the future course of theology. This is all the more remarkable because his pontificate was relatively brief but, during this time, he convened four consistories and five synods and wrote three encyclicals and four apostolic exhortations. In addition, he published an apostolic constitution and eleven *motu proprios* and delivered seventy-four major speeches and lectures, all of which probably came from his own pen. To these one must add the Wednesday audiences and countless sermons given either in the eternal city, during thirty pastoral visits in Italy and three World Youth Days, or in the course of his no less than twenty-three apostolic visits that brought him to almost every continent. He beatified three persons and canonized forty. Worth highlighting are the theologian Blessed John Henry Newman (1801–1890; beatified 2010) and the philosopher-pope St. John Paul II (1920–2005; beatified 2011), as he feels intellectually and spiritually close to both thinkers. Certainly, the pontificate of Benedict XVI will be recorded by historians as the theologically deepest and most productive since Leo the Great (440–461) and Gregory the Great (590–604). This is shown especially in his homilies, which set a standard for many a century to come. As well as could a saint or Church Father, he could present even the most complex of issues eloquently and succinctly yet simply and, at times, even in hauntingly beautiful language.

---

[3] *The Tablet*, March 9, 2013, 32.

[4] *La Documentation Catholique*, February 28, 2013 (no. 2507), 225–46.

The breadth and quality of his thought is truly astonishing. Under the burden of the Petrine office, he continued to write learnedly and copiously. The long-term legacy of the papacy of Benedict XVI can be summed up by noting that it leads to a Christocentric shift (or turn) within the Church. This has several elements:

1. Benedict teaches one to see and to interpret one's entire existence from the salvific mysteries of Christ.
2. The ongoing reception of the Second Vatican Council has been greatly deepened and rendered easier through his speeches and catechesis by reminding everyone of Jesus Christ being *the* self-revelation of God (see *Dei Verbum* 2). A seeming contradiction between "the spirit of the Council" and the Council's actual texts is thereby denied.
3. Due to the constant emphasis on the Church Fathers, the liturgy, the martyrs, the mystics, and the saints during his Wednesday catecheses, Christian faith becomes visible afresh as something organically growing in time and space in concrete human beings under the sure guidance of the Holy Spirit.
4. The emphasis on Christ as *the Logos* confirms human reason and philosophy as essential components of faith and roots the latter also in the integrity of the human nature of the person in Jesus Christ. Thus, fundamentalism as a possibly viable option is rejected.
5. The liturgy is perceived as an organically grown whole in legitimate diversity (see his letter *Summorum Pontificum* [2007] and his apostolic constitution *Anglicanorum Coetibus* [2009] for his solemn manner of celebrating liturgies).
6. "Canonical exegesis" leads to a rehabilitation both of John's Gospel and of the elements of Church and Tradition as sources for understanding the Gospel message.
7. The importance of historical-critical exegesis is confirmed and incorporated into the faith of the Church.
8. Henceforth, any effort for reform within the Church must be one of yet greater loyalty to the figure of Jesus Christ.
9. The combination of all the preceding points creates a still broader and deeper basis for ecumenical dialogue and for a future union of Christendom.

It would be a bold undertaking if one wanted to attempt to pay proper tribute within the context of only one essay to a pontificate so rich and blessed with different theological accents. Here, only a few outlines will be shown in broad strokes. For this purpose, Ratzinger's position in the intellectual history of theology and his accomplishments prior to ascending the Chair of Peter will be briefly summarized (1951–2005). Upon this canvas the theological outlines of his pontificate (2005–2013) will be sketched on the basis of his encyclicals, some selected speeches, and the *Jesus of Nazareth* trilogy.

The Achievements of the Scholar Joseph Ratzinger and Their Historical *Locus*

To his mind, a personal relationship with the Holy Trinity and the realization of the centrality of the Incarnation are the critical axes of Christian existence and of any kind of theological knowledge. Ever since his seminary days (1945–1951), he has opted against an up until that time prevalent intellectualistic and propositional presentation of faith as practiced by baroque manualists and nineteenth-century teachers of neo-Scholasticism. Contrary to the Koran—where little historical data is processed—the Christian Holy Scripture is intentionally rich in historical contexts. Resulting from the concrete events of revelation, Christians celebrate consistently a historization of faith as the constant Incarnation of the divine Word, Jesus Christ. This epochal shift to a personal attestation to faith misled not a few Christian thinkers, particularly in the second half of the twentieth century, to surrender the content of Christian faith altogether in favor of subjectivism—but not the priest and theologian Ratzinger. He has dared to undertake the balancing act between (1.) the theology of Christianity's complete intellectual heritage, bypassing manualists such as Suárez, Molina, Cajetan and neo-Scholasticism. (2.) current theological scholarship, which decidedly approaches issues only historically and contextually, and to a certain extent in a personalist manner. Trusting in the continued presence of the Holy Spirit *in* history, the consonance of a Christian's personal faith with the whole of the Church's faith becomes apparent: the unity of Scripture, the testimony of the martyrs, the Fathers, mystics, and saints, as well as of liturgy and the life and the teachings of the Church, steps into the foreground. In keeping with the Second Vatican Council (1962–1965), Ratzinger argues that the self-communication of the absolute and sovereign God cannot be reduced or shackled to the immanent categories of the German Idealist philosopher Immanuel Kant (1724–1804). While he affirms ever anew the intelligibility of the *fides quae*—the Catholic beliefs—he enriches these with the subjective dimension of the *fides qua*, the necessarily personal acts of faith. By ignoring this almost unique achievement of balancing and integrating the subjective dimensions of faith with its objective components, some parties refer to his theology as supposedly "progressive" before and "conservative" after the Second Vatican Council. Borrowing terms from an alien arena—namely, that of politics—they ignore not only the very essence of theology and the Christian faith in general; they in fact do grave injustice to the greatness of the theologian Ratzinger. In the same breath, his critics imply that faith is merely a subjective product of the here and now, lacking any binding orientation to God's definitive self-revelation in Jesus Christ. In fact, Ratzinger's outlook from his early seminary days until now has remained remarkably consistent and free of contradictions.

As a young seminarian, he was the first ever to translate Thomas Aquinas's *De caritate* into German. This notwithstanding, he soon turned away from Thomas's more abstract, propositional thinking as expressed in the *Summa theologiae*. In the writings of St. Augustine (354–430), he discovered a theologian who thinks all of life and being as grounded in God's initiative. In unexpected ways, God enlightens the human spirit. From that point onward, Ratzinger belongs to an *illuminatory mindset*: an arch spanning from Plato and Paul's Damascus experience, via Augustine (*tolle et lege*), Anselm of Canterbury, Bonaventure, and John Henry Newman (*cor ad cor loquitur*), to Romano Guardini.[5]

One of Ratzinger's lasting achievements is his use of the Church Fathers and Scripture as the indispensable common bases for all Christians. It proves fruitful now in ecumenical dialogue. The successes in the Catholic–Orthodox or Catholic–Oriental dialogue would have been unthinkable without the insistence of Ratzinger on the crucial nexus between Scripture and Tradition—or at least less easily obtainable. As a *peritus (advisor)* to the influential archbishop of Cologne, Cardinal Josef Frings (1887–1978), Ratzinger contributed significantly to the course and final documents of the Second Vatican Council. In *Dei Verbum*, he is in a decisive way responsible for Christian revelation being perceived as a lively, dynamic process.[6] Revelation is not a condescending sharing of information on the part of God with humankind, but the personal self-communication of God in and through His only-begotten Son, Jesus Christ. Jesus

5 De Gaál, *Theology of Benedict XVI*, 33–36.

6 See Emery de Gaál, "The Theologian Joseph Ratzinger at Vatican II: His Theological Vision and Role," *Lateranum* 78, no. 3 (2012): 515–48, at 524–30.

Christ is the definitive revelation of God. As Henri de Lubac (1896–1991) had done previously, so Ratzinger likewise insists during the Council that, together, Scripture and Tradition attest to revelation, yet without being identical to it.[7] Unlike Hermes and Mercury, only transmitters of a divine message in ancient pagan religions, Jesus is himself the divine message. This deepening of the understanding of revelation determines the Christocentric trajectory of the Second Vatican Council. Such insight is also the lasting legacy of the theologian, prefect, and pope. In addition, he collaborated in decisive ways in the final drafts of *Lumen gentium* and *Ad gentes*. Stimulated also by Benedict, many denominations issuing forth from the Reformation have discovered afresh or for the first time the Church Fathers and Tradition. In the process, many of their theologians have come to appreciate a much richer common ground with the Roman Catholic Church.

Along with the anthropocentric shift, Ratzinger rejects a one-sided emphasis on bloodless creedal statements and on an abstract summary ontology, as well as on an unreflective appeal to Church authority alone.[8] However, in pronounced opposition to the anthropocentric shift (oftentimes given to populist slogans), alongside the *ressourcement* movement, and with the whole Church, Ratzinger emphasizes the ever-greater continuity of the self-revelation of the triune God in Jesus Christ in the sacramental Church, existing now for two thousand years.[9] Precisely in agreement with Johann Adam Möhler (1796–1838) and de Lubac, he thinks the self-identity of the Church in time and space through to its ultimate consequence. This allows for—and in fact is the *conditio sine qua non* for—genuine development and reform, as was argued and presented

[7] See Second Vatican Council, Dogmatic Constitution on Divine Revelation *Dei Verbum* (November 18, 1965), 2, available from http://www.vatican.va (hereafter cited in text as DV). See also Kurt Koch, "Der Treue Sohn des Vaters," in *Das Geheimnis des Senfkorns: Grundzüge des theologischen Denkens von Papst Benedikt XVI* (Regensburg: Pustet, 2010), 146–58.

[8] Worth reading, as it was written under the immediate impression of this change in method, is Walter Kasper, *Die Methoden der Dogmatik: Einheit und Vielfalt* (Munich: Kösel, 1967).

[9] For a good portrayal of the *ressourcement* current, see Gabriel Flynn and Paul D. Murray, *Ressourcement: A Movement for Renewal in Twentieth-Century Catholic Theology* (Oxford: Oxford University Press, 2012). There one finds some discussion concerning the question of whether Ratzinger may be considered a member of this movement, particularly in Lewis Ayres, Patricia Kelly, and Thomas Humphries, "Benedict XVI: A *Ressourcement* Theologian?" (423–39).

by Newman in classical fashion.[10] Otherwise, one would have to deal with a random catenation of unrelated creeds.

With one of the founders of the seminal *Sources Chrétiennes* series,[11] the future Cardinal Jean Daniélou (1905–1974), Ratzinger locates Christian faith not in being (*ens*) and essences (*essentiae*), but in the concrete existence of persons. As personally called to freedom, man is invited, within the order of creation, to participation with the second Person of the triune God in inner-Trinitarian life by way of incorporation into the mind frame and earthly fate of Jesus Christ. As the then-rector of studies in the Freising seminary, Alfred Läpple (1915–2013), recalled the seminarian Ratzinger remarking to him: "A *Summum Bonum* (highest good) does not require a mother."[12] This foundational insight was decisive to leading Ratzinger to turn to Newman, Augustine, and the Jewish religious philosopher Martin Buber (1878–1965). Much influenced by Romano Guardini (1885–1968), he now accessed St. Bonaventure (c. 1217–1274) and Josef Pieper (1904–1997). Consonant with Augustine, Christianity is for Ratzinger essentially the unity of love and reason, which is lived ever anew in the Church's Eucharistic communion.

The anthropocentric shift includes a change in method from a classical, deductive approach to a historical, inductive one. This new method sometimes places beliefs at the discretion of the individual believer. Such a paradigm shift leads to a profound crisis both of Christian faith in general and of Catholic faith in particular, as it jeopardizes the definitive revelation of God in Jesus as formulated in Vatican II (*Dei Verbum*). At the same time, virulent since the Enlightenment, liberalism (which trusts the give and take of immanent entities to determine the content of truth) celebrates

---

10 See: Johann Adam Möhler, *Unity in the Church or the Principle of Catholicism* (Washington, DC: Catholic University of America, 1996); Henri de Lubac, *Corpus Mysticum: The Eucharist and the Church in the Middle Ages*, trans. Gemma Simmonds, C.J., with Richard Price and Christopher Stevens, ed. Laurence Paul Hemming and Susan Frank Parsons (Notre Dame, IN: Notre Dame University, 2006); John Henry Newman, *An Essay on the Development of Christian Doctrine* (New York: Longmans and Green, 1949).

11 *Sources Chrétiennes*, multiple vols., ed. Claude Mondésert, Jean Daniélou, and Henri de Lubac (Paris: Cerf, 1942–).

12 Alfred Läpple, "'That New Beginning That Bloomed among the Ruins': Interview with Prof. Dr. Alfred Läpple by Gianni Valente and Pierluca Azzaro," *30DAYS* 24, nos. 1–2 (2006): 54–66, at 60 (accessed October 12, 2017, http://www.30giorni.it/articoli_id_10125_l3.htm). See also: Joseph Ratzinger, *Milestones: Memoirs 1927–1977*, trans. Erasmo Leiva-Merikakis (San Francisco: Ignatius Press, 1998), 41–60; Koch, *Das Geheimnis des Senfkorns*; and *Christliche Antworten auf die Fragen der Gegenwart: Grundlinien der Theologie Papst Benedikts XVI*, ed. Josef Kreiml (Regensburg: Pustet, 2010).

its definitive entry into the consciousness of people from all walks of life from the 1960s onward. Subcutaneously, this epochal development seems to lead to a *de facto* abolition of the *homo religiosus* in general, as well as to the denial of man being created in the image and likeness of God (Gen 1: 26) and, within Christianity, to an outright negation of the *Chalcedonense* (Jesus Christ as true God and true man). This is the essence of Cardinal Frings's talk, which he delivered in Genoa, Italy, on the eve of the Council in 1961. The talk had been written by Ratzinger who, at that time, was professor of theology at the University of Bonn.[13] Increasingly, the Incarnation of God cannot be thought, let alone existentially lived. The redemptive nature of faith no longer is appropriated. Is not a historically unparalleled depersonalization of people the result, with the invariable attendant consequences of people becoming invariably incapable of both participating in liturgy and contributing to a vibrant democracy, thereby losing the ability to live in any kind of friendship and solidarity?

Ratzinger recognizes in the Church's conscious *Entweltlichung* ("detachment from the world"; see his Freiburg homily of 2011) and in a Christ-centered refocusing of human life the only ways to avert such a danger. His Christological *ceterum censeo* is an eloquently presented corrective that, in the long term, must prevail in all of Christendom. Much like Leo the Great or the abbot Benedict, he will go down in Church and world history as a prophetic visionary.

Neither a Kantian reduction of men's horizon to the pure idea of Christianity—à la Karl Rahner's *Foundations of Christianity: An Introduction to the Idea of Christianity*[14]—nor a naïve confidence in an immanentistically understood self-perfection of humanity by virtue of the forces of the here and now—be it in the benign forms of G. W. F. Hegel (1770–1831), Teilhard de Chardin (1881–1955), Ernst Bloch (1885–1977), and liberation theology[15] or in National Socialism or Communism—offer vi-

---

[13] Heinrich Denzinger, *Enchiridion Symbolorum: Compendium of Creeds, Definitions, and Declarations on Matters of Faith and Morals*, ed. Peter Hünermann, 43rd ed., English edition, ed. Robert Fastiggi and Anne Englund Nash (San Francisco: Ignatius Press, 2012), 301–2. For the Genua talk, see Josef Frings, "Kardinal Frings über das Konzil und die moderne Geisteswelt," *Herderkorrespondenz* 16 (January 1962): 168–74. See also Emery de Gaál, "Joseph Ratzinger at Vatican II," 519–24.

[14] Karl Rahner, *Foundations of Christian Faith: An Introduction to the Idea of Christianity*, trans. William V. Dych (New York: Seabury, 1978).

[15] As representative of these, see: Teilhard de Chardin, *The Heart of Matter* (New York: Harper and Row, 1966); Ernst Bloch, *The Principle of Hope* (Cambridge, MA: MIT, 1986); Gustavo Gutiérrez, *A Theology of Liberation: History, Politics and Salvation* (Maryknoll, NY: Orbis, 1973).

able solutions. Man is infinitely greater than such projects of mere human contrivance—and all the more so God. In the midst of the heady student revolt, the professor of theology serenely conveyed this to a wider and surprisingly receptive audience in 1968 in lectures at Tübingen University. They turned into the celebrated classic *Introduction to Christianity*,[16] an international bestseller, appearing in at least seventeen languages and in numerous editions since then. In 1972, he cofounded the theological journal *Communio*, which is now published in fourteen languages around the world. The seminal Pontifical Biblical Commission documents *The Interpretation of the Bible in the Church* (1993) and *The Jewish People and Their Sacred Scriptures in the Christian Bible* (2002), which Ratzinger published as president of the Commission and prefect of the Congregation for the Doctrine of the Faith, are likewise pioneering. The *Catechism of the Catholic Church* (1992), the *Joint Declaration on the Doctrine of Justification* (1999; in conjunction with the Lutheran World Federation), and the Congregation for the Doctrine of the Faith's *Dominus Iesus* (2000) are of long-term importance—published during his time as prefect. In all these texts, an incarnational humanism is in evidence. Although he is by no means the only important contributor to the last Council, he will certainly go down in history as its single most important and influential interpreter.[17] Over against any superficial reading of *Gaudium et spes*, and in agreement with such noted theologians as Hans Urs von Balthasar (1905–1988), Avery Dulles (1918–2008), Bernard Lonergan (1904–1984), and Romano Guardini (1885–1968), Ratzinger sees not only Christ *in the world*, but also the world redeemed and granted a home *in Christ*.

The decisive issue for the global human family in the coming decades will be the question of which worldview is Enlightenment-resistant. Is perhaps only Christianity genuine enlightenment? What or who can save people from themselves? Is there something beyond the *dictatorship of relativism*, and therefore something beyond cold, economic pragmatism, that can inspire people and provide a justification for human existence? Gradually, all peoples are confronted with these and similar questions throughout the world in the twenty-first century. In his *Jesus of Nazareth* trilogy, Pope Benedict XVI anticipates the answer. Equal to the father of Western monasticism, St. Benedict, who laid the foundations for the flourishing of Christian culture during the Middle Ages in Europe after the dark ages of

[16] Joseph Ratzinger, *Introduction to Christianity*, trans. J. R. Foster (San Francisco: Ignatius Press, 2004).

[17] Tracey Rowland, "Always Christ at the Centre," *The Tablet*, February 16, 2013, 11.

the migration of peoples, could not Pope Benedict XVI have laid the foundations for a future, genuine world community grounded in the profession of faith in the triune God?

The Pontificate of Pope Benedict XVI

One is better able to understand the labors of the nearly eight-year pontificate of Benedict XVI when one calls to mind that the Church Father Augustine was the subject of his dissertation. As did the Fathers of the Church, Benedict uniquely combines theology, exegesis, ministry, and contemplation, but in a manner that reflects the current state of scholarship. When visiting the grave of Augustine in Pavia in 2007, he noted that this African saint experienced his "second conversion" when he was ordained a priest and gave up his studies in private, monastic seclusion to go into public ministry. Henceforth he devoted himself to instructing ordinary people in the most sublime mysteries of faith.[18] He did not cease being a theologian. Rather, he gave up only the academic language and lifestyle of a scholar. But his deep theology and clear language now impressed and convinced simple people and scholars alike.

The beatification of John Henry Newman (2010), the visit to the Ecumenical Patriarch Bartholomew in Constantinople (2010), and the brief visit in 2011 to Martin Luther's (1483–1546) Augustinian monastery in Erfurt—the first made by any pope—were significant exterior, theological accents of this pontificate.

Three Encyclicals—Invitations to Faith

In his first encyclical, *Deus caritas est* (2005), Benedict XVI addresses the most vulnerable aspect of contemporary culture. With this choice, Ratzinger reveals himself as an Augustine expert, possessing deep knowledge of Scripture, the saints, the Church Fathers, and theologians alike. He points to the intrinsic interrelatedness of nature and grace. Therefrom arises such a strong link between faith, worship, and ethos that they together make divine *Agape* (charity) tangible: "God is love" (1 John 4:16).[19] As elsewhere, so

[18] For his visit to Augustine's grave, see materials in *Zenit*, April 22, 2007.

[19] Pope Benedict XVI, Encyclical Letter on Christian Love *Deus Caritas Est* (December 25, 2005), 14, available from http://www.vatican.va (hereafter cited in text as DCE). See Christoph Binninger, "'Deus caritas est': Versuch einer Entfaltung und Ausdeutung der theologischen Grundaussagen der ersten Enzyklika von Benedikt XVI," in Kreiml, *Christliche Antworten auf die Fragen der Gegenwart*, 169–85.

also in this text, Benedict discusses the interrelation between philosophy and faith. Much has been misunderstood in past years with the nonchalant refrain "God is love," thereby intellectually and existentially levelling down the drama of human existence. For the Pope, Christian faith is the result of an event, an encounter with God as a person. It is not so much the consequence of an ethical option. "For God so loved the world that he gave his only-begotten Son, that whoever believes in him should not perish but have eternal life" (John 3:16). This gift of God turning to human beings is experienced in the Eucharist. The pope speaks of "sacramental 'mysticism'" (DCE 13).[20] Earlier, he stated: "The imagery of marriage between God and Israel is now realized in a way previously inconceivable." Because human marriage is a parable and sign of the unconditional fidelity of God to his people, it calls for an exclusive and definitive character of its own (DCE 11). This makes comprehensible for the reader the words of Augustine: "If you see charity, you see the Trinity" (DCE 19).[21] The indissoluble unity of faith, worship, and ethical lifestyle describes effectively the Church in its entirety. Its members are joyfully duty-bound to give this love expression ever anew. The ultimate goal of such *charity* is not only the betterment of the world, but more importantly, the personal message of love, which has its origin in the triune God. No human entity on its own—such as a nation or commercial enterprise—can ever aspire to, let alone achieve, such affection (DCE 28). The human person is intrinsically ordered to such love, but only a three-in-one God can open the human eyes to such a perspective and, in fact, enable it. Attempts to eliminate such a perspective amount to eliminating humankind. Against this background, his words at the opening of the conclave of 2005 can be better understood: the "dictatorship of relativism" not only excludes objective truth but also, and more precisely, denies the possibility of defining God as love, ultimately abolishing the human person at the same time.[22]

Against this sobering description of contemporary culture, Christian dogmas and moral teachings appear not as arbitrary statements or capricious prohibitions, but as expressions of divine, salutary affection to every human being in his unique historical situation. Thus, they become the bases enabling a response on the part of people to God's initiative. The dynamics of divine charity in Christ Jesus highlight the identity of truth and love as possessing a divine origin, toward which every man, *qua homo*, is

---

20 See also Kurt Koch, "Gott ist Liebe," in *Das Geheimnis des Senfkorns*, 266–75.

21 See Augustine, *Confessions* 3.6.

22 Joseph Ratzinger, Homily at the Mass pro Eligendo Romano Pontifice (April 18, 2005), available from http://www.vatican.va.

oriented. Benedict underscores that *vera caritas* (true love) and *cara veritas* (beloved truth) issue forth from intra-Trinitarian life.[23]

The triune God liberates people from the labor of identifying themselves and, by extension, of justifying their existence before the court of utilitarianism. Friedrich Nietzsche (1844–1900) and Martin Heidegger (1889–1976) glorified the project of human self-determination. Rudolf Bultmann (1884–1976)—and other theologians in his wake—claimed to liberate people for a better understanding of the self through a program of demythologization. All these efforts result only in an erosion of the Christian message—and *l'ennui* (boredom) is the corresponding reaction on the part of human beings. Apparently, it is useless for Benedict to demonstrate the absurdity of Kant's transcendental aesthetics. The radical otherness of God utterly surprises. Expressed in Augustinian terms: it is divine love that, as it were, enlightens and illuminates people to their actual purpose. [24] "God's will is no longer for me an alien will, something imposed upon me from without. . . . [It] is now my own will, based on the realization that God is in fact more deeply present to me than I am to myself (DCE 17)."[25] This leads to true humanism (DCE 9).

This facilitates access to his second encyclical, *Spe salvi* (2007). He finds Christian hope is important for a healthy self-criticism of modernity, which domesticates,[26] degrades, and inhumanely immanentizes, and which can be only an eschatological hope such as was proclaimed by the French Revolution in 1789 and by Marxism since the publication of the *Communist Manifesto* in 1848. He points out that the German thinkers Theodor Adorno (1903–1969) and Max Horkheimer (1895–1973) concede that the project of removing fear from this world failed.[27] The pope reaffirms that reason, even apart from and before faith, needs faith to reach its intended goals (SS 23). Otherwise one would only encourage and re-invite crude social Darwinism (SS 26). Also, among non-Christian religions

[23] See Augustine, *De Trinitate* 4.*prooemiun*.39, *De civitate Dei* 11.28.29, and *Confessions* 7.10.12.

[24] Roch Kereszty, "Deus Caritas Est: A Potential to Renew Christian Life and Thought," *Communio* 33 (Fall 2006): 473–90, at 490.

[25] See Augustine, *Confessions* 3.6.11.

[26] Pope Benedict XVI, Encyclical Letter on Christian Hope *Spe Salvi* (November 30, 2007), 22, available from http://www.vatican.va (hereafter cited in text as SS).

[27] See Max Horkheimer and Theodor Adorno, *Dialectic of Enlightenment: Philosophical Fragments* (Stanford, CA: Stanford University Press, 2002). For this encyclical in general, see: Kurt Koch "Der Mensch braucht Gott, sonst ist er hoffnungslos," in *Das Geheimnis des Senfkorns*, 276–79; Rudolf Voderholzer, "'Spe salvi'—eine zu Unrecht fast vergessene Enzyklika," in Kreiml, *Christliche Antworten zu Fragen der Gegenwart*, 186–211.

and in secular society, hope remains a central topic of human existence, but it lacks its deepest content. In his customarily lucid manner, the Pope formulated that hope is experienced and is sustained in community and is only thereby true and authentic: "Our hope is always essentially also hope for others; only thus is it truly hope for me too" (SS 48; see CCC 1032). Hope is an indelible *datum* (given) of human existence. Already in the Pelagian heresy, he perceives the danger: instead of living eschatological hope—that is, toward eternal life—an attempt is made to assure oneself of such already in this world.[28]

He reminds the reader of Dostoevsky's novel *The Brothers Karamazov*. There, the Russian author protested against a God who redeems people regardless of whether they practiced the supernatural virtue of hope and thereby gained merits (SS 44). Hope as a supernatural virtue must be practiced by each generation anew. It never automatically arises: never is it the facile distillate of pure reason (in contrast to Kant and Rahner), and neither can it mindlessly, without having been appropriated by every generation afresh, be handed down (SS 24).

The next papal encyclical, *Caritas in veritate* (2009), is premised on Paul VI's *Populorum progressio* (1967) and John Paul II's *Sollicitudo rei socialis* (1987). Tellingly, the starting point here is not an external occasion, such as the global economic crisis of 2008. The revelation of God in Jesus Christ is the decisive *point d'appui*. The unity of truth and love as beheld in the form of Jesus compels people to labor for a just economic and social order.[29] "A Christianity of charity without truth would be more or less interchangeable with a pool of good sentiments, helpful for social cohesion, but of little relevance." The supernatural virtue of faith is required for this task (CIV 4). Thus does one become acutely aware of the priority of obligations vis-à-vis rights (CIV 43), of the intrinsic connection between moral education and ethics (CIV 15),[30] and of the interdependence of "human ecology" and environmental ecology (CIV 51).

---

[28] Joseph Ratzinger, *Behold the Pierced One: An Approach to a Spiritual Christology*, trans. Graham Harrison (San Francisco: Ignatius Press, 1986), 42–43.

[29] Pope Benedict XVI, Encyclical Letter on Integral Human Development in Charity and Truth *Caritas in Veritate* (June 29, 2009), 1–5, available from http://www.vatican.va (hereafter cited in text as CIV).

[30] See also: Kurt Koch, "Im Dienst einer ganzheitlichen Entwicklung," in *Das Geheimnis des Senfkorns*, 280–288; Benedict XVI, *Creation and Evolution: A Conference with Pope Benedict XVI in Castel Gandolfo*, ed. Stephan Horn and Siegfried Wiedenhofer (San Francisco: Ignatius Press, 2008); Josef Spindelböck, "Die Sozialenzyklika 'Caritas in veritate,' Ein Wort zur rechten Zeit'" in Kreiml, *Christliche Antworten auf Fragen der Gegenwart*, 212–49.

Adorno observed that there could be no higher form of affection than preventing someone from dying of hunger.[31] Benedict XVI indirectly rejects as cruel such banal materialism, for man is considerably greater than this and hungers for more than just maintaining his vegetative system. True brotherhood is achieved in Christian humanism, which reflects divine mercy and invites everyone to enter into divine mercy. Christ defines human hunger in a much grander and more realistic way. Love lived in truth produces true freedom and forms the foundation for an "integral human development" (CIV 18). It is this personified unity of love and truth that motivates Christian engagement in the world and invites contributions to the causes of peace and justice.[32] It is the beautiful vocation of Christians to proclaim the love of Christ through, among other things, the establishment of the earthly city as a city characterized by unanimity and peace that anticipates the heavenly Jerusalem.

Four Speeches—High Points of European Intellectuality

Among the numerous speeches that Benedict XVI delivered, four stand out: 2006 in Regensburg, 2008 in Paris, 2010 in London, and 2011 in Berlin. They have been given at a time when the European continent resembles a huge construction site—but without any discernible master plan—and is mired in a deep, historically unparalleled political, economic, and cultural crisis.

In Regensburg, his last post as a professor of theology (1969–1977), he delivered what is probably—at least as judged by its media reception—his most famous speech. On this occasion, he opposes a domestication of faith in the sense of Adolf von Harnack's (1851–1930) plan of contextualizing Christian faith within the horizon of religious studies, a plan that thereby implicitly denies Christianity being God's definitive self-revelation to humankind. It is rather foolhardy for people to seek happiness without the assistance of divine grace, the Pontiff argues. Only a reason related to God rejects violence, terror, and totalitarianism on good, reasonable grounds, as it alone knows positively that voluntarism is diametrically opposed to what humankind is called to. At the same time, Benedict voices unquali-

[31] Theodor W. Adorno, *Minima Moralia: Reflections from a Damaged Life* (New York: Verso, 2006), 109.

[32] See Congregation for the Doctrine of the Faith, Instruction on Christian Freedom and Liberation *Libertatis Conscientia* (March 22, 1986), 2–4, available from http://www.vatican.va.

fied opposition to the Harnackian project of a de-Hellenization of Christianity. There exists substantial agreement and complementary congruence between the ancient Greek understanding of the world and the biblical faith in God,[33] since the latter demonstrates in a constitutive manner that human reason always reaches beyond itself. Here the *Vernunftpotential*[34] (the potential of rationality) of Christian monotheism is anticipated and prominently underscored. Alas, the self-dynamics of the media age quite successfully sublimated this indispensable insight by celebrating the Muslim violence this lecture unintentionally unleashed. Referencing a question the Byzantine emperor Manuel II Palaeologus addressed to a Muslim concerning whether Islam intends spreading by way of recourse to coercion was the occasion for violent Muslim reaction. However, this speech did provoke numerous Muslims to ask whether Islam actually is a religion of violence. Since the first letter of thirty-eight Muslim scholars and representatives to Benedict in October 2006, an unprecedented, respectful, and fruitful Catholic–Muslim dialogue had become well established.

In the French capital of Paris, he spoke in front of 700 artists in the historic *Collège des Bernardins*, a former Cistercian Monastery that the late Cardinal Jean-Marie Lustiger (1926–2007) had transformed into a place of encounter between Christian faith and French intellectuals. Here, the Pope discussed the values monastic spirituality offers for contemporary Europe. Christian wisdom as sought by the monks is a *quaerere Deum*, a seeking of God:

> Amid the confusion of the times, in which nothing seemed permanent, they wanted to do the essential—to make an effort to find what was perennially valid and lasting, life itself. They were searching for God. They wanted to go from the inessential to the essential, to the only truly important and reliable thing there is.[35]

---

[33] Pope Benedict XVI, "Regensburg Lecture: Faith, Reason and the University," University of Regensburg, September 12, 2006, accessed December 8, 2017, https://w2.vatican.va/content/benedict-xvi/en/speeches/2006/september/documents/hf_ben-xvi_spe_20060912_university-regensburg.html.

[34] See Alfons Knoll, "Vernunft oder Gewalt? Gegenwärtige Monotheismuskritik im Licht der Regensburger Papstrede," in *Die "Regensburger Vorlesung" Papst Benedikt XVI: im Dialog der Wissenschaften*, ed. Christoph Dohmen (Regensburg: Pustet, 2007), 47–57. See also Thomas Heinrich Stark, "Glaube und Vernunft: Eine Relecture der Regensburger Vorlesung von Papst Benedikt XVI," in Kreiml, *Christliche Antworten auf Fragen der Gegenwart*, 35–65.

[35] Pope Benedict XVI, Address at Collège de Bernardins (September 12, 2008), available from http://www.vatican.va.

Man enters into dialogue with the Word of God. This is done through studying Scripture and prayer, and it culminates in monastic prayer having become music: "Coram angelis psallam Tibi, Domine" (Ps 138:1). In this movement of the soul to God, the divine Word is present in the midst of countless human words. As the *Catechism of the Catholic Church* also teaches, the Word of God is not precisely the same as Holy Scripture (CCC 108). Exactly this allows ever afresh the interior movement of the human being to encounter the dynamic whole of Scripture as a book in which the *Logos* speaks directly to him. Meditating on the Word is never reduced to a mechanical process, but evokes and obliges knowledge and charity. This renders present a tension-filled unity between obligation and freedom that draws on the monastic lifestyle and forms the basis for all of Western culture. It is the misfortune of present-day Europe to no longer countenance such unity as indispensable for a civilized body politic: "It would be a disaster if today's European culture could only conceive freedom as absence of obligation, which would inevitably play into the hands of fanaticism and arbitrariness." Such an exemplarily lived vivification of the Word by monks leads to culture, to the *labora* of the order's founder, St. Benedict. Europe would be unthinkable without this alliance of *ora et labora*. Must not a tearing asunder of the two lead to a destruction of the world? Hope has a name, the Pope says, because our hope is the *Logos*, the incarnate reason of God, Jesus Christ (1 Pet 3:15). The plenitude of rich meanings contained in the term *Logos* is decisive. In continuity with Greek *Logos*-philosophy, for Christians of late antiquity, the *Logos* is *the* primordial ground of all being that vouches for the reasonableness of its constituents. It both lays out and restores humankind's original harmony: "*Quaerere Deum*—to seek God and to let oneself be found by him, that is today no less necessary than in former times." A civilization that transfers the *quaerere Deum* into the private sphere inevitably leads to a denial of human reason's greatest skills.[36]

Benedict XVI pursued an analogous concern in Westminster Hall in London in 2010: "I would suggest that the world of reason and the world of faith—the world of secular rationality and the world of religious belief—need one another and should not be afraid to enter into a profound and ongoing dialogue, for the good of our civilization."[37] This was already

[36] See Rudolf Schnackenburg, "Die Herkunft und Eigenart des joh. Logos-begriffs," in *Das Johannesevangelium 1–4*, Herders theologischer Kommentar zum Neuen Testament 4/1 (Freiburg im Breisgau: Herder, 1979), 257–69. See also Kurt Koch, "Gott ist Logos und Liebe," in *Das Geheimnis des Senfkorns*, 14–44.

[37] Pope Benedict XVI, Address to the Representatives of British Society at Westminster Hall (September 17, 2010), available from http://www.vatican.va.

the thesis espoused by the then-prefect of the Congregation for the Doctrine of the Faith in 2004 in the grand Bayeux Cathedral on the occasion of the sixtieth anniversary of the allied landing in Normandy. When faith and reason remain unrelated to one another, "a pathology of reason" and "a pathology of religion" can be the unwelcomed result. After he praised England for its "common law tradition" and after touching on the "dilemma" between Caesar and God that St. Thomas More († 1535) suffered through, he finds that religion is not tasked with providing the *polis* with standards, but rather with contributing to "the search for objective moral principles to the cleansing and elucidation of the reason effort."[38] Hence, the task for religion is to serve as a corrective for reason, for unrelated to belief, human reason is prone to go astray. Therefore, his listeners are encouraged to promote dialogue between reason and faith on all levels so that an "integral" development of the human person might come about. Only on such a basis can freedom of belief, freedom of conscience, and freedom of assembly be ensured.

In Berlin in 2011, in front of the German parliament, the *Bundestag* (the former *Reichstag*), Benedict chose the image of the "listening heart" of King Solomon (1 Kgs 3:9) as a point of departure. Along with Augustine, he notes that without justice the state falls prey to thieves. Benedict repeats: no specific public order can be derived from revelation. This notwithstanding, he reminds his audience that:

> [The] pre-Christian marriage between law and philosophy opened up the path that led via the Christian Middle Ages and the juridical developments of the Age of Enlightenment all the way to the Declaration of Human Rights and to our German Basic Law of 1949, with which our nation committed itself to "inviolable and inalienable human rights as the foundation of every human community, and of peace and justice in the world."[39]

These words were spoken, ironically, in the very location where Hitler had suspended democratic principles in 1933 and denied the German people their Christian heritage.

Both the image of the listening heart of Solomon and the reference to natural law underscore that conscience references a reality that both

---

[38] Joseph Ratzinger, *Values in Time of Upheaval* (San Francisco: Ignatius, 2007), 117–122

[39] Pope Benedict XVI, Address to the Bundestag (September 22, 2011), available from http://www.vatican.va.

historically and materially precedes the political process. However, if human reason is reduced to positivism—as is being done currently—then one does without the classical sources for law and ethics. In such case, man is himself perceived as greatly foreshortened. In time, society will lack culture and radical tendencies will assert themselves. Implicitly, the successor of Peter raises the question of whether the ecological movement points to an empty void if it does not perceive the environment as God's deliberate creation: "The conviction that there is a Creator God is what gave rise to the idea of human rights, the idea of the equality of all people before the law, the recognition of the inviolability of human dignity in every single person." Europe must not sever herself from the symbiosis of Athens and Jerusalem.

In these four speeches in major capitals of the European Union, Benedict XVI recommended a tension-filled union of faith and reason as the salutary corrective to a Europe suffering from a lack of inspiring ideas. Far from any pathos and/or eye-catching gestures, he invites and warns at the same time—similar to an Old Testament prophet—arguing in a sober and factual manner without giving the impression of being condescending or even being embittered. It is indicative of the quality of current mass media, with technology-controlled public discourse, that there was hardly any discussion doing justice to the ideas he advanced, let alone an appreciation of the same thereafter. The theologian-pope is not creative, but original, faithful to the origins: he draws from the wellsprings of faith. He draws on existing teaching, and in a particularly eloquent way on Matthew 22:15–22, with parallels to the two-swords teaching of Pope Saint Gelasius I (492–496). As this remedy is unpalatable, the public square proved incapable of acknowledging that there is no alternative in sight.

The Jesus of Nazareth *Trilogy*

The success of this series, unprecedented in the Jesus literature, is based on the fact that Benedict challenges Christian theology in its entirety to appreciate itself anew as a decidedly ecclesial vocation. "The rift between the 'historical Jesus' and the 'Christ of faith'"[40] must be overcome. Far from an unreflective reprise of the Gospels, this trilogy is a call to contemporary theology to continue in the spirit of the Church Fathers. Scientific research and textual criticism are essential for a solid portrayal of

[40] Joseph Ratzinger / Benedict XVI, *Jesus of Nazareth*, vol. 1, *From the Baptism in the Jordan to the Transfiguration*, trans. Adrian J. Walker (New York: Doubleday, 2007), xi.

Jesus Christ. In paradigmatic fashion, Benedict uses the current findings of various disciplines to draw his picture of Jesus. But the Pope insists that if God is actually love and he invites people to take part in this eternal affection, then theologians are also called to articulate these mysteries of faith accordingly. As a rigorous science, theology should inspire people to a Christian way of life. Otherwise, "intimate friendship with Jesus, on which everything depends, is in danger of clutching at thin air."[41]

In this respect, Benedict provides in his trilogy a synthetic picture of the mystery of Christ. The prayer of Jesus shows something of the nature of the inner-Trinitarian communion of Father and Son in the Holy Spirit. The disciples are involved in this relationship. Thus, ecclesiology and anthropology are centered on the figure of Jesus. This forms the basis for a "positive secularity." Once human volition is united with the will of Christ, it becomes creative, varying according to different cultural conditions, to reshape the world in Christ.

For this reason, this trilogy by no means represents an illegitimate blending of theology and personal prayer.[42] There exists an inner connection between Creator and creation. As Benedict is inspired by the Church Fathers, theology invariably leads to contemplation for him. This perspective enables him to overcome earlier neo-Scholastic Christologies, which rested heavily on a conceptual grasp of the mystery of Christ constructed upon abstract categories that, in isolation, could have theoretically been a hindrance to an immediate encounter with the person of Christ.[43] As everything essential is biographical to him, he notes: "Concerning this book about Jesus . . . I've been internally on its road for a long time."[44] Every turn

---

[41] Ratzinger, *Jesus of Nazareth*, 1:xii. For different reactions, see: *Ein Weg zu Jesus: Schlüssel zu einem tieferen Verständnis des Papstbuches*, ed. Thomas Söding (Freiburg im Breisgau: Herder, 2007); *Annäherungen an "Jesus von Nazareth": Das Buch des Papstes in der Diskussion*, ed. Jan Heiner Tück (Ostfildern: Matthias-Grünewald, 2007); *"Jesus von Nazareth" Kontrovers: Rückfragen an Joseph Ratzinger*, ed. Karl Lehmann (Münster/Berlin: LIT, 2007); Josef Kreiml, "Der Glaube an Jesus Christus in der Theologie Benedikt XVI: Zum Jesus-Buch des Papstes," in *Christliche Antworten auf Fragen der Gegenwart*, 152–68.

[42] The interpretation that it is such a blending was expressed in Stefan Schreiber, "Der Papst und der Teufel: Ein Exeget liest Joseph Ratzingers Jesus-Buch," *Theologische Revue* 103 (2007): 355–62.

[43] Due to the rich forms of devotional life and the greater interiority of past centuries, this emphasis on faith's intelligibility by way of a propositional presentation was seen at that time as demonstration of the superior rationality of Catholic faith, rather than as a shortcoming.

[44] Ratzinger, *Jesus of Nazareth*, 1:x (translation modified by present author).

in the road has been undergirded by a personal, meditative, and prayerful mindset. Everything depends on whether the Christian can call out with the apostle Thomas: "My Lord and my God!" (John 20:28). This alone allows Christians—along with Christ—true "communion" with the Father, who is the true center of the person of Christ.

Given its foundational perspective, this trilogy has the potential to lead the way to a reinvigorated theology in the twenty-first century. Like that of the Fathers of the Church, this theology does not engage only an imaginary academic forum, but serves to enrich the entire Church. Thanks to his synthetic powers, the theologian Ratzinger offers a model for how the oftentimes lamented postmodern fragmentation of theology can be overcome. The guiding principle is not a merciless "publish or perish" for the sake of academic laurels, theology as a solipsistic *l'art pour l'art*—which can barely provide an overview of the theological discipline—but rather a deep mystagogical concern: to lead the seekers and believers to behold the Father in Christ, and thus to participate in the intra-Trinitarian life. A Christology thus defined rekindles, and indeed liberates, human rationality in an almost revolutionary way to become doxological.

In the very extensive commentary on the Our Father, Benedict reveals that the only possible access to Jesus Christ is achieved through prayer.[45] Methodologically, he is using the "canonical exegesis" introduced by the Protestant exegete Brevard Childs (1923–2007): reading "individual texts within the totality of the one Scripture, which then sheds new light on all the individual texts."[46] This is significant because it leads the historical-critical method forward, thereby allowing it to become "theology in the proper sense."[47] He is convinced that both the decision in favor of faith and historical reason legitimize a "Christological hermeneutic which sees in Jesus Christ, the key of the whole."[48] The post-Easter profession of faith as formulated by the Church is inescapable and irreducible. There is simply no other access to Scripture and to Jesus Christ.[49] Consequently, he begins the series with the Baptism of Jesus in the Jordan River. Only theology—literally taken to mean "speaking with Jesus, the *Logos*, from the Father"—unlocks the figure of Jesus. Not *against* the ecumenical councils

---

[45] Ratzinger, *Jesus of Nazareth*, 1:128–68.

[46] Ratzinger, *Jesus of Nazareth*, 1:xviii. See Brevard S. Childs, *Biblical Theology of the Old and New Testaments: Theological Reflections on the Christian Bible* (Minneapolis, MN: Fortress, 1993).

[47] Ratzinger, *Jesus of Nazareth*, 1:xix.

[48] Ratzinger, *Jesus of Nazareth*, 1:xix.

[49] See Ratzinger, *Jesus of Nazareth*, 1:303.

of Nicaea (325) and Chalcedon (451), but *with* them, the biblical figure of Jesus becomes comprehensible. Jesus is the Son of God and therefore God himself: "of the same substance" with the Father.[50] Addressing every human being of every epoch, it is only the eternal Person of Christ that grants the individual dignity. Benedict recognizes such lived freedom in Mary's faith and life.[51] Together with the Son of God, he recommends the Virgin Mary as the key for anthropology and as a corrective for a misunderstood freedom.[52]

Significantly, he rehabilitates the Gospel of John, which has been ignored by numerous exegetes between 1960 and 2000.[53] Time and again, one discovers with John:

> It is never a merely private remembering, but a remembering in and with the "we" of the Church. . . . Because the personal recollection that provides the foundation of the Gospel is purified and deepened by being inserted into the memory of the Church, it does indeed transcend the banal recollection of facts.[54]

All this occurs mindful of "the rationalization of the world" through the eternal *Logos*, Jesus, who overcomes both the ageless "wiles of the devil" and postmodern "chaos theory."[55] The exchange of ideas conducted with the American rabbi Jacob Neusner enriches this work.

The *Jesus of Nazareth* trilogy sets standards equally for exegesis and for the theological enterprise in general in the twenty-first century. It is consistently modern and "enlightened." It takes seriously Kantian epistemology, with its thesis of the unattainability of the *thing in itself*, and overcomes it at the same time. In the 1988 Erasmus Lecture, Ratzinger had expressed hope for a renewal, a "new synthesis" of biblical scholarship.[56] In fact, he himself achieved some remarkable feats of insight with this trilogy.

---

50 Ratzinger, *Jesus of Nazareth*, 1:320.

51 Joseph Ratzinger and Hans Urs von Balthasar, *Mary: The Church at the Source*, trans. Adrian J. Walker (San Francisco: Ignatius Press, 2005), 13ff.

52 Ratzinger and von Balthasar, *Mary: The Church at the Source*, 1:37ff.

53 Ratzinger, *Jesus of Nazareth*, 1:218–86.

54 Ratzinger, *Jesus of Nazareth*, 1:231.

55 Ratzinger, *Jesus of Nazareth*, 1:174.

56 Joseph Cardinal Ratzinger, "Biblical Interpretation in Crisis: On the Question of the Foundations and Approaches of Exegesis Today," in *Biblical Interpretation in Crisis: The Ratzinger Conference on Bible and Church*, ed. Richard J. Neuhaus (Grand Rapids, MI: Eerdmans, 1989), 1–23.

(1) Access to Jesus Christ occurs only through prayer. (2) Christology has to take the eternal, divine Sonship of Jesus as its starting point. (3) Only a balanced Christology, namely, one that takes seriously Jesus's pre-existence and unity with the Father and his Incarnation, is able to think the unity of Scripture (e.g., the correlation between Matthew 1:25–27, Luke 10:21–22, and John 10:14–15 is crucial because it apprehends the consonance between the synoptic understanding of Christ and that of the Gospel of John). (4) Against this background, much of the understanding of Scripture, the Fathers, and the Middle Ages appears remarkably consistent and invites Christians to a *relecture.* (5) Faith is a legitimate form of knowledge. (6) When complemented by a hermeneutics of canonical exegesis, the historical-critical method better appreciates its own intrinsic value within the Church. (7) Ever since Pentecost, the Church is part of a living *continuum* called Tradition. Finally (8), in continuation of the *ressourcement* movement, this trilogy integrates Scripture, liturgical practice, cosmology, ethics, Patristics, spirituality, and the testimony of the Saints. In fact, contours of a renewal of Patristic theology become visible.[57]

Conclusion

In the section entitled "The Shepherd" in the first volume of the *Jesus of Nazareth* trilogy, Ratzinger writes:

> Jesus' own "I" is always opened into "being with" the Father; he is never alone, but is forever receiving himself from and giving himself back to the Father. "My teaching is not mine"; his "I" is opened up into the Trinity. Those who come to know him "see" the Father; they enter into this communion of his with the Father. It is precisely this transcendent dialogue, which encounter with Jesus involves, that once more reveals to us the true Shepherd, who does not take possession of us, but leads us to the freedom of our being by leading us into communion with God and by giving his own life.[58]

---

[57] See Benedict XVI, *The Fathers of the Church*, ed. Joseph T. Lienhard, S.J. (Grand Rapids, MI: Eerdmans, 2009); Benedict XVI, *Jesus, the Apostles, and the Early Church*, trans. *L'Osservatore Romano* (San Francisco: Ignatius Press, 2007); Benedict XVI, *A School of Prayer: The Saints Show Us How to Pray*, trans. *L'Osservatore Romano* (San Francisco: Ignatius Press, 2013).

[58] Ratzinger, *Jesus of Nazareth*, 1:283.

The undramatic resignation of Pope Benedict XVI in 2013 and his subsequent turn to deeper contemplation in the seclusion of the former monastery "Mater Ecclesiae" in the Vatican Gardens are grounded in the inner logic of his priestly existence, his theology, and his high understanding of the papal office. There, he enters deeper into the mystery of Christ and invites us to do likewise, to follow the same path. Precisely thereby he continues to serve the Church as shepherd in her geographic heart.

CHAPTER 2

The Theologian Joseph Ratzinger at Vatican II

His Theological Vision and Role[1]

> At the Council the proponents of this theology [on the basis of Sacred Scripture, the Fathers of the Church, and the great liturgical heritage of the universal Church] had been concerned about nourishing the faith, not only of the last hundred years, but on the stream of tradition as a whole. . . . For the time being, this attempt seems to have failed; it had little effect in comparison with the more comprehensible programs that have replaced it since. Nevertheless, there are more and more indications that the impulse of this theology was not spent in a vacuum.
>
> —J. Ratzinger, *Dogma and Preaching*[2]

THE ABOVE DESCRIBES the grand vision of *ressourcement* theology—a loose current intentionally eschewing systematization—which had been

1 This essay was originally published in *Lateranum* LXXVIII, no. 3 (2012): 515–548. Used by permission.

2 Joseph Ratzinger, *Dogma and Preaching: Applying Christian Doctrine to Daily Life*, trans. Michael J. Miller and Matthew J. O'Connell (San Francisco: Ignatius Press, 2011), 382. This text was written roughly ten years after the Council's first session. See also p. 380: "The debate about the true heritage of Vatican II today cannot be conducted in terms of the documents alone. A decisive factor for its progress will be whether an intellectual defense can be found not only for an anti-historical–utopian interpretation of the Council, but also for a creative spiritual understanding of it in living union with the true tradition."

all but ignored and forgotten soon after the Council.[3] Frequently, a deconstructivist view isolates a text from its intellectual, historical, and ecclesial context. But can one comprehend the Council without the contributions to the Council Fathers by the representatives of this current as *periti*, such as Yves Congar, O.P., Alois Grillmeier, S.J., Marie-Dominique Chenu, O.P., Henri de Lubac, S.J., Jean Daniélou, S.J., Otto Semmelroth, S.J., Josef Andreas Jungmann, S.J., and, last but not least, Joseph Ratzinger? History attests well the observation that an ecumenical council proves its "creative spiritual" worth not via a momentary utopian interpretation, but by its integration into the Church's organic, living unity and her true, Spirit-sustained Tradition. There is no gainsaying that, as the Church commemorates the fiftieth anniversary of the Second Vatican Council (1962–1965), an examination of the theological vision and role of one of this council's major *periti* is in order. This is all the more justified because he fortuitously became Pope Benedict XVI. At this juncture, one is in the felicitous position to have sufficient documentation as regards professor Ratzinger's contributions to Cardinal Josef Frings's (1887–1978) important interventions during the Council and the cardinal's proposals for various conciliar documents.[4] However, it remains difficult to ascertain Ratzinger's actual share in the genesis of individual texts the Council passed,[5]

---

3 Indicatively, to the present author's knowledge, Ratzinger never uses the term *ressourcement* to predicate his own position.

4 The Cologne priest and historian Norbert Trippen (1936–2017) has written a thoroughly researched two-volume biography of Cardinal Josef Frings on the basis of his access to the cardinal's personal archive. Frings had not handed over his conciliar estate to the Cologne archdiocesan registry, as all Roman drafts had been categorized *sub secreto* (Trippen, *Josef Kardinal Frings (1887–1978)*, vol. 2, *Sein Wirken für die Weltkirche und seine letzten Bischofsjahre*, Veröffentlichungen der Kommission für Zeitgeschichte, ser. 2 [Forschungen], 104 [Paderborn: Schöningh, 2005], 21). The German text cited in the footnotes is from this volume, as it may capture a nuance not always present in the Latin. Much credit is also due to the careful study of Jared Wicks, S.J., "Six Texts by Prof. Joseph Ratzinger as *Peritus* before and during Vatican Council II," *Gregorianum* 89, no. 2 (2008): 233–311. Unless otherwise noted, all English translations from original languages are the present author's own work.

5 Probably never will the complete genesis of the conciliar texts be reconstructable. In addition, it is unknown to the present author whether Ratzinger had written a personal diary. The diaries of other *periti* shed some light on this process. The completion of the publication of Tromp's diary is keenly awaited. His diary as it has been published up to now is contained in: S. Tromp, S.J., *Konzilstagebuch mit Erläuterungen und Akten aus der Arbeit der Theologischen Kommissionen*, vol. 1, *Commissio Praeparatoria (1960–62)*, ed. A. von Teuffenbach (Rome: Gregoriana, 2006); Tromp, *Konzilstagebuch mit Erläuterungen und Akten aus der Arbeit der Theologischen Kommissionen*, vol. 2, *Vatikan-*

since numerous theologians collaborated on the revisions and redactions of the texts.[6]

The Stature of Cardinal Frings

Cardinal Frings had selected three trusted and highly competent advisors for the Council: for procedural issues, Hubert Jedin (1900–1980);[7] for pastoral and canonical questions, his vicar general, Joseph Teusch (1902–1976);[8] and for all matters theological, Joseph Ratzinger. Significantly, the last advised him both during the Council's preparatory phase and for its full duration. After considering the suggestions of his advisors, Frings would either dictate to or review with his personal secretary, Hubert Luthe (1927–2014), his upcoming vote or speech. Not infrequently he simply made Ratzinger's drafts or suggestions his own. Insofar as the speeches or

---

isches Konzil (vols. 2.1 and 2.2 [1962–1963]), ed. A. von Teuffenbach (Nordhausen: Bautz, 2011).

6 This investigation is not concerned with the postconciliar analyses and interpretations of Vatican II. See Joseph Ratzinger, *Theological Highlights of Vatican II*, trans. Henry Traub, S.J. (part I), Gerard C. Thompson (parts II and III), and Werner Barzel (part IV) (Mahwah, NJ: Paulist Press, 1966). See also: Ratzinger's commentary in *Commentary on the Documents of Vatican II*, ed. H. Vorgrimler (New York: Herder and Herder 1967–1969), 1:297–305, 3:155–98 and 262–71, 5:115–63; W. Repgen, "Das Konzil und der frühe Ratzinger," *Renovatio* 51 (1995): 193–203; G. Marchesi, S.J., "Benedetto XVI e il Concilio Vaticano II," *La Civiltà Cattolica* 157 (2006): 381–90; J. Komonchak, "Benedict XVI and the Interpretation of Vatican II," *Cristianesimo nella Storia* 28 (2007): 323–37. In contrast, cf. the analysis offered by P. Blanco Sarto, "Joseph Ratzinger, Perito del Concilio Vaticano II (1962–1965)," *Anuario de Historia de la Iglesia* 15 (2006): 43–66. More recently, see: Pope Benedict XVI, "Interpreting Vatican II," *Origins* 35, no. 32 (January 26, 2006): 534–39; M. Hauke, "Das Zweite Vatikanum und die Überlieferung. Eine wichtige Wegweisung von Papst Benedikt XVI," *Katholische Monatsschrift* 36 (2006): 90–94.

7 Born to a Catholic father and a baptized Jewish mother, his *venia legendi* was withdrawn by the Nazi regime in 1933 and he was forced to live in exile in Rome from 1939 to 1945. A noted expert on the Council of Trent, he became professor for Church history in Bonn in 1949 (K. Repgen, "Der Geschichtsschreiber des Trienter Konzils," *Zeitschrift der Savigny-Stiftung für Rechtsgeschichte: Romanistische Abteilung* 70 [1984]: 356–93). For a more general overview, see: *History of Vatican II*, 5 vols., ed. G. Alberigo and J. A. Komonchak (Maryknoll, NY: Orbis, 1995–2006); *Herders theologischer Kommentar zum Zweiten Vatikanischen Konzil*, 5 vols., ed. P. Hünermann and B. J. Hilberath (Freiburg im Breisgau: Herder, 2005).

8 Teusch had directed the Cologne archdiocesan office countering Nazi propaganda from 1934 until 1945. (N. Trippen, *Rheinische Lebensbilder*, vol. 15 [Cologne: Bachem, 1995], 223–46).

papers fall within the preparatory phase, they are published in the *Acta et Documenta*. Those delivered during the Council are printed in the *Acta Synodalia*. The speeches of the Cologne cardinal stand out in the *Acta Synodalia*, as they always bear the remark *Textus scripto traditus*. Since the almost completely blind Cologne ordinary was unable to read his carefully composed speeches, he delivered them by heart and in generally intelligible Latin[9]—this was one of his fortes—sometimes interspersed with ironic remarks. This may not, however, imply a lack of independence on part of the Cologne archbishop. Frings had the schemata read to him and would pose critical questions, thereby forming his own opinion while also displaying humble eagerness to learn. His judgment thus formed, he would confront his advisors and ask them to compose a response or a speech. Nothing could be written in his name unless he fully identified himself with its content.[10]

Hubert Jedin—a celebrated Church historian, and one of Frings's *periti,* and an on-site witness—relates that, toward the end of the Council, the Louvain canonist Wilhelm Onclin (1900–1980) shared with him his firm impression that Cardinal Frings had been "the most respected father of the Second Vatican Council." Jedin notes that when a speech to be delivered by Frings was announced, the naves of Saint Peter emptied—including the bars!—as nobody wanted to miss that cardinal's statements, which were considered always significant.[11] Quite naturally, this amplified the influence of his theological advisor, Joseph Ratzinger.

In addition, one must take into consideration the prestige enjoyed both by the Archdiocese of Cologne and by the person of Frings within the global Church in order to assess somewhat the influence Ratzinger exercised prior to and during the Council. Ever since purloining the relics of the three magi in 1164, the Archdiocese of Cologne numbers itself among the world's wealthiest dioceses. Moreover, its centuries-old struc-

---

[9] Trippen, *Frings*, 2:21.

[10] Joseph Ratzinger, "Kardinal Frings und das II. Vatikanische Konzil," in *Kardinal Frings: Leben und Werk*, ed. D. Froitzheim (Köln: Weinand, 1979), 191–205, at 202–3.

[11] H. Jedin, "Kardinal Frings auf dem Zweiten Vatikanischen Konzil," in *Festgabe für Bernhard Stasiewski zum 75: Geburtstag*, ed. G. Adrianyi (Leverkusen: Borengässer, 1980), 7–16, at 16: "Gegen Ende des Konzils hat der Löwener Professor Onclin mir gegenüber einmal gesagt, nach seiner Ansicht sei Kardinal Frings der angesehenste Vater des Zweiten Vatikanums. . . . Aus eigener Beobachtung kann ich bezeugen, dass, wenn der Generalsekretär des Konzils eine Rede des Kölner Kardinals ankündigte, die Seitenschiffe von St. Peter (einschließlich der Bar) sich leerten, weil man diesen Redner nicht verpassen wollte. Denn Kardinal Frings hatte stets etwas Wichtiges zu sagen—und er hatte den Mut, es zu sagen."

tures and close proximity to both France and the Netherlands provide it with remarkable cosmopolitan acumen, established theological resources, and a global perspective. Well prior to the Council, Frings had initiated annual collections for the needy in the world: *Adveniat* and *Misereor*, held ever since in all German dioceses. As a result, cosmopolitan Cologne entertains friendly relations with a great number of sees abroad. It is thus little wonder that the exquisitely educated Cardinal-Archbishop Frings had been appointed a member of the preparatory commission in 1960. In 1962 he became member of the *praesidium*, and when the leadership of the conciliar deliberations was handed over to the moderators in 1963, he remained a member of that *praesidium*. Of not less significance is the following: as president of the (West) German (Fulda) bishops' conference, he regularly convened on Mondays—precisely at 5 p.m. and for the complete duration of the Council—a consultation of all German-speaking bishops at the Santa Maria dell'Anima, the college for German-speaking priests in Rome. This included bishops from Austria, Luxembourg, and the German parts of Switzerland and Italy, the German mission bishops, and those of Scandinavia. Frings would preside *ex officio* at these gathering.[12] The significance of these consultations for the Council's course cannot be overstated. Not by deliberate design, but *nolens volens*, they created a German structure paralleling the official conciliar commissions—operating often in tandem with the corresponding French and/or Benelux groups—that would ultimately prevail on many points during the Council.[13]

One must bear in mind that in this matrix of pivotal roles the Cologne archbishop played, Ratzinger was his all-important theological collaborator. A comparison between Ratzinger's preceding opinions and Frings's subsequent speeches or votes confirms this.[14] While it is impossible to ascertain who may have been the most influential *peritus* during the Council, it is reasonable to assume the still young professor Ratzinger must be counted among its twenty, if not ten, most significant *periti*.

THE VISION ENUNCIATED AT GENOA IN 1961

In his memoirs, Frings supplies the background to the memorable and much noted lecture he gave in Italian on November 20, 1961, at the *Teatro Duse*

---

[12] Trippen, *Frings*, 2:210–11.

[13] Alberigo and Komonchak, *History of Vatican II*, 2:85. See also R. Wiltgen, *The Rhine Flows into the Tiber: The Unknown Council* (New York: Hawthorn, 1967).

[14] Trippen, *Frings*, 2:244.

in Genoa.[15] The context was the *Columbianum*, an institute founded by the Jesuit Father Angelo d'Arpa for questions regarding future developments. Father d'Arpa had organized a series of four papers by different eminent cardinals and had asked Frings to talk on the announced council and the contemporary situation as it differs from that at the eve of the First Vatican Council (1869–1870). However much he was intrigued by the topic, Frings considered himself incapable of addressing this theme in "a foundational way" (*grundlegend*). During a concert at Gürzenich (a festive concert hall in central Cologne), he had met Joseph Ratzinger, professor of fundamental theology at the University of Bonn since 1959. Aware of his stellar reputation, Frings requested him to draft the talk for him. Presented with a draft soon thereafter, Frings immediately considered it superb and "retouched it only at one location" ("nur an einer Stelle eine Retuschierung").[16] The attending Cardinal Giuseppe Siri (1906–1989) of Genoa was thoroughly satisfied. When Cardinal Julius Döpfner (1913–1976), archbishop of Munich—and subsequently one of four moderators during the Council (1963–1965)—was shown the text, he remarked, "Well, a historic document," regretting that it would never materialize.[17] The Genoa talk marks the be-

---

15 The detailed paper was first presented during a meeting of the German bishops' conference in Fulda. See protocol of the plenary conference of the bishops of the German dioceses in Fulda from August 29 until 31, 1961 (*Historisches Archiv des Erzbistums Köln*—Cabinetts-Registratur [henceforth, CR], II:2.19,25, and CR, III:2.19,51[2]). See also Emery de Gaál, *The Theology of Pope Benedict XVI: The Christocentric Shift* (New York: Palgrave Macmillan, 2010), 88–89.

16 See J. Frings, *Für den Menschen bestellt, Erinnerungen des Alterzbischofs von Köln* (Köhln: Bachem, 1973), 248–49: "Er fragte mich, ob ich bereit sei, über das Konzil auf dem Hintergrund der Zeitlage im Unterschied zum Ersten Vatikanischen Konzil zu sprechen. Das Thema reizte mich, und ich sagte zu. Aber ich sah, dass ich allein nicht imstande sein würde, dieses Thema grundlegend zu besprechen. In einem Gürzenich-Konzert traf ich Professor Joseph Ratzinger, der kurz vorher als Fundamentaltheologe nach Bonn gekommen war und der sich bereits einen großen und guten Rufes erfreute. Ich bat ihn, ob er mir bei der Bearbeitung dieses Themas behilflich sein wollte, und auch ihn schien diese Themenstellung zu reizen. Er lieferte mir bald einen Entwurf, den ich so gut fand, dass ich nur an einer Stelle eine Retuschierung vornahm."

17 Frings, *Für den Menschen bestellt*, 248–49. It is unknown whether Ratzinger's *Doktorvater*, Gottlieb Söhngen, a priest of the Cologne archdiocese, had a hand in his becoming Frings's *peritus*. He did certainly influence his student becoming professor in Bonn, a part of the Cologne archdiocese. In his memoirs, Ratzinger relates another event as the cause for their collaboration: "Cardinal Frings heard a conference on the theology of the Council that I had been invited to give by the Catholic Academy of Bensberg, and afterward he involved me in a long dialogue that became the starting point of a collaboration that lasted for years" (Joseph Ratzinger, *Milestones: Memoirs, 1927–1977*, trans. Erasmo Leiva-Merikakis [San Francisco: Ignatius Press, 1998], 120).

ginning of a long and fruitful collaboration between Frings and Ratzinger. The Cologne Church historian Norbert Trippen (1936–2017) relates having heard the talk read aloud in Frings's presence during lunch at the Cologne seminary. Deflecting all praise from himself, the cardinal quipped at the end: "Has not Ratzinger acquitted himself superbly?"[18]

To his surprise, Pope John XXIII asked Frings for a private audience on February 23, 1962. There the pope at once embraced him and said he had read the Genoa talk and wanted to express his gratitude for the beautiful thoughts it contained.[19] Frings's personal secretary, Luthe, remembers the pope exclaiming, "Che bella coincidenza del pensiero!" These spontaneous words imply a material agreement between the vision of the Council as Ratzinger had expressed in the paper and the pope's own wishes for the Council he was about to convene. Characteristic for his person, the cardinal replied modestly that a certain theology professor at Bonn, Joseph Ratzinger, had composed the text for him. The pope's very favorable verdict encouraged Frings to rely henceforth on Ratzinger's theological acumen throughout the Council.[20]

The lecture was published as "Kardinal Frings über das Konzil und die moderne Geisteswelt" ("Cardinal Frings on the Council and the Modern World of Thought").[21] As an *ouverture*, Ratzinger first stresses the incarnational nature of Catholic truth and that councils always are in some way influenced by "contemporary circumstances." Pope John XXIII's term *aggiornamento* is interpreted as a call "to examine the cultural and intellectual world of today, in the midst of which the Council intends to place the Gospel not under a bushel basket but on a lamp stand, so that it might enlighten everyone living in the house of the present age (cf. Mt 5:15)."[22] The author registers profound changes vis-à-vis Vatican I, such as "an acceleration of time," but prophetically discerns "liberalism surging anew" as a reaction to Marxism and an already-defeated "romanticizing nationalism(s)" in Italy and Germany.[23] While much in the present age may be considered incipiently manifest already at the eve of Vatican I, he warns against facilely assuming a return of the past. Neither nineteenth-century fideism nor rationalism has been fully overcome. Also, he notes secularism in Latin

---

18 Trippen, *Frings*, vol. 2, 241.

19 Frings, *Für den Menschen bestellt*, 249.

20 Trippen, *Frings*, 2:262.

21 J. Frings, "Kardinal Frings über das Konzil und die moderne Geisteswelt," *Herderkorrespondenz* 16 (January 1962): 168–74 (slightly abridged in Wicks, "Six Texts," 253–61).

22 Wicks, "Six Texts," 254.

23 Frings, "Kardinal Frings über das Konzil," 168.

America gaining momentum and American Catholicism coming of age.

This prologue allows him to turn to the upcoming Council and modern thinking. Along with the world becoming smaller, a hitherto unknown, novel sense of the unity of humankind develops. Individual national cultures are cloaked by a technically unified culture, and a unified language of European-American provenience arises, which he describes as "another *koiné*." He compares the eve of Vatican II with the Hellenistic time of early Christianity. It is the special divine summons, the singular, privileged *kairos* of our age urging us and the Church to transform "humanity's new *koiné* into a Christian dialect" as the apostles and martyrs had done in the first centuries. But he adds a cautionary note: after two world wars caused by Christians, "the non-Christian world harbors a deep skepticism against Christianity and its ability to change the world."[24] Ratzinger could have written the following passage in 2012: "The emergence of new worldwide perspectives has left Westerners disillusioned and aware of the limited significance of their own culture and history."[25] This leads to a relativism that denies all absolutes and admits only relativities. Such relativism may occasion Christianity to part ways with seeming absolutes, but also to discover better the true purity of Christian faith. The Council should strive to open the Church "as the truly spiritual people born of the Spirit and water (Jn 3:5)" to "the total fullness of the human spirit." The local episcopal authority should be "strengthened in order to meet the needs of the particular churches, while keeping bishops together in the unity of the whole episcopate around its stable center, the Chair of Peter."[26]

Reminiscent of Romano Guardini's (1885–1968) prescient and now classic analysis of the relentless ascendance of the technical age,[27] which Ratzinger himself had personally experienced in Munich while still a student and later as an associate pastor, Ratzinger discusses in the next section the impact of technology on contemporary religiosity. Previously, human beings lived "in a close and direct dependence on nature," but now the world bears everywhere the marks of human labor and organization that cover up the world as God's creation. The technical milieu of the industrial laborer leads to atheism and the inconsistencies inherent in capitalism. While cautioning against demonizing technology per se, from its

[24] Frings, "Kardinal Frings über das Konzil," 169.

[25] Wicks, "Six Texts," 256.

[26] Wicks, "Six Texts," 257.

[27] Romano Guardini, *Letters from Lake Como: Explorations in Technology and the Human Race* (Grand Rapids, MI: Eerdmans, 1994).

omnipresence follows inexorably that "die Selbstvergöttlichung der Menschheit löst die Vergöttlichung der Natur mit innerer Notwendigkeit ab" ("humankind's self-divinization replaces the divinization of nature with inner necessity"). This is amplified by the sciences offering only *prima vista* viable responses to even deep (spiritual) human desires. This occasions a profound change in the role of religion. As the human person remains "the great abyss" (Augustine) and "the unknown" (A. Carrel),[28] it must be the Council's task now to spell out again "the enduring right religion holds on man." The Church should demonstrate that true progress and God's truth are not mutually exclusive realities.[29]

These considerations lead to a further point: a reflection on "the phenomenon of ideology." Marxism, existentialism, and neoliberalism are defined as "surrogate religions." Seemingly, ideology offers a comprehensive meaning for life. In one sentence, the beguiling nature of a world *etsi Deus non daretur* ("as if God does not exist") is captured:

> It is in its essence the exact product of a world in which old paganism is definitively overcome by the technical situation, in which the gods have become impossible, which, however, also shies away from the wager of a faith in God and creates itself a religion without religion—for precisely this is the nature of ideology, which promises to fulfill the task of religion—i.e., providing meaning—without being religion.[30]

The technical environment produces the Augustinian *homo in se ipso incurvatus* (the self-absorbed human being). Despite Marxism and existentialism being then much in vogue, Ratzinger makes out neoliberalism as the underlying current and as the enduring ideology outlasting these

---

[28] Awarded the Nobel Prize in Physiology or Medicine in 1912, Alexis Carrel (1873–1944) oscillated between Catholic faith ("including devotions to Our Lady of Lourdes, "supporting eugenics"), fascism, and atheism (supporting eugenics). He returned to the faith in 1939. In 1935, he authored *Man, The Unknown* (New York: Harper, 1935), which appeared in German as *Der Mensch, Das Unbekannte Wesen* (Stuttgart: Deutsche Verlags-Anstalt, 1955). The book's German title became a popular quotation in Germany.

[29] Frings, "Kardinal Frings über das Konzil," 171.

[30] Frings, "Kardinal Frings über das Konzil," 172: "Sie ist also ihrem Wesen nach das genaue Produkt einer Welt, in der das alte Heidentum durch die technische Situation endgültig überholt ist, in der Götter unmöglich geworden sind, die aber auch das Wagnis des Glaubens an einen Gott scheut und sich eine Religion ohne Religion schafft—denn das ist genau das Wesen von Ideologie, welche verspricht die Aufgabe der Religion—die Sinngewährung—zu erfüllen ohne Religion zu sein."

philosophies. Here the Church's positive task is to present Christian faith as the true answer to the human spirit's quest.

Ad intra, Ratzinger and Frings ask self-critically whether such a situation is caused also by nineteenth-century Christianity neglecting universal hope in favor of individual salvation. Does not the index of forbidden works smack of "totalitarian practices" stifling a genuine struggle with spiritual/intellectual questions ("geistigen Fragen") he asks? Need the Church not reevaluate her own relevant praxes? The Council is a welcome opportunity to make "the edifice Church accessible to modern man as his Father's house in which he can live joyfully and feel safe and secure."[31]

The lecture concludes on a rather positive note: the charismatic gifts of the Holy Spirit now seem concrete to a degree, but altogether unthinkable at the eve of Vatican I. These promptings he sees manifest in Marian piety, the liturgical movement, a rediscovery of Scripture and a fresh appropriation of the Church Fathers by theology, and the advent of the ecumenical movement. Essentially, he detects two complementary movements: (1) an objective-sacramental one—namely, liturgical piety; and (2) the subjective-personal one of Marian piety. They are summarized as *per Christum ad patrem* and *per Mariam ad Christum*. Jointly, these currents lead to a rediscovery of the Church in the concept of the *mater ecclesia* as the total Christ, head and members (Augustine).[32] Marian piety refers to the Church and her martyrs. The present age can take heart from the fact that it produces martyrs. The future task is to unite the Marian and liturgical movements. To encourage such witness of Christian faith in today's world must be the Council's task, rather than issuing doctrinal statements:

> [The Marian movement] should impart to the liturgically minded person something of its warmth of heart, interiority and *Ergriffenheit* (touched by the sublime) and deep willingness to repent and atone, and vice-versa it could receive from the liturgical movement something of the holy sobriety and clarity, the luminosity and the strict earnestness of the old laws of Christian prayer and thought, which keep in check the exaggerated imagination of the loving heart and direct it to its proper place."[33]

---

[31] Frings, "Kardinal Frings über das Konzil," 174.

[32] See J. Ratzinger, *Volk und Haus Gottes in Augustins Lehre von der Kirche: die Dissertation und weitere Studien zu Augustinus und zur Theologie der Kirchenväter* [originally published in 1951], in *Gesammelte Schriften*, vol. 1 (Freiburg im Breisgau: Herder, 2011).

[33] Frings, "Kardinal Frings über das Konzil," 174: "Sie sollte dem liturgischen Menschen

These two notable movements should be integrated so that Mary shines forth as the icon and original image of the believing Church celebrating the liturgy.

This text reflects the author's own Marian piety (in particularly to Lourdes and Fatima), sympathies for the liturgical movement originating in Benedictine monasteries, and appreciation of the Charismatic Renewal movement then still nascent. He envisions broadening the cultural basis of the Catholic Church by better integrating non-Latin cultures. Episcopal collegiality must be strengthened. This notwithstanding, the Genoa talk also expresses (1) a self-critical view of the Church, (2) an unvarnished, broad, perceptive analysis of relativism and then-reigning ideologies, and (3) a prescient understanding of world affairs. With the benefit of hindsight, one can only confirm the text's prophetic nature. While one is witness to the demise of crude ideologies, their underlying assumptions are as powerful as ever: the hold of technology on man has become far stronger, thereby pervasively diminishing the role of religion in private lives. At the beginning of the twenty-first century, relativism and liberalism seem to rule supreme the world over.

Dei Verbum—the Neo-Scholastic Paradigm Overcome—Christ is Revelation

On November 14, 1962, the Second Vatican Council's general congregation met in St. Peter's Basilica. On the agenda was a prepared schema *De fontibus revelationis* (*On the Sources of Revelation*), related by Cardinal Alfredo Ottaviani (1890–1979), president of the preparatory commission and prefect of the Holy Office.[34] First, the archbishop of the French city of Lille, Cardinal Achille Liénart (1884–1973), criticized it.[35] Cardinal

etwas von ihrer Herzenswärme, von ihrer persönlichen Innigkeit und Ergriffenheit, von ihrer tiefen Bereitschaft zu Buße und Sühne geben, und sie könnte umgekehrt von dort her etwas von der heiligen Nüchternheit und Klarheit, von der Helligkeit und dem strengen Ernst der großen alten Gesetze christlichen Betens und Denkens empfangen, das die allzu beflügelte Phantasie des liebenden Herzens in Grenzen hält und ihr den richtigen Ort anweist."

[34] Significantly for the Council's subsequent course, he was the last representative of the *Ius publicum ecclesiasticum* tradition, which maintained the Church's independent judicial sovereignty vis-à-vis the state (see J. Listl, *Kirche und Staat in der neueren Katholischen Kirchenrechtswissenschaft* [Berlin: Duncker & Humblot, 1978]).

[35] Known in France as "the Red Bishop," he had supported labor unions and labor priests, as well as courageously opposed, as archbishop of Lille (1928–1968), both Nazi occupation and allied aerial bombardments. He had been a member of the Council's prepa-

Frings immediately followed by raising similar objections. This contrasts sharply to the prevailing atmosphere during the First Vatican Council. Ratzinger observed it began *im Fortissimo*.[36]

Frings delivered a forceful *non placet* on account of two factors. The schema's tenor was too professorial for a conciliar document and suffered material deficits. The documents prepared by the Roman curia reflected too much a magisterial positivism that failed to incorporate the fullness of Catholicism: using sources of different dogmatic and magisterial quality uncritically as if they were all equal but ignoring the rich patristic patrimony and especially the Greek Church Fathers.[37] More significantly, nineteenth-century historicism produced the notion of two seemingly static sources for revelation: Scripture and Tradition. Frings lamented that undue emphasis was placed on *how* revelation is transmitted and less on what revelation actually *is*: namely, Jesus Christ, the *Logos*. Rather, one should speak of Scripture and Tradition as *fontes cognoscendi* (sources of insight). Such a view does not reduce God to mere historical or human categories. It would require the labors of three years for the final version on revelation to be approved on November 18, 1965, and it would stress the Christocentric nature of revelation.

What is the background for Frings's unheard of, truly historic intervention, daring to face up to the omnipotent cardinal-prefect of the Holy Office? Frings's famous speech had been prepared by Ratzinger and had been submitted in advance to the Cardinal Secretary of State in September of 1962. There the theologian from Bonn argued that the document should be revised "to make it no longer prejudicial to internal disputes of Catholic theologians."[38] In a speech delivered by Ratzinger to the German-speaking bishops on October 10, 1962, the eve of the solemn inauguration of Vatican II, in the *Anima*, one can see the reasoning behind Frings's arguments. It must have lasted at least an hour.[39]

---

ratory commission (1961–1962) and of the Council's *praesidium* (1962–1965); see G. Alberigo, "Liénart," in *Lexikon für Theologie und Kirche*, 3rd ed., vol. 6 (Freiburg im Breisgau: Herder, 2006), 927.

[36] Joseph Ratzinger, "Kardinal Frings und das II. Vatikanische Konzil," in *Kardinal Frings: Leben und Werk*, ed. D. Froitzheim (Köln: Wienand, 1979), 191–205, at 196.

[37] Joseph Ratzinger, "Buchstabe und Geist des Zweiten Vatikanums in den Konzilsreden von Kardinal Frings," *Communio* 16 (1987): 251–65, at 253–54. What popular opinion perceives as "Progressismus des Kölner Kardinals" is in fact merely an insistence on bringing the Holy Spirit as it works throughout Church history fully to bear on the Council.

[38] Wicks, "Six Texts," 267.

[39] For a brief summary see Trippen, *Frings*, 2:324.

There, in his masterly *tour d'horizon* of dogmatic history, he detects an "astounding narrowing of the concept of revelation" in the Roman curia's schema. Neither Scripture nor Tradition are the source of revelation, but only God is the *unus fons* (one source). Ratzinger attributes this reversal of sequence to historicism, which is a rather late phenomenon in Church history—having as ultimate consequence reducing Scripture to *in illo tempore*, ultimately to subjective human standards. But God and his revelation transcend text and a collection of human customs: God does not reveal sentences about himself, but rather reveals himself. Ratzinger pleads for a dynamic understanding of revelation, rather than a static or intellectualistic one, as implied in manualist neo-Scholasticism with its anti-modernist stance. Such a mindset prevents one from appreciating the true nature of revelation. He reminds his listeners that during the Middle Ages Scripture was considered a *fons scientiae* (source of insight), but never a *fons revelationis* (source of revelation). Revelation is not the outcome or conjunction of Scripture and Tradition as its two *rivuli* (creeks), but rather the condition for the possibility of their coming into being. Temporally, revelation precedes both.[40] Otherwise, he argues, one runs the danger of succumbing to a *sola scriptura* (only Scripture) principle, which he considers scripturalist and positivist. Already, his studies in Munich under the guidance of Gottlieb Söhngen (1892–1971)[41] on St. Bonaventure's understanding of history had acquainted him with the concept of God as the

---

40 He predicates the temporal precedence of Christ vis-à-vis Scripture and Tradition as "ontological" but grants a "gnoseological" reversal of order (Ratzinger, "Buchstabe und Geist," 256).

41 The Cologne priest and Munich professor's influence on Ratzinger in 1947–1958 for fundamental theology and philosophical propaedeutics can hardly be overstated. Söhngen did not publish much. However, he was one of the most original theologians of his time. Going back to the Augustinian tradition, he attempted to widen neo-Scholasticism by embracing history as salvation history and integrating Anselm of Canterbury, Bonaventure, and John Henry Newman. In dialogue with Protestant thinkers Karl Barth and Emil Brunner, he advanced the centrality of natural theology and the concept of *analogia entis* to Catholic faith. In a personalist way, he apprehends Jesus Christ as *the* mystery enlivening all of history and mankind: ergo, all time is Christ-centered. See Gottlieb Söhngen, "Christi Gegenwart in uns durch den Glauben" and "Das Mysterium des lebendigen Christus und der Glaube (ein Beitrag zu einer kategorialen Analysis fidei)," in *Die Einheit der Theologie* (Munich: Zink, 1952), 324–41 and 342–69 (respectively). In a certain way, Ratzinger's theology is but a grand expansion on Söhngen's vision. See also J. Graf, *Die Suche nach der "Einheit der Theologie": Gottlieb Söhngens Beitrag zum Durchbruch des heilsgeschichtlichen Denkens* (Frankfurt am Main: Peter Lang, 1991).

primary actor in the event of revelation.[42] This has him propose a different title for the document on revelation. Rather than *De fontibius revelationis*, he suggests either *De revelatione* or, even better, *De Verbo Dei* as title for this dogmatic constitution. In fact, the Council would adopt the title *Dei Verbum*—very close to what Ratzinger had favored. Of course, he does not intend denigrating divine revelation's propositional content (*fides quae*). For this reason he perceives Scripture and Tradition as being the "material principles of our knowing revelation," but "not revelation itself."[43]

This question had gained topicality in the years prior to the Council. The Catholic Tübingen dogmatic theologian Josef Rupert Geiselmann (1890–1970),[44] had discovered that during the Council of Trent (1545–1548, 1551–1552, and 1562–1563) the question had been left open as to how to relate Scripture and Tradition to one another.[45] While writing his *Habilitationsschrift* on Bonaventure, Ratzinger had heard Geiselmann expound his theory of Scripture being sufficient for revelation ("materielle Vollständigkeit der Schrift")[46] at a conference in Königstein in 1956, prompting his own investigations into this matter.[47] Ratzinger argued that if the title and the content of the draft were left unchanged, then the Council would come out in favor of a *partim–partim* ("partially [and] partially") position, a position claiming that revelation is contained partially in Scripture and partially in Tradition. Ratzinger, however, maintained that Scripture and Tradition are kept constantly anew in a mutually life-giving tension by being involved in the labors of the Holy Spirit *in* temporality. It is upon such a pneumatological background alone that the dogma of 1950

[42] See Joseph Ratzinger, *The Theology of History in St. Bonaventure*, trans. Zachary Hayes, O.F.M. (Chicago: Franciscan Herald, 1971), 57–58, 62–63, 66, and 71.

[43] Wicks, "Six Texts," 272.

[44] As professor for scholastic philosophy and apologetics and later for dogma in Tübingen, Geiselmann contributed to studies on the Tübingen School of Theology's understanding of Tradition (see L. Scheffczyk, "Josef Rupert Geiselmann—Weg und Werk," *Theologische Quartalschrift* 150 [1970]: 385–95).

[45] Josef R. Geiselmann, "Das Konzil von Trient über das Verhältnis der Heiligen Schriften und der nicht geschriebenen Traditionen," in *Die mündliche Überlieferung: Beiträge zum Begriff der Tradition*, ed. Michael Schmaus (Munich: Max Hueber 1957), 123–206. Geiselmann expounds his theory in greater detail in *Die Heilige Schrift und die Tradition* (Freiburg im Breisgau: Herder, 1962). Ratzinger reacts to it in Joseph Ratzinger and Karl Rahner, *Revelation and Tradition*, trans. W. J. O'Hara, *Quaestiones Disputatae* 17 (New York: Herder and Herder, 1966).

[46] In 1987, Ratzinger described such a postion as "unsinnige Tautologie"—i.e., nonsensical tautology ("Buchstabe und Geist," 255).

[47] Ratzinger, *Milestones*, 124–28.

is viable.[48] Backed by such authorities as Tertullian, Bonaventure, and Thomas Aquinas, he showed that a dynamic concept of *paradosis* (Tradition) was elemental to the thoughts of the Church Fathers. Scripture and Tradition are co-constitutive elements in the one Spirit-filled Church, and only so are both true to themselves.[49] Furthermore, such understanding of revelation does justice to the pluriformity of the historic forms Catholic faith can take on. This has the theologian from Bonn conclude:

> Scripture, Tradition, and the Church's Magisterium are not static entities placed beside each other, but have to be seen as one living organism of the Word of God, which from Christ lives on in the Church.[50]

Not perceiving revelation thus entails subscribing to something akin to Greek mysticism—à la Philo and Augustine—where the human object is simply overpowered by divine action. But inspiration is historical, not

---

[48] "From its perspective, the concept of 'tradition' had itself become questionable," Ratzinger explains in 1997, "since this method will not allow for an oral tradition running alongside Scripture and reaching back to the apostles—and hence offering another source of historical knowledge besides the Bible. This impasse is indeed what had made the dispute on the dogma of Mary's bodily assumption into heaven so difficult and insoluble" (Ratzinger, *Milestones*, 124). For this reason, his dissertation director, Söhngen, had opposed the dogma of Our Lady's Assumption prior to its solemn proclamation in 1950; he then accepted it immediately thereafter, but without being able to provide the dogmatic rationale for it. This historical context provides the background for his student's remark some years thereafter in an article. The collaboration of the personal and ecclesial dimensions of the one faith in giving it greater verbalization is further elaborated when its cooperation with the Petrine ministry is described: "Damit dürfte das Zusammenspiel der . . . drei ursächlichen Kräfte von Neudogmatisierungen (fides veritas—periculi necessitas—ecclesiae auctoritas) deutlich geworden sein: Die vorgegebene Glaubenswahrheit ist als innerlich ermöglichende Ursache tätig, die häretische Gefahr als äußerlich bewegende, die im Papst konzentrierte kirchliche Autorität aber ist das eigentlich aktive Prinzip" (Joseph Ratzinger, "Offenbarung—Schrift—Überlieferung: Ein Text des heiligen Bonaventura und seine Bedeutung für die gegenwärtige Theologie," *Trierer Theologische Zeitschrift* 67 [1958]: 13–27 at 17 [this article is the portion of his *Habilitationsschrift* published separately]). The vivacity of revelation is described as possessing both an exterior, objective moment and an interior, actual moment. Thus, revelation can never be completely objectified in Scripture (ibid., 26–27). For an analysis of Ratzinger's understanding of revelation, see R. Voderholzer, "Offenbarung, Schrift und Kirche: eine relecture von 'Dei Verbum' im Licht vorbereitender und rezipierender Texte Joseph Ratzingers," *Internationale katholische Zeitschrift Communio* 39 (2010): 287–303.

[49] Wicks, "Six Texts," 275.

[50] Wicks, "Six Texts," 277.

denying free human nature collaborating in the divine-human milieu. Consonant with this view, he rather emphatically insists Christianity is not a religion of the book. In the *Itinerarium mentis ad Deum*, Bonaventure—the subject of Ratzinger's *Habilitationsschrift*—demonstrated that every age and every human being is capable of encountering the living Christ. Ergo, it is not exaggerated to state that Ratzinger advocates something analogous to Johann Adam Möhler's (1796–1838) notion of the Church as the ongoing Incarnation: while revelation is complete in Jesus Christ, it awaits ever again both a personal and an ecclesial appropriation in the sense of becoming present again and again.[51] Reminding one indirectly of St. Augustine's personal conversion experience—*tolle, lege* ("take and read")—he writes:

> The Bible differs from the holy books of Hinduism, Buddhism, or Islam, precisely in this[:] that these are taken to be timeless divine dictation, whereas the Bible is the result of God's historical dialogue with human beings and only from this history does it have meaning and significance.[52]

Falling back to a static understanding would be all the more infelicitous because one is now able to formulate "the authentic biblical character" of revelation.[53] In addition, an understanding of revelation as arising solely from Scripture is too great a burden for Scripture, as it sometimes errs in matters of history. Ratzinger points out Mark referring to the High Priest Abiathar (Mark 2:26) when meaning actually his father Achimelech. Matthew and Luke correct this error in their Gospels. In his intervention on November 14, 1962, Frings would echo this caution against up-

---

[51] "Wenn im Neuen Testament de facto nun doch auch Schrift gewachsen ist, so kann sie nicht mehr jenen abschließenden und ausschließenden Sinn haben, der ihr nach paulinischer Auffassung im Alten Testament zukam, sondern sie ist eher das Werkzeug der Eröffnung des Alten in den offenen Raum des Christusgeschehens hinein. Sie ist gleichsam der stehengebliebene Vorgang der neuen Auslegung der Schrift von Christus her" (Karl Rahner and J. Ratzinger, *Offenbarung und Überlieferung*, Quaestiones Disputatae 25 [Freiburg im Breisgau: Herder, 1965], 38).

[52] Wicks, "Six Texts," 278–79. This dimension is elaborated thus: "Damit dürfte das Zusammenspiel der . . . drei ursächlichen Kräfte von Neudogmatisierungen (*fides veritas—periculi necessitas—ecclesiae auctoritas*) deutlich geworden sein: Die vorgegebene Glaubenswahrheit ist als innerlich ermöglichende Ursache tätig, die häretische Gefahr als äußerlich bewegende, die im Papst konzentrierte kirchliche Autorität aber ist das eigentlich aktive Prinzip" (Ratzinger, "Offenbarung—Schrift—Überlieferung," 17).

[53] Wicks, "Six Texts," 278–79.

holding biblical inerrancy in matters historical.[54] There Ratzinger warns against delving into details concerning the historical truth of Jesus, such as treating the "infancy narrative, resurrection from the dead, and ascension beside each other on the same level." The task of a council is distinct from that of a textbook.[55] No one subscribes to verbal inspiration, and the "ghost of modernism" should not allow one to blunder. While not simply inventing at random, the evangelists and eyewitnesses were overpowered by the effulgence of divine presence. It was not their claim to hand it down *verbatim*: "Instead they transmitted them in the power of the Holy Spirit as words of a living person—of the Christ of today by the process we call tradition." Echoing again Augustine, he argues that the Old Testament is not simply relating in vague terms a Christological message, but requires on the believer's part the personal existential effort to pass the text "through a Christological transformation," seeing therein contained "the *ecclesia ab Abel* (the Church from Abel)."[56] The believer's heart knows that Christ made himself known in the one history of salvation, the history of Israel and the Church. Ratzinger reminds the assembled bishops and theologians of Augustine's comprehensive understanding of salvation.[57] Eusebius of Caesarea related how Emperor Constantine convened the Council of Nicaea (AD 325) as a *militia Christi* for the Council Fathers to "fight together against the powers of darkness," not so much against heretics. With such a patristic perspective, Ratzinger urges that the Council should rise above "settling internal theological issues" and give "a common witness of faith against the unbelief of the world."[58]

Revelation has a "Thou" as its subject—Jesus Christ—and revelation occurs through his body, which is also the Church.[59] This is kept alive in

---

[54] *Acta Synodalia Sacrosancti Concilii Oecumenici Vaticani II* [henceforth, *Acta Synodalia*] (Vatican City: Typis Polyglottis Vaticanis, 1970–1980), 1/3:36.

[55] Wicks, "Six Texts," 281.

[56] Wicks, "Six Texts," 283.

[57] Augustine, Epistola 102 (*Patrologia Latina* [PL], 33:374).

[58] Wicks, "Six Texts," 284. In a personal letter addressed to Cardinal Ottaviani and dated February 15, 1963, Cardinal Frings attempts to communicate the theological "state of art" as regards revelation. See Nachlass Josef Kardinal Frings's *Historisches Archiv des Erzbistums Köln*— [henceforth, NF], 141. There one finds also Ratzinger's draft with his personal remarks. The delay was caused by Frings having undergone eye surgery in Vienna (Trippen, *Frings*, 2:353–55).

[59] "Denn wenn dann weiterhin gilt, dass das Lebendige, die Offenbarung selbst, Christus ist und dass Christus noch immer lebt, nicht nur *in illo tempore* gelebt hat, dann ist klar, dass das Subjekt der Offenbarung eben dieser Christus selber ist und dass er es durch seinen Leib ist, mit dem er uns unverrückbar an jenen Anfang *in illo tempore* bindet und zugleich bis zu seinem ‚Vollalter' hin weiterführt. Dann müssen also andere Methoden

the new draft, which represents a merger of Ratzinger's and Karl Rahner's (1904–1984) thoughts, now titled *De revelatione Dei et hominis in Iesu Christo facta* (*The Revelation of God and Man in Jesus Christ*).[60] The phrase *vivum Dei Verbum quaerens nos* ("God's living Word seeking us out") is certainly indebted to Ratzinger. It is Christ taking the initiative in revealing both God to mankind and mankind to itself. This will find eloquent expression both in *Dei Verbum* 2 and in *Gaudium et spes* 22.

Reminiscent of Bonaventure, chapter III gives Jesus Christ the role of the *one* Truth revealing all truths. Church and Scripture are perceived as mutually dependent realities. Israel's and the Church's faith inform Scripture, but the Church in turn submits to Scripture, as it is the *ancilla verbi*, the handmaid of the Word. Through Christ abiding Eucharistically in the Church, the living ambience of the Church in turn becomes *the* interpretament for Scripture, as Christ is the *clavis Scripturarum*, *the* key for accessing the Sacred Texts par excellence.[61]

As council *peritus*, Ratzinger assisted the doctrinal commission in the spring of 1964 in revising what would evolve into *Dei Verbum* 21–26, chapter VI, which promotes Sacred Scripture in the life of the Church.[62] The final text of the constitution no longer speaks of statements of faith and sources of revelation. Rather, it presents what revelation is: "It pleased God, in his goodness and wisdom, to reveal himself and to make known the mystery of his will (cf. Eph 1:9)" (DV 2). Accordingly, a definition of faith follows as man freely committing his entire life to God (DV 5).

The vivacity of Christian faith is based on God's divine initiative to communicate himself. This is now the overriding concern of the Council

---

mit in die Auslegung eintreten, und vor allem gehört dann der Lebenszusammenhang und der Erfahrungszusammenhang mit hinzu, in dem die Schrift Schrift, und mehr als Schrift ist. Dann sind die Spekulationen um die materielle Vollständigkeit von selbst gegenstandlos, weil ein anderes Formalprinzip waltet. Die Offenbarungskonstitution hat genau diese Sicht formuliert aber ihre Botschaft ist bis zur Stunde ungehört geblieben" (Ratzinger, "Buchstabe und Geist," 257).

[60] For an overall description of the collaboration between Ratzinger and Karl Rahner during the Council and their later respective interpretations of this event, see Santiago Madrigal, S.J., *Karl Rahner y Joseph Ratzinger: Tras las huellas del Concilio* (Santander, ES: Sal Terrae, 2006).

[61] The Latin text with a parallel English translation is found under its heading in B. Cahill, "The Renewal of Revelation Theology (1960–1962): The Development and Responses to the Fourth Chapter of the Preparatory Schema De depositione Fidei," in *Tesi Gregoriana*, Serie Teologia *51* (Rome: Gregorian University Press, 1999), 300–17.

[62] Jared Wicks, S.J., *Professor Ratzinger at Vatican II: A Chapter in the Life of Pope Benedict* (New Orleans, LA: Loyola University, 2007), 13.

Fathers. Indeed, *Dei Verbum* 1 emphasizes God's initiative in revealing himself, and *Dei Verbum* 2 stresses Christ as the "mediator and sum total of revelation." *Dei Verbum* 11 refrains from suggesting divine dictation or describing how texts become inspired but, rather, mentions God calling and aiding biblical authors in composing Scripture. Nevertheless, the former *peritus* notes, as prefect in 1987, that the postconciliar era is almost completely unaware of this revolutionary presentation of revelation. Indeed, the era is wholly owned by a biblicism of sorts and can no longer see any value in Tradition and dogma—thus the contemporary crisis of faith to no small part.[63]

Lumen Gentium—the Identity of Church and the Eucharistic Lord

Within the horizon established by *Dei Verbum*, *Lumen gentium* thematizes the nature of the Church. Already in the preparatory phase, on May 8 and 9, 1962, the schema on the Church under the heading *De Ecclesiae Militantis eiusdemque necessitate ad salutem* was discussed by the central commission.[64] Frings had given Ratzinger all the fascicles for review. At first, Ratzinger supplied his observations in small handwriting on the borders. Thereupon, either Frings or his secretary, Luthe, had requested Ratzinger to compose a comprehensive text that would be better understood by the nearly blind Frings and Teusch. This was presented in June.

The schema had been composed in the spirit of Roman, curial theology. Immediately, the beginning of chapter I, *De Ecclesiae Militantis natura*, provoked Frings to vote *placet iuxta modum*, adding: "The term *militantis ecclesia* seems little suitable—perhaps 'the Church on the way' or 'the on earth journeying Church' would be better." Here one detects the first use of a concept that will mature to the notion of "the people of God on pilgrimage."[65]

In the same vein, he registered his *non placet* for chapter III, *De membris Ecclesiae eiusdemque necessitate ad salutem*, as the topic had not been sufficiently discussed with Cardinals Bea, König, and Döpfner. In addition, one ought not establish in the outset who the actual members of the

---

63 Thus in Ratzinger, "Buchstabe und Geist," 256.

64 *Acta et Documenta Concilio Oecumenico Vaticano II Apparando*, ser. 2 (Praeparatoria [henceforth, *Acta et Documenta* II]), vol. 2/3 (Vatican City: Typis Polyglottis Vaticanis, 1964–1969 and 1994), 986ff.

65 *Acta et Documenta* II, 2/3:986–90 (text) and 1026 (Frings's vote). See also *De Ecclesiae Militantis Maturae*, in NF, 73.

Church are. Also, nothing was being said regarding the "Christian dignity" of those communities separated from the Church yet holding fast to the sacraments, which are predicated as Church in diverse previous ecclesial documents.[66]

Concerning chapter IV, *De episcopis residentialibus*, Frings admonishes his fellow bishops to be mindful that the images of "body" and "head" are reserved for the Church and Christ. Never throughout Church history are they applied to the college of bishops or the popes. In fact, it would be silly to speak of a body within a body. Moreover, this may give rise to confusion as to who is actually the head, Christ or the pope. In the sentence beginning "potestas tamen huius corporis," he also suggested changes. The delimiting phrase "exclusively on the initiative of the head" does not do justice to the weighty role of the college of bishops. This college exercises its role not only in an extraordinary but also in an ordinary manner.

For this reason he suggested that the modified text should incorporate this significant nuance and read:

> The unanimous teaching and proclamation of this college is an ordinary path to explain Christ's truth in the Church and to preserve it; the extraordinary path to exercise this authority is the ecumenical council, which can be convened only by the pope and which requires his confirmation in order to be valid.[67]

On June 19, 1962, Ottaviani presented two chapters of the schema on the Church: *De Ecclesiae Magisterio* (on the teaching office) and *De auctoritate et oboedientiae in Ecclesia* (on authority and obedience in the Church). Ratzinger suggested to Frings that one should add to the section on the teaching office a brief explanation delineating "the moral boundaries of the primacy of jurisdiction." This he considered called for, as many non-Catholics believe the pope to be viewed by Catholics as competent to act arbitrarily. He refers to Rahner mentioning the hypothetical, but nevertheless canonically permissible, possibility, of the Pontiff forcing Uniat Catholics to adopt the Latin rite. Frings's decision will go yet further by

---

[66] NF, 73. See also *Acta et Documenta* II, 2/3:990–993 (text) and 1026–27 (Frings's vote).

[67] "Die einmütige Lehre und Verkündigung dieses Kollegiums ist ein ordentlicher Weg, die Wahrheit Christi in der Kirche zu erklären und zu bewahren; der außerordentliche Weg, diese Vollmacht auszuüben, ist das Ökumenische Konzil, das nur durch den Papst einberufen werden kann und seiner Bestätigung bedarf, um gültig zu sein" (*De Episcopis Residentialibus*, in NF, 73; see also *Acta et Documenta* II, 2/3:1039–49 [Frings's *animadversio* on 1048–49]; and Trippen, *Frings*, 2:284).

voting *non placet.* He questioned whether it was the Council's task to collect papal constitutions, encyclicals, and addresses "in a barn" (i.e., in the fashion of a catalogue) and argued that "our theologians are much too introverted, preoccupied with the idea Church, her nature, her teaching office and the obedience due her." Rather, they should discuss God, his greatness and goodness, and Jesus Christ, our redeemer. Only briefly should one provide a definition of the Church, the relationship of bishops among each other, their college, and the pope. Chapter VIII, concerning the Church's authority and obedience, required "public denunciations of evils in the Church" receiving guidance from Matthew 18:15–17. In this context, Ratzinger suggested also adding "protection of the individual against anonymous accusations," which had previously been neglected. Rather than being negative and defensive, the text should encourage Christian initiatives arising from a genuine sense of responsibility for Catholic faith. Alluding to fellow *peritus* Rahner, he reminded Frings that "the Church" does not mean belonging to a group of totalitarian states exerting exterior force, imposing "mortal silence," and devaluing "freedom and charity." On the contrary, "a call to freedom and charity, within the bounds of obedience and service," should not "be totally missing in the document" because, he reminds them, freedom and charity come to flourish precisely in this ecclesial context of obedience and service.[68] These two proposals Frings would argue on June 19, 1962, in his speech at the central commission:

> This is also the place to raise one's voice according to Mt 18:15–17 against anonymous denunciations of individual Christians. . . . Also, something needs to be said about fostering Christian initiatives amongst the faithful, because not only fear may not reign, but rather the freedom of the children of God, charity and magnanimity."[69]

---

[68] "Die Kirche gehört ja (um Karl Rahner zu zitieren) nicht zu jenen 'totalen Staaten, bei denen die äußere Macht und ein in tödlichem Schweigen geschehener Gehorsam alles, und Freiheit und Liebe nichts ist'; so sollte ein Anruf an Freiheit und Liebe, die mitten im Raum des Gehorsams und des Dienens, ja gerade dort leben können, in einem solchen Dokument nicht gänzlich fehlen" (Ratzinger's typed comments to *De Ecclesiae Magisterio: De Auctoritate et Oboedientiae in Ecclesia*, in NF, 97; see also *Acta et Documenta* II, 2/4:621–35 [drafts]).

[69] "Hier scheint auch der Ort zu sein, gemäß Mt 18,15–17 ein Wort gegen anonyme Denunziationen einzelner Christen zu sagen. . . . Auch werde ein Wort gesagt über die Pflege christlicher Initiative bei den Gläubigen, weil in der Kirche nicht nur die Furcht herrschen darf, sondern die Freiheit der Kinder Gottes, Liebe und Großmut" (Frings's speech in *Acta et Documenta* II, 2/4:638–39; see also Trippen, *Frings*, 2:292).

This is a good case illustrating the fruitful collaboration between Frings and Ratzinger. It also demonstrates how Christian responsibility and freedom differ fundamentally from a well-intentioned but naïve emancipatory pathos capturing the imagination of the generation of 1968.

When rejecting the schema *De Ecclesia* on December 4,1962, Frings would remind his fellow Council Fathers to integrate not only the last few centuries of Western Catholic theology into the conciliar documents but also both the Greek and older Latin traditions. This objection does not tangate merely the surface. Rather, Frings faults the schema's juridical-sociological language. In addition, reflecting the broad *Ressourcement* vision of his advisor Ratzinger, he finds not a trace of Greek Eucharistic ecclesiology in the schema—so precious to the Oriental brethren. Further, he asks why the teaching office is treated separately from the chapter on the bishops. Are not the *doctores et magistri* bishops instituted by and in union with the Holy Father, and is not the Holy Father himself a bishop? He also critiques the text for not mentioning the Word of God, which—together with the sacraments, as two pillars—supports the whole Church edifice. While the chapter dwells on the Church's duty to proclaim the Gospel, it fails to mention the mission of the Son of God to humankind, issuing forth from the Father and continuing through the Church and her ministry. The fact that the Church has "the right to preach to all peoples" does not make the Gospel more acceptable to these peoples. He misses the breadth, depth, and universality—and therefore the Catholicity—that are the outstanding features of ecumenical councils. A comparison between Ratzinger's handwritten comments on the schema and Frings's speech in front of the bishops assembled in St. Peter's reveals their material identity.[70]

On September 13, 1963, during the second session, Ratzinger (in all probability) would report to Luthe that patristic thought now dominates in *De Ecclesia* while sources from the Middle Ages and modernity are well represented.[71] Accordingly, Frings's speech to the bishops lauds the new text. Nevertheless, toward the end, he faults it for emphasizing papal infallibility too much while discussing episcopal responsibilities in matters of the teaching office too little.[72] On September 29 of the same year, Frings developed a spiritual understanding of collegiality, rooted in the sacra-

---

70 See NF, 125, for Ratzinger's handwritten text; and *Acta Synodalia*, 2/4:218–20, for Frings's actual speech (*textus scripto traditus*). See also Trippen, *Frings*, 2:339–40.

71 NF, 179.

72 NF, 178. *Acta Synodalia*, 2/1:343–46.

mentality of the Church as *Ursakrament* (primordial sacrament).[73] Christ is the dynamic reality collecting all of humankind for his Second Coming. Christ's Passion and poverty find their parallels in the Church's poverty and relationship to the poor.[74]

Shortly thereafter, on November 8, 1963, Frings would cause a historic, upsetting sensation in an address to the aula by fustigating the Roman curia for carrying over outdated ways of governance from the days of the Inquisition. He insisted that persons accused of doctrinal error be presumed innocent unless proven otherwise. This produced *plausus in aula* (applause among the bishops assembled in the aula of St. Peter). Frings would add seven sharper lines to the intervention drafted by Ratzinger, but not without consulting with the respected Munich canonist Klaus Mörsdorf (1909–1989).[75] In spite of Ottaviani's negative public reaction, Paul VI requested on the evening of that very day that Frings submit a memorandum on a possible reform of the curia, which he did with the aid of Wilhelm Onclin, a canonist from Louvain.

Along with Rahner, J. Salaverri, S.J., and M. Maccarone, Ratzinger also served between November 1963 and early 1964 as council *peritus* assisting the doctrinal commission revising the text on episcopal collegiality, which would become *Lumen gentium* 21–23, affirming the college of bishops participating with the pope as their head in governing the Church together as successors to the college of the Apostles.[76] This notwithstanding, on November 13, 1963, Frings made an impassioned but, as later history will show, also prescient appeal: "Venerable Fathers, preserve in the national (bishops') conferences the individual's freedom and the charity of all. So that the letter may not kill, but the Spirit may vivify."[77]

It had been a concern for Ratzinger to balance an ecclesiology based on the Augustinian notion of people of God with a lasting Eucharistic

---

[73] This term was coined by fellow *peritus* Otto Semmelroth prior to the Council in *Church and Sacrament* (Notre Dame, IN: Fides, 1965 [German original in 1953]).

[74] *Acta Synodalia*, 2/1:343–46 and 2/2:493ff, respectively.

[75] Wicks, "Six Texts," 121. See also: NF, 181; *Acta Synodalia*, 2/4:616–18; Trippen, *Frings*, 2:383–85.

[76] See: G. Wassilowsky, *Universales Heilssakrament Kirche: Karl Rahners Beitrag zur Ekklesiologie des II. Vatikanums* (Innsbruck-Wien: Tyrolia, 2001), 243–45; P. Martuccelli, "Episcopato e Primato nel Pensiero di Joseph Ratzinger," *Rassegna di Teologia* 48 (2007): 501–48; Martuccelli, "Forme concrete di Collegialità Episcopale nel pensiero di Joseph Ratzinger," *Rassegna di Teologia* 50 (2009): 7–24; Martuccelli, "Forme di Collegialità Episcopale nel pensiero di Joseph Ratzinger, Concilio, Sinodo dei vescovi, Conferenze episcopali," *Rassegna di Teologia* 50 (2009): 377–401.

[77] *Acta Synodalia*, 2/5: 66.

structure as the *conditio sine qua non* for the Church to exist at all. In contrast, Robert Bellarmine, S.J. (1542–1621), had famously emphasized the Church's institutional visibility ("the Church is as visible as the republic of Venice"). Now, the Last Supper is perceived as the foundation of the Church. It is Christ celebrating his Pasch who is the center forming the unity and identity of the new people of God. This becomes apparent in the Cross, when Jesus proves himself the new and true Paschal lamb. The ecclesial community no longer comes about via the Temple in Jerusalem or by commemorating the exodus, but by Christ present in the Eucharist enabling the unity of the world Church, the parish community, and any Christian liturgical gathering.[78] In a dictionary entry prior to the Council, Ratzinger wrote concerning these three moments of being Church:

> These [three constitutive elements] transition into one another in such a manner, that the respective local community is a concrete representation of the total reality ekklesía, and the cultic gathering again is perceived as the concrete realization of being parish. So as Israel executed its unity through the Temple and every year in the Pasch feast in and around the Temple, so the locally dispersed communities of Christian believers became one from the new Temple, from the Lord's body. . . . They are one as ekklesía, i.e. as God's cultic gathering, by eating the one bread, that makes them one body (1 Cor 10:17); they no longer need the local connecting link of the common Temple and the bond of the common blood, because they possess the deeper unity of the new bread, through which the Lord unites them amongst themselves and with Him in the cultic celebration."[79]

---

[78] See P. A. Franco, "The Communion Ecclesiology of Joseph Ratzinger: Implications for the Church of the Future," in *Vatican II Forty Years Later*, ed. W. Madges (Maryknoll, NY: Orbis, 2006), 3–25.

[79] ". . . gehen in der Weise ineinander über, daß die jeweilige Ortsgemeinde als konkrete Darstellung der einen Gesamtgröße ekklesía erscheint und daß wiederum die Kultversammlung als die konkrete Realisierung des Gemeindeseins aufgefaßt wird. So wie Israel eins geworden war durch den Tempel und jedes Jahr in der Passah-Feier im und um den Tempel seine Einheit vollzog, so wurden die örtlich verstreuten Gemeinden der Christusgläubigen eins vom neuen Tempel, vom Herrnleib . . . her: Sie sind eins als ekklesía, d.h. als Kultversammlung Gottes, in der sie das eine Brot essen, das sie zu einemLeib macht (1 Kor 10,17); sie brauchen das lokale Bindemittel des gemeinsamen Tempels und das Band des gemeinsamen Blutes nicht mehr, weil sie die tiefere Einheit des einen Brotes haben, durch das in der Kultversammlung der Herr sie untereinander und mit sich selbst vereint" (Joseph Ratzinger, "Kirche III," in *Lexikon für*

This understanding of the Lord's Last Supper as the origin and purpose of the Church is most foundational to understanding the systematic substratum of Ratzinger's theology. The identity as congruency of Church and liturgical gathering is plausible for him only if it is related to the Son of God.[80] Consonant with this perspective, *Lumen gentium* 2 states that God "chose to raise up men to share in his own divine life . . . [through] Christ, the redeemer, 'who is the image of the invisible God,'" and *Lumen gentium* 9 adds that "Christ instituted . . . the new covenant . . . in his blood . . . he called a race . . . not from flesh but from water and the Holy Spirit (cf. Jn 3:5–6) . . . the People of God' (1 Pet 2:9–10)."[81]

Mary—The Church at Her Origin

A much debated issue had been whether to issue a separate document on Our Lady or to integrate the figure of Mary into the Dogmatic Constitution on the Church. In the summer of 1962, the schema of Ottaviani's commission on faith offered a conventional approach: a separate treatment of Mary with the title *De Beata Maria Virgine Matre Dei et Matre hominum* (*On the Blessed Virgin Mary, Mother of God and of humankind*).[82] As both Frings[83] and Ratzinger were known for their joyful Marian piety, it is worth pondering whether they agreed on the schema. This can never be fully answered, as Frings did not vote on this issue; his ballot lies unused in his personal files. However, Ratzinger's position is well known. In his typed advice to Frings, one reads:

> I believe, for the sake of the Council's goal one should desist from this Marian schema. If the Council should be in its total effect a *suave incitamentum* [a gentle incentive] to the separated brethren *quaerendam unitatem* [seeking unity], then it must also take into account to a degree a pastoral consideration and let it be guided

Theologie und Kirche, 2nd ed., vol. 6 [Freiburg im Breisgau: Herder, 1961], 174–83, at 175–76).

80 This view would resonate in numerous subsequent writings, such as Ratzinger's *Principles of Catholic Theology: Building Stones for a Fundamental Theology*, trans. Sr. Mary Frances McCarthy, S.N.D. (San Francisco: Ignatius Press, 1987), 27–55; and *The Spirit of the Liturgy*, trans. John Saward (San Francisco: Ignatius Press, 2000).

81 Second Vatican Council, Dogmatic Constitution on the Church *Lumen Gentium* (November 21, 1964), available from http://www.vatican.va (hereafter cited in text as LG).

82 *Acta et Documenta*, 2/4:746–72.

83 Trippen, *Frings*, 1:469–87.

> by *caritas* [charity] in the selection of the to be declared *veritates* [truths].[84]

Further on in the same text, Ratzinger suggests adding a simple prayer addressed to the Mother of God for Christian unity at the conclusion of the document on the Church, formulated in the robust language of Tradition and desisting "from using undogmatized terms such as *mediatrix*."[85] This position would prevail during the Council, and *Lumen gentium* has, indeed, a lengthy section devoted to Our Lady as the formative center of ecclesial existence (LG 55–69).

It should be noted, however, that the German cardinals Frings and Döpfner, archbishops Jaeger and Schäufele, and bishops Höffner and Volk jointly undertook an intervention in material agreement with Ratzinger's position addressed directly to Pope Paul VI, who had let it be known on November 19, 1965, that he would declare—contrary to the will of the majority of the Council Fathers—Our Lady *Mater Ecclesiae* on November 21, 1965:

> We also welcome Mary being designated *Mater fidelium*, as in the schema *De ecclesia*. We also wish for the title *Maria, Mater Ecclesiae*. Yet it is not in every nuance comprehensible. Obviously for this reason the theological commission could not decide to accommodate the wishes expressed in the *modi*, to propose *Maria, Mater Ecclesiae* as a conciliar text, . . . [but] rather to designate Mary as *Matrem Christi et matrem hominum, maxime fidelium*. . . . If *Maria, Matrem Ecclesiae* is understood at *Mater fidelium*, then this is biblically well founded; for as Abraham is described as

[84] Trippen, *Frings*, 1:481.

[85] "Ich glaube, man sollte um des Ziels des Konzils willen auf dieses marianische Schema verzichten. Wenn schon das Konzil in seiner Gesamtwirkung ein *suave incitamentum* an die getrennten Brüder *ad quaerendam unitatem* sein soll, dann muss es auch ein gewisses Maß an seelsorglicher Rücksicht nehmen und sich bei der Auswahl der zu deklarierenden *veritates* von der *caritas* leiten lassen. . . . Den Katholiken wird kein neuer Reichtum gegeben, den sie nicht schon hätten (der Anhang betont dies eigens!), den Außenstehenden (besonders den Orthodoxen) wird ein neues Hindernis gesetzt, zurückzufinden. Das Konzil würde mit der Verabschiedung eines solchen Schemas seine ganze Wirkung gefährden. Ich würde vorschlagen, man möge unter völligem Verzicht auf ein doktrinelles *caput* (dieses Opfer müssen die Romanen einfach bringen) ein schlichtes Gebet an die Gottesmutter um die Einheit an den Schluß der Ekklesiologie setzen und dieses Gebet ganz aus der kraftvollen Sprache der Tradition formen, die doch voller Reichtümer ist und dabei ganz auf undogmatisierte Termini wie *mediatrix* u. dgl. zu verzichten . . ." (NF, 96).

Pater omnium credentium at the beginning of the Old Covenant (Rom 4:11), Mary stands at the beginning of the New Covenant: "Blessed are you because you believed" (Luke 1:45; author's translation). In this sense *Maria, Mater Ecclesiae* is well grounded and an enrichment for both ecclesiology and Mariology and a new incentive for the piety of the faithful.

If, however, the title *Maria, Mater Ecclesiae* is understood as [predicating] the institution Church, then it would be difficult to justify this. Because in the *ordo salutis maternitas* and *paternitas* correspond, whereby *paternitas* in the order of nature precedes *maternitas*. Mary would not be Our Mother, were not first God Our Father; Mary would not be *Regina*, if Christ not *Rex*; she would not be *Domina*, if Christ were not *Dominus*.

Now, as far as can be surveyed, nobody calls the heavenly Father, Christ or the Holy Spirit *Pater Ecclesiae*. This also seems rather impossible for the following reason: the graces of office, which the Church as *Institutio* constitute [*sic*], contain *per se* not the *gratia filiationis*. This is always given with the *gratia sanctificans*, but not with the office as such. For this reason one cannot easily perceive of Mary as the *Mater Ecclesiae* in the sense of the institution.

Therefore we *humillime* request to combine the title *Maria, Mater Ecclesiae* with the title *Mater fidelium* and to interpret it in this sense.[86]

---

[86] "Wir begrüßen es auch sehr, wenn Maria als *Mater fidelium* bezeichnet wird wie im Schema De Ecclesia. Der Titel *Maria, Mater Ecclesiae* ist uns auch erwünscht. Jedoch ist er nicht in jedem Sinne verständlich. Darum hat sich die theologische Kommission offenbar nicht entschließen können, den in den Modi geäußerten Wünschen zu entsprechen, *Maria, Mater Ecclesiae* als konziliaren Text vorzuschlagen, . . . vielmehr Maria als *Mater Christi et matrem hominum, maxime fidelium* zu bezeichnen. . . . Wenn *Maria, Mater Ecclesiae* verstanden wird als *Mater fidelium*, dann ist dies biblisch gut begründet; denn wie Abraham am Anfang des Alten Bundes stehend als *Pater omnium credentium* bezeichnet wird (Röm 4,11), so steht Maria glaubend am Anfang des Neuen Bundes: 'Selig bist Du, weil Du geglaubt hast' (Luk 1,44). In diesem Sinne ist *Maria, Mater Ecclesiae* bestens begründet und eine Bereicherung der Ekklesiologie wie der Mariologie und ein neuer Ansporn für die Frömmigkeit der Gläubigen.Der Titel *Maria, Mater Ecclesiae* könnte aber auch von der Kirche als Institution verstanden werden, und so ist er schwer zu begründen. Denn im *ordo salutis* korrespondieren *maternitas* und *paternitas*, wobei die *paternitas*, der Natur nach früher ist als die *maternitas*. Maria wäre nicht *Regina*, wenn Christus nicht *Rex*, sie wäre nicht *Domina*, wenn Christus nicht *Dominus* wäre.

"Nun nennt aber, so weit zu sehen ist, niemand den himmlischen Vater, Christus oder den Heiligen Geist *Pater Ecclesiae*. Das scheint auch nicht gut möglich zu sein

This memorandum deserves our special attention, as the carefully and stringently argued text suggests Ratzinger as its sole author. It is part of the history of this Council that it did not prevail.

Ad Gentes—Mission as the Whole Church's Participation in the Inner-Trinitarian Missions

The third period of the Council in 1963 sees Ratzinger collaborating with one of the theological luminaries of the twentieth century to supply the doctrinal basis for missionary work. Yves Congar, O.P. (1904–1995), would famously observe in his memoirs: "Heureusement qu'il y a Ratzinger. Il est raisonnable, modeste, désintéressé, d'un bon secours" ("Fortunately there is Ratzinger. He is reasonable, modest, disinterested, a good help").[87] Together, they would convince the Council that mission is not something limited to distant territories under the jurisdiction of the *Propaganda Fide*, but an essential and indispensable feature for the Church to be at all Church—from the times of the Apostles onward. Mission is an inalienable *proprium* of the Church.

On November 7, 1964, Frings spoke as first Council Father in reaction to propositions for a document including aspects of missionary work. He suggests "ein eigenes und umfassendes Schema" ("a separate and comprehensive schema") on mission as it is of constitutive relevance to the whole of the Church and criticizes the previous draft as too superficial. Also, he considers the term mission "as evangelization shining forth in its original splendor" when the *Sanctissimum et Dulcissimum Nomen Jesu* (the most holy and sweetest name of Jesus) is proclaimed in areas not yet Christianized, citing Paul: "Woe to me if I do not preach the gospel" (1 Cor 9:16). Finally, he supports the proposal to have the Pope organize a comprehensive mission strategy and institute a *consilium generale* to launch such a project. He also supports an initiative to have all dioceses donate money regularly for the missions.[88]

---

aus folgenden Grunde: Die Amtsgnaden, welche die Kirche als *Institutio* konstituieren, enthalten *per se* nicht die *gratia filiationis*. Diese ist mit der *gratia sanctificans* immer gegeben, aber nicht mit dem Amt als solchem. Darum ist Maria nicht leicht als *Mater Ecclesiae* in dem Sinne der Institution zu verstehen.

"Darum bitten wir *humillime*, den Titel *Maria, Mater Ecclesiae* mit dem Titel *Mater fidelium* zu verbinden und in diesem Sinne zu interpretieren" (NF, 281; Trippen, *Frings*, 2:447–48).

[87] Yves Congar, O.P., *Mon Journal du Concile*, vol. 2 (Paris: Cerf, 2002), 355–56.

[88] See NF, 245; *Acta Synodalia*, 3/6:374–76; Trippen, *Frings*, 2:437–38.

Soon thereafter, in January of 1965, Ratzinger drafted a longer Latin text, lost in the 1960s and rediscovered in the 1980s in the personal archive of Congar, illustrating the motivation for missionary activity to lie in the inner-Trinitarian outpouring of God's charity, expressed in the two missions of the Son and the Holy Spirit:

> One has to look above all to the Christology of the Gospel of St. John, in which *missus* (the one who is sent) is almost a title of Christ. . . . For this reason this Christological foundation is as well and inseparably a Trinitarian foundation. . . . As it is living from Christ, the Church is also necessarily *missa* (sent) and *missio* (mission).[89]

Thus, missionary zeal has nothing at all to do with the conquest of a person or people, but rather with enabling all to give their lives the deepest and most joyful meaning possible. The Church but reflects Christ's light and permits people to experience in the Eucharist God's presence in Christ's sacrifice, and thereby the divine invitation to adore and glorify Him, the triune God. *Metanoia*, "conversion," is indispensable for "the planting of the Church" to occur. It allows evangelization to be seen not as an isolated occurrence, but as the dynamic and constant self-description of the Church. Like Pentecost, evangelization thus understood continuously gathers people to unite the Old and New Testaments, and thereby overcomes the vanity of the Tower of Babel, which had led to incomprehension and dispersal. By her very nature, the whole of the Church is but one missionary endeavor: "One carries out mission so that the glory and power of God may be shown forth in the world. Mission is done so that God may be adored."[90] As a consequence, it is the joyful responsibility not only of the Supreme Pontiff but also of all bishops to promote the work of the missions. He proposes every bishops' conference have a secretariat dedicated solely to missionary work.

Frings expressly welcomed the text drafted jointly by Congar, Ratzinger, and Seomois in Nemi under the direction of the vice president of the subcommission on the missions, Johannes Schütte (1913–1971), superior general of the Society of the Divine Word. In the aula, he praised the profound and broad presentation of the theological foundations of missionary activities. As the text already did, he also stressed that mission is nothing

[89] Wicks, *"Six Texts,"* 286.

[90] Wicks, "Six Texts," 287.

short of the Church's participation in and continuation of Christ's own mission on earth. Yet, perhaps, he added, the text could speak more of how missionary activities contribute to the salvation of humankind. While non-Christians can also hypothetically be saved, humankind cannot reach definitive salvation without the missionary works of Christians. Going beyond the draft, he reminded everyone that native clergy are entrusted not only with the task of ministering to Christians, but likewise with participation in the Church's global missionary efforts.[91] This would inform the final shape of the decree *Ad gentes*.[92]

Unitatis Redintegratio—Ecumenical Dialogue as Work of the Holy Spirit

In a letter dated September 17, 1962, to the secretary of state, Cardinal Amleto Cicognani (1883–1973), Frings criticizes the schema on ecumenism, *Ut omnes unum sint*, for concerning itself exclusively with the Eastern Churches. It should state this clearly in the preamble, he said, and mention that a separate text will be issued for those denominations issuing forth from the Reformation. Ratzinger proposed the first text be composed also in Greek![93]

Again, Frings delivered a memorable, though short, talk on ecumenism in the aula on November 28, 1963. It consists of a compilation of arguments from various *periti*. Ratzinger's contributions, if any, cannot be determined.[94] But Ratzinger definitively influenced his speech on September 28, 1964. There, Frings would advocate including again in the text a reference to Ephesians 2:11–22 that had been omitted in the schema at hand, underlining the fact that Jesus Christ unites Jews and Gentiles in *pulcherrima et admirabilis theologia* ("that beautiful and admirable theology"). He also regretted that the draft omits the sentence stating that not all Jews were responsible for Jesus's violent death. When speaking of other religions, the drafted text mentioned the splendor of truth reflected in these, which illumines every human being. Ratzinger suggested modify-

---

[91] See: NF, 329; *Acta Synodalia*, 4/3:739–40.

[92] J. B. Anderson, *A Vatican II Pneumatology of the Paschal Mystery: The Historical-Doctrinal Genesis of Ad Gentes I, 2–5*, Analecta Gregoriana 250 (Rome: Gregorian University Press, 1988), 301–4 (reprint of Ratzinger's original Latin draft for *Ad gentes*).

[93] Wicks, "Six Texts," 264–68, at 265. See also *Acta Synodalia*, appendix (Vatican City: Typis Polyglottis Vaticanis, 1983), 74–77 (reprint of Latin letter submitted by Frings and composed by Ratzinger).

[94] Trippen, *Frings*, 2:394–95.

ing this to read "although imperfect and infiltrated with many human errors, . . . but in much the splendor of that truth shines forth, that illumines every human being coming into this world."[95] In addition, he urged the Council not "to determine" (*bestimmt*) that Christians should love not only their neighbors but also their enemies. At the same time, it should call to mind that this Christian duty fulfills Jesus Christ's command to practice such love.[96] He also pointed out that the one, holy, catholic, and apostolic Church is not an abstract super-church still to be fashioned, but is found in the abiding Lord, the Truth of Jesus Christ among us: the Catholic Church around Peter.[97] This would furnish building stones for the declaration *Nostra aetate*.

VIEWS THAT CONTRIBUTED TO *GAUDIUM ET SPES*

Ratzinger proposed a revision of section 9 of the schema *De Ecclesia in mundo huius temporis* in October 1965. It reminds the reader that human beings know that "their own good will, . . . inventions and external progress" are insufficient and that "they find no equilibrium." The Church trusts in "that man who is at the same time true God and in whom the kingdom of God and the human kingdom coincide." With hauntingly poetic language distinguishing the author, he writes:

> In the face of Jesus Christ crucified, moreover, the Church knows that humans are not only wounded by that divine love that embraces them and makes their hearts restless, but they are wounded as well by their own infidelity, by which they turn away from God to seek only their own gain and not seldom bite and devour each (cf. Gal 5:15). Thus the Church believes that the definitive answer to the pressing questions of the human race is found in Christ, true God and true man. Therefore she intends to respond to the questions of today in the light that God makes resplendent in the face of Christ (2 Cor 4:6).

---

[95] NF, 250. See also *Acta Synodalia*, 3/2:582–84; and Trippen, *Frings*, 2:424–25: "Doch scheint mir richtiger zu sagen, dass in anderen Religionen, obgleich unvollkommen und mit vielen menschlichen Irrtümern durchsetzt, über religiöse Dinge gesprochen werde, jedoch in vielem der Glanz jener Wahrheit aufscheine, die jeden Menschen erleuchtet, der in diese Welt kommt."

[96] Trippen, *Frings*, 2:425.

[97] *Acta Synodalia*, 3/2:583 (*textus scripto traditus* on 584).

> Thus the Church invites all people to hear the message that she brings forth from her faith and she wants to hear the questions and answers of all those with whom she forms one human race and one history.[98]

In this text, Ratzinger alerts the reader to the inextricable post-lapsarian state of humankind and affirms the difference between the world and the Church. Far from giving rise to Platonic aloofness, it is *the* inner cause for solidarity with, charity toward, and concern for all, precisely by spelling out Chalcedonian Christology.

During the fourth session, on September 24, 1965, Frings intervened again. Ironically, the secretary general, Cardinal Pericle Felici (1911–1982), who was not partial to Frings, was forced to read the speech, as Frings had no time to commit to memory the text Ratzinger had prepared for him.[99] He faulted the schema for insufficiently explaining the text's goal:

> In the first part it speaks of the Church's sincere collaboration with humankind in order to achieve greater fraternity of all; in the second part this thesis is being illustrated with words describing the innermost mission of Christ, namely the supernatural salvation of humankind. This is a case of a highly dangerous confusion between human progress, for the sake of which dialogue should be instituted, and divine salvation, which is being achieved by faith's obedience. It comes as no surprise that this confusion marks the whole schema, as its goal is being defined in such a confusing way. For this reason I propose and *demand*, that the terms people of God and Church be clarified and used in the same meaning [consistently] throughout the schema and that the schema's goal be clearly presented. In order to achieve this, marginal changes—that are being interspersed here and there—do not suffice, but rather a revision of the whole in its substance is required.[100]

---

[98] Wicks, "Six Texts," 292–93. See also *Acta Synodalia*, 4/1:440; and Joseph Ratzinger, "Angesichts der Welt von heute: Überlegungen zur Konfrontation mit der Kirche in Schema XIII," *Wort und Wahrheit* 20 (August–September 1965): 493–504.

[99] The diaries of both Hubert Jedin and Wolfgang Große, secretary to Bishop Franz Hengsbach from the diocese of Essen, confirm this (Trippen, *Frings*, 2:473).

[100] "Im ersten Teil ist die Rede von der aufrichtigen Zusammenarbeit der Kirche, mit dem Menschengeschlecht, um eine größere Brüderlichkeit aller zu bewirken; im zweiten Teil wird diese These mit Worten illustriert, die die innerste Sendung Christi, nämlich das übernatürliche Heil des Menschen, bezeichnen. Hier handelt es sich um eine höchst

The world's *tristesse* can be dispersed only by Jesus Christ, by the mystery of his Cross and Resurrection. A clearer distinction between the natural and supernatural orders is called for.[101] One senses here how urgent for Ratzinger a thorough revision of the text was, lest there be a lack of differentiation between salvation—which is brought about exclusively by God's grace and immanent perfection—and the result of human, contingent, and post-lapsarian efforts. Alas, this prophetic voice (implicitly against a crude Hegelian reinterpretation of history), however much based on sound biblical scholarship and Christian anthropology, met "the anger of French theologians," such as Congar and Daniélou.[102]

CONSIDERATIONS LEADING TO *DIGNITATIS HUMANAE*

Along with *De Ecclesia*, Cardinals Ottaviani and Bea submitted jointly a sub-proposal titled "On the Relationship between Church and State, and on Religious Freedom." In chapter IX, Ottaviani maintained that the state is duty-bound to respect and enforce the truth of Catholic faith and support the one true Church. It should assist people in attaining spiritual goods. Chapter X, composed by Cardinal Augustin Bea, S.J. (1881–1968), diverged markedly from this view. This tension would lead to a crisis in the Council in 1964.[103]

---

gefährliche Verwirrung zwischen menschlichem Fortschritt, um dessentwillen der Dialog gestiftet werden soll, und göttlichem Heil, das durch den Gehorsam des Glaubens erlangt wird. Es verwundert nicht, dass diese Verwirrung das ganze Schema durchzieht, weil dessen Ziel so verwirrend definiert wird. Deshalb schlage ich vor und *fordere*, dass die Begriffe Volk Gottes und Kirche geklärt und durch das ganze Schema im gleichem Sinne gebracht werden und auch das Ziel des Schemas deutlicher dargelegt wird. Um das zu erreichen, genügen nicht marginale Veränderungen, die da und dort eingestreut werden, sondern es bedarf einer Überarbeitung des ganzen Textes in seiner Substanz" (NF, 339; emphasis added by present author). See also *Acta Synodalia*, 4/2:405–6. Otto Semmelroth confirms, in his diary for September 24, 1965, that Frings's invention was composed by Ratzinger (Trippen, *Frings*, 2:472–73; see also Ratzinger, *Theological Highlights of Vatican II*, 147–71).

[101] Only ten years after the Council, he observes public opinion to perceive in the term "world" an "anti-syllabus" and the world as it evolved since the French Revolution of 1789, with Teilhardian optimism. Thus, contemporary society is unable to appreciate *Gaudium et spes* (Joseph Ratzinger, "Der Weltdienst der Kirche heute: Auswirkungen von Gaudium et Spes im letzten Jahrzehnt," in *Zehn Jahre Vaticanum II*, ed. A. Bauch, A. Gläßer, and M. Seybold [Regensburg: Pustet, 1976], 36–53, at 40).

[102] Trippen, *Frings*, 2:473.

[103] "De Relationibus inter Ecclesia et Statum necnon de Tolerantia/Libertate Religiosa," in *Acta et Documenta* II, 2/4:657–88.

Ratzinger reacted to the first text:

> In every regard the argumentation of section 3 seems to me problematic. . . . Everyone acknowledges that *in principle* Catholic truth is accessible to man, however, in fact the conditions of people vary fundamentally, so that one cannot accuse non-Catholics of malice. What one cannot expect of an individual human being, this one may not impose upon those who exercise the *Potestas civilis*. . . . Hence one must register gravest doubts against the sentence: "Cultui . . . publico ab Ecclesia praestitio Civitas sese associare debet non tantum per cives, sed etiam per illos, qui auctoritate praediti Societatem civilem repraesentant."

Concerning sections 2 and 3 of the same schema, he observes:

> The state *as* state is called to make a profession of faith: it is this that makes the claim so dangerous, that the *Potestas civilis* . . . might recognize Catholic truth. However, such a cult and faith cannot exist. The subject of faith can only be a person. . . . Never can the *Potestas civilis* believe and perform cult. . . . The idea of a state religion, as it practically appears, is not only unreal, but in fact from within [the very nature of] Christian [faith] improper.[104]

[104] "Die Argumentation des Abschnitts 3 scheint mir in jeder Hinsicht bedenklich zu sein. . . . Jedermann anerkennt, dass dem Menschen zwar *grundsätzlich* die katholische Wahrheit zugänglich ist, dass aber faktisch die Bedingungen der Menschen grundverschieden sind, sodass man die Nichtkatholiken nicht der Böswilligkeit zeihen kann. Was man aber vom Einzelmenschen nicht verlangen kann, das darf man auch nicht den Menschen auferlegen, die *Potestas civilis* verwalten. . . . Größte Bedenken sind daher gegen den Satz anzumelden: 'Cultui . . . publico ab Ecclesia praestito Civitas sese associare debet non tantum per cives, sed etiam per illos, qui auctoritate praediti Societatem civilem repraesentant.'. . . Der Staat *als* Staat hat ein Bekenntnis zum katholischen Glauben abzulegen; das ist es auch, was die Behauptung so gefährlich macht, die *Potestas civilis* . . . könne die katholische Wahrheit erkennen. Einen solchen Kult und Glauben kann es aber nicht geben. Subjekt des Glaubens kann immer nur eine Person sein. . . . Es kann also niemals die *Potestas civilis* glauben und Kult erweisen. . . . Die Idee einer Staatsreligion, wie sie praktisch hier auftaucht, ist nicht nur irreal, sondern gerade vom Inneren des Christlichen her unsachgemäß" (Ratzinger's typed remarks in NF, 97 [Frings's vote on June 19, 1962]; see also *Acta et Documenta* II, 2/4:657–88 [text], at 692–93, and 725 [Frings's vote]).

This line of argumentation positions the state in something akin to "constructive neutrality" vis-à-vis the Church. Ratzinger continues:

> The state must on the one hand grant freedom of religion and may never coerce towards any one religion, no matter what historical claims it (a particular religion) might have therein; it must not protect all religions equally, but give preference to those whose moral strength are proven.

This thought leads him to conclude:

> The positive, edifying character of Catholic faith is so unambiguously obvious to every human being, that no state is morally legitimized to deny her the freedom to flourish due her.[105]

The extent to which Frings was influenced by his *peritus* Ratzinger is once again evidenced by his vote on the chapter concerning the Church–state relationship in the schema *De Ecclesia*, where he calls for the complete elimination of number 3, reasoning in the vein of Ratzinger:

> In the New Testament divine revelation is not directed to human communities, but rather to individual human beings, who have to decide as individuals according to their well-informed consciences. . . . [And] there does not exist in the strict sense a Catholic state nowadays—if it ever had existed—and [in the draft] the determined rights due to the present-day close integration of peoples cannot be exercised without great harm for the common good and the Church.[106]

---

[105] "Dass der Staat einerseits Gewissensfreiheit zu gewähren hat und niemals zu einer bestimmten Religion, welche geschichtlichen Ansprüche sie in ihm auch haben möge, zwingen darf; dass er aber nicht alle Religionen gleichmäßig schützen muss, sondern jenen Vorzug gewähren wird, die ihre sittliche Kraft bewiesen haben; dass der positive, aufbauende Charakter des katholischen Glaubens heute so eindeutig für jeden Menschen sichtbar ist, dass kein Staat moralisch legitimiert ist, die ihm gebührende Freiheit zur Entfaltung zu versagen" (NF, 97).

[106] "Weil sich im Neuen Testament die Verkündigung der göttlichen Offenbarung nicht an menschliche Gemeinschaften richtet, sondern an einzelne Menschen, die sich als einzelne entsprechend ihrem gut gebildeten Gewissen entscheiden müssen. . . . Weil es einen katholischen Staat im strengen Sinne heute nicht gibt—wenn es ihn je gegeben hat—und die hier festgestellten Rechte wegen der heutigen engen Verflechtung der

He continues by saying that the Church neither requires protection from the state nor requests the state to act against the dissemination of religious errors. At the same, he insists religion has the inalienable right to prosper in its mission, profane structures, and social works. There is, however, only one religious truth that *eo ipso* has the inalienable right to spread to all peoples. He underlines that there can be no pluralities of conflicting religious truth claims:

> All human persons possess the personal right to profess their faith also in public, which they recognized as true after having carefully formed their conscience, [they have the right] to propagate it, even when their view is in error. . . . Freedom of religion defined as the right to profess and to disseminate it, must be granted to all denominations, insofar as they do not violate the foundations of the state or the fundamental rights of people. Greater rights can be granted to those [religions] which have proven themselves in the world as beneficial to the wellbeing of people. . . . In matters of common concern (*rebus mixtis*), relating to terrestrial and spiritual wellbeing, one should strive for an agreement between Church and state, be it official or de facto.[107]

Regarding the two schemata *De ordine sociali* and *De communitate gentium*, Ratzinger argued for far-reaching modifications, as the two documents get lost in technical detail that smacks of a (neo-Scholastic) "treatise on social dogmatics hovering above and beyond time." Instead, he advised to refer to the papal social encyclicals. Accordingly, Frings voted *non placet* on both drafts.[108]

During the fourth period, Frings submitted four pages of emendations to the text on *Libertas religiosa*. He welcomed the emphasis on the nonviolent way of exercising one's faith and suggested improving the text by shortening it to its essential message and changing its literary genre. The declaration, he said, should refrain from arguing, which is the task "of philosophers and theologians." Some corrections were also, he

Völker nicht ausgeübt werden können ohne großen Schaden für das Gemeinwohl und für die Kirche" (NF, 97).

[107] *Acta et Documenta* II, 2/4:657–88, 692–93, and 725.

[108] See *De Communitate Gentium*, in NF, 104 (text with Ratzinger's remarks on the border and Frings's vote on August 20, 1962); and *De Ordine Sociali*, in NF, 105 (text along with Ratzinger's position and Frings's vote August 20, 1962). Neither is published in *Acta et Documenta* II. See Trippen, *Frings*, 2:296–97.

thought, in order, as "in the final analysis divine revelation and Catholic faith place in luminous light the transcendence of religion above and beyond the state."[109] Furthermore, the proposed text was not correct in its presentation of the history of religion. Later in the text, the term "freedom" was used in confusing ways that run the danger of conflating radically different realities. Choosing between good and evil is one form of freedom of choice given man by his Creator. The perfect freedom of the children of God is given us exclusively by Christ liberating us from sin and the Holy Spirit providing the requisite strength to overcome temptation, and one has to set the juridical notion of religious freedom apart from this.[110]

One senses in Ratzinger's arguments and Frings's interventions the outline of a new paradigm that would later in the Council bear the name *Dignitatis humanae*, the Declaration on Religious Freedom. Ratzinger's thoughts arose not so much from ecumenical or interreligious dialogue, but from a profound reflection on the nature of personal faith in Christ and the dignity inherent to each individual believer's act of faith. One cannot help but be surprised at the congeniality of his thoughts with thinkers who had pondered the issue of religious freedom at greater length, such as Cardinal Bea, Max Pribilla, S.J. (1874–1954), and fellow *peritus* John Courtney Murray, S.J. (1904–1967), who would prove instrumental for the final shape of *Dignitatis humanae*.

Conclusion: Vatican II as the Christocentric Shift

There is no gainsaying that much more light must be shed on this topic—especially on the genesis of *Sacrosanctum concilium*. However, clear contours of Ratzinger's theological vision and role during the epochal Second Vatican Council emerge that permit one to draw definitive conclusions. His influence was decisive in numerous areas. In fact, the degree of his influence was so considerable that one cannot ignore Ratzinger's contributions and still do justice to the spirit and message of Vatican II. For a proper evaluation and reception of the Council, this insight is significant.

[109] "Weil letztendlich die göttliche Offenbarung und der katholische Glaube die Transzendenz der Religion über den Staat in ein helles Licht setzen" (unsigned copy of speech found in NF, 351; text of speech delivered, *textus scripto traditus* and *emendationes additae*, in *Acta Synodalia*, 4/1:201–3; see also Trippen, *Frings*, 2:467–68).

[110] This is the criticism of an insufficiently nuanced use of the term "freedom" that Hubert Jedin and Joseph Ratzinger drafted jointly for Frings (Trippen, *Frings*, 2:468n686).

Ratzinger shared in the optimistic atmosphere and mood characteristic of the Council, while also acting as a voice of caution.

He contributed in central ways to overcoming an overly hierarchical and juridical fixation. He also assisted in expressing the Catholic faith in language more personalist and Christ-centered. He advanced the overhaul of the theological idiom—from a historistic nineteenth-century and manualist neo-Scholastic outlook to one that perceives the whole of Church history as one single salvation-historic trajectory or arch: God's abiding presence through the Eucharistic Lord in the power of the Holy Spirit in time and space.[111] He represented thereby a loose movement one calls *ressourcement*. It resists quite deliberately systematization or forming a school, as it practices principled openness to the whole of Catholic heritage. Attentiveness to the promptings of the Holy Spirit means also transcending facile, oftentimes unspiritual, political categories, such as "progressive" or "conservative," to describe the Council itself or the faith held by an individual believer. Drawing from the living waters of such Tradition (John 4:10), the *periti* of this movement proved pivotal for the Council not becoming subservient to a particular philosophy, system, school, or, let alone, ideology.

Determinative for Ratzinger's theological vision as expressed in his contributions to the Council are the Pauline words "that Christ may dwell in your hearts" (Eph 3:17). This defines the new people of God, "built into it for a dwelling place of God in the Spirit" in history (Eph 2:22; see 2:19–21). The mystery of the living Christ takes on cosmic features in his body the Church—is *factum historicum*, as Ratzinger's *Doktorvater*, Gottlieb Söhngen, phrased it.[112] Far from lifeless, Überlieferung—or "Tradition," in contradistinction to mere human "custom" in English—is indispensable for believers to apprehend and live who they are.[113] Tradition is Christ's footprints among us that enable us to become participants in his life.[114] Thus comprehended, Catholicity becomes Christ's very own invit-

---

[111] See Walter Kasper, *Die Methoden der Dogmatik: Einheit und Vielheit* (Munich: Kösel, 1967). In this book, a short description of this profound change of theological perspectives is supplied.

[112] Söhngen, *Die Einheit der Theologie*, 347.

[113] See the quotation from Ratzinger, *Dogma and Preaching*, 382, at the outset of this article.

[114] Söhngen develops this on a broad canvas in four steps in *Die Einheit der Theologie*: "Vom Wesen des Christentums" (288–304); "Überlieferung und apostolische Verkündigung (eine fundamentaltheologische Studie zum Begriff des Apostolischen)" (305–23); "Christi Gegenwart in uns durch den Glauben (Eph. 3,17)" (324–41); and "Das Mysterium des lebendigen Christus und der lebendige Glaube (ein Beitrag zu einer kat-

ing gesture and—via inclusion—that of the Blessed Trinity to the world. Most importantly, Christians may participate in this gesture. Tradition enables ever again living "friendship with God."[115] This explains the continual youthfulness and enduring attractiveness of Ratzinger's theology—and *a fortiori* that of Vatican II.

egorialen Analysis fidei)" (342–69). In countless books, articles, and homilies, Ratzinger unfolds this *point d'appui* in great detail.

[115] Gregory of Nyssa, *De Vita Moysis* (*Patrologia Graeca*, 44:429CD). See also Ratzinger, "Buchstabe und Geist," 265.

CHAPTER 3

Joseph Ratzinger's Early Contributions to Fundamental Theology: 1955–1961[1]

THERE IS A MAGIC to every beginning. This applies also to Pope Benedict XVI's beginnings as professor of theology. This article wishes to turn the reader's attention to select early (1955–1961), in part unpublished, contributions of the young professor of theology, Joseph Ratzinger, to the then-nascent academic discipline called "fundamental theology."

All Great Theology is Biographical —and a Hypothesis

As regards what is commonly called *Weltanschauung*, something heretofore unprecedented and truly cataclysmic had occurred with the end of World War I in the year of 1918. The common narrative that had formed the organizing principle of a private person, and bonded a community into one of a shared fate and common destiny in central Europe since roughly the Middle Ages, had violently dissolved, the narrative of the triad of God, ruler (emperor/king/lord), and home (country/one's native soil), heretofore considered unseverable. Joseph Ratzinger was born in Germany in 1927 between the years of the Second (Wilhelmic) Reich (1871–1918) and the Third Reich (1933–1945), in a period of constantly changing, weak central governments struggling to reach an often elusive democratic con-

[1] This essay was originally published in *Josephinum Journal of Theology* 21, no. 2 (Summer/Fall 2014) (appeared May 2016): 263–291. Used by permission.

sensus, a period of onerous reparations, hyperinflation, and depression. The *Reichstag* (the German Diet) resembled "a house divided." Nobody knew who would fill the void the Great War (1914–1918) had caused, and many were left bereft of a personal compass to master life. In a sense, this historically unparalleled lack of a common intergenerational metanarrative continues to characterize Europe to this day, but in an ironic twist, it is nowadays declared an altogether rightful *Lebensgefühl* (awareness of life)—in fact, the *only* legitimate norm: postmodernity.[2]

Ratzinger's parents acutely sensed this unprecedented political, social, and cultural uncertainty and invariably contrasted it with their idyllic Bavarian landscape and their joyful belief in Bavaria's world of singular harmony between thought, sentiment (*Gemüt*), nature, and Catholic faith. Wisely, Ratzinger's father, the senior Joseph, familiarized his family with *De civitate Dei*, Augustine's Christocentric reading of human history composed after the sacking of Rome, the center of human civilization, by Alaric's Visigoths in AD 410. By suggesting an ominous parallel between 410 and 1918, he assisted his family in understanding the *Zeichen der Zeit* ("interpret the present time," from Luke 12:56): an impending war, the ideological suppression of Christian faith at the hands of a wholly materialistic Nazi regime, and growth of confidence in God. Also to this end, they read Catholic spiritual literature and romantic poets. In 1943, the two Ratzinger boys, Georg and Joseph, were thrust into another epic war as forcibly conscripted, although as *unarmed* helpers/soldiers in the German *Wehrmacht*. They found answers in their Catholic faith to the troubling questions provoked by war: pointless death, unimaginable suffering, and increasingly futile military measures. Arising from these wartime experiences and as a remarkably fitting answer to them, both Ratzinger brothers would offer a seemingly rudderless world a salutary answer—the mystery of the Incarnation of God's Word—the one through the arts and the other as a stellar thinker. One would excel as a musician and the other as a theologian, penetrating the Christian faith in a fresh way. Significantly, both reacted to the atrocities produced by ideologies by freely sacrificing their lives as priests. Their respective biographical experiences predestined them for a lifelong program of recovery of the intellectual, cultural, and

---

2 Joseph Ratzinger, *Milestones: Memoirs, 1927–1977*, trans. Erasmo Leiva-Merikakis (San Francisco: Ignatius Press, 1998), 7–40. See also Emery de Gaál, *The Theology of Pope Benedict XVI: The Christocentric Shift* (New York: Palgrave MacMillan, 2010), 13–20.

religious pillars upon which human civilization needed to be (re)built.[3]

Tellingly, already early on, Georg was nicknamed by fellow seminarians the *Orgel-Ratz* (organ Ratzinger) and Joseph the *Bücher-Ratz* (book Ratzinger).[4] Fundamental theology may have been especially appealing to Joseph Ratzinger, as it thematizes numerous central theological concepts, bringing "fragments" into dialogue with "the whole of the faith." There the foundations of Catholic faith are spelled out.

Important Elements for a Promising Theologian

Joseph Ratzinger studied briefly with his brother on Freising's somewhat secluded and dreamy *Domberg* (Cathedral Mountain), and studied theology in the Munich archdiocesan seminary, but he soon moved to the baroque *Fürstenried* Palace and finally to the Ducal Georgianum in Munich, where only the most promising of Bavarian seminarians were living "that new beginning that bloomed among the ruins," as Ratzinger-biographer, fellow priest, and professor of theology Alfred Läpple (1915–2013) later observed.[5] While studying the various disciplines of theology in Freising and subsequently at Munich University, Ratzinger was exposed to the neo-Scholastic variant of Thomas Aquinas's thoughts. Initially, he considered it too cerebral to answer the existential questions war invariably forces upon people. More convincing for him was the personal or "illuminatist" approach of Augustine, Bonaventure, Blaise Pascal, John Henry Newman, and Romano Guardini.[6] This first impression was reinforced by the personalist thought of contemporaries such as Martin Buber (1878–1965), Ferdinand Ebner, Wilhelm Adam, and Josef Pieper (the last, surprisingly, a Thomist). In addition, Joseph Pascher (1893–1979), the professor of liturgy at Munich's *Ludwig-Maximilians-Universität* and rector of the adjacent Georgianum, instilled in the young student a lasting appreciation

---

3 Ratzinger, *Milestones*, 13–20. Alfred Läpple, *Benedikt XVI und seine Wurzeln: Was sein Leben und seinen Glaube prägte* (Augsburg: St. Ulrich, 2006).

4 Manuel Schlögl, *Am Anfang eines grossen Weges* (Regensburg: Steiner & Schnell, 2014), 17.

5 Ratzinger, *Milestones*, 41–45. See also Alfred Läpple, "'That New Beginning That Bloomed among the Ruins': Interview with Prof. Dr. Alfred Läpple by Gianni Valente and Pierluca Azzaro," *30DAYS* 24, nos. 1–2 (2006): 54–66, accessed October 12, 2017, http://www.30giorni.it/articoli_id_10125_l3.htm.

6 Such a reading of Ratzinger's basic theological approach is confirmed in Joseph Ratzinger, "Licht und Erleuchtung: Erwägungen zu Stellung und Entwicklung des Themas in der abendländischen Geistesgeschichte," *Studium Generale* 13 (1960): 368–78.

for the close nexus between liturgy, prayer, Scripture, theology, and life.[7]

Most importantly, already in 1947, Ratzinger found in Gottlieb Söhngen (1892–1971) a fundamental theologian attempting to give expression to faith in an unconventional way. From that time onward, Ratzinger remained especially interested in the area of fundamental theology. Distinct from apologetics, it was then a novel way of reflecting on Catholic faith.[8] Söhngen, coming from the cosmopolitan Rhineland, was capable of conversing with equal facility on a wide range of topics. He could discuss the Church Fathers and John Henry Newman, as well as Immanuel Kant's (1724–1804) epistemology and Anselm of Canterbury. In addition, he was highly knowledgeable about music. All these circumstances certainly contributed to the attraction that the discipline of fundamental theology exerted upon the seminarian Ratzinger. Under Söhngen's direction, Ratzinger wrote both his prize-winning doctoral dissertation on Augustine's ecclesiology[9] and his *Habilitationsschrift* (terminal paper) on Bonaventure's understanding of history.[10] Both represent original contributions to theology and prefigure important insights Vatican II would soon expound upon, such as "People of God" (*Lumen Gentium* 13 and 32) and the essential correlation between the Church and the Eucharist. Sensitized to this correlation since 1949 by the writings of Henri de Lubac (1896–1991), he discovered the *communio* structure of the Church, especially by way of this French Jesuit's works *Corpus Mysticum* and *Catholicism*.[11]

---

7 Ratzinger, *Milestones*, 47–60. See also de Gaál, *Theology of Benedict XVI*, 33–45.

8 Joseph Ratzinger, "Das Ganze im Fragment: Gottlieb Söhngen zum Gedächtnis," *Christ in Gegenwart* 23 (1971): 398–99. See also de Gaál, *Theology of Benedict XVI*, 33–36.

9 Joseph Ratzinger, *Haus und Volk Gottes in Augustins Lehre von der Kirche*, in *Gesammelte Schriften*, vol. 1 (Freiburg im Breisgau: Herder, 2011), 43–550.

10 Joseph Ratzinger, *The Theology of History in St. Bonaventure* (Chicago: Franciscan Herald Press, 1971). For the reunited text, see Joseph Ratzinger, *Offenbarungsverständnis und Geschichtstheologie Bonaventuras*, in *Gesammelte Schriften*, vol. 2 (Freiburg im Breisgau: Herder, 2009), 53–659.

11 Ratzinger, *Milestones*, 98. Reflective of this *communio* ecclesiology, see: Joseph Ratzinger, "Grundgedanken eucharistischer Erneuerung im 20. Jahrhundert," *Klerusblatt* 40 (1960): 208–11; Ratzinger, "Kirche und Liturgie/vollzogene Gemeinde im Leben: Zwei Vorträge auf der Österreichischen Theologenwoche vom 14. bis 20. Juli, 1958 in Salzburg," *Mitteilungen des Instituts für Österreichische Geschichtsforschung* (2008): 13–27. See also Thomas Weiler, *Volk Gottes—Leib Christi: Die Ekklesiologie Joseph Ratzingers und ihr Einfluß auf das Zweite Vatikanische Konzil* (Mainz: Grünewald, 1997); Henri de Lubac, *Catholicisme: Les aspects sociaux du dogme* (Paris: Cerf, 1947); de Lubac, *Corpus Mysticum: l'Eucharistie et l'Église au Moyen Âge, Etude historique* (Paris: Aubier, 1949).

Ratzinger uncovered in Bonaventure's theology that revelation is not the communication of supratemporal propositions, but rather nothing less than, ultimately, divine self-communication. Importantly, in this light, revelation is perceived as historically mediated, an insight that *Dei Verbum* would incorporate with far-reaching consequences. Thus, human beings discover themselves now as personally called by God in and to freedom. The meaning in which a people had collectively participated in a more or less unreflective way prior to World War I should now be accessed directly and personally by the individual believer. Since 1918, society and the state had abandoned their role as preservers and transmitters of truth and meaning; so, in this new paradigm, the Church is to "awaken in the souls" of the believers —a paradigm programmatically captured by Romano Guardini (1885–1968), who greatly impressed Ratzinger shortly after World War I.[12] Now wholly without state or social support, the Church was considered by some as called to provide a life-sustaining metanarrative, serving both the individual and society.[13]

Beginning in the summer of 1952, as docent at the archdiocesan Freising Seminary, Ratzinger taught an eclectic mix of courses, first in sacraments and then also in dogmatics and fundamental theology. Many an hour he spent in the well-stocked seminary library copying Latin, Greek, and French primary texts—including from the first volumes of the pioneering series *Sources Chrétiennes*.[14] This would serve as the indispensable scholarly basis for someone destined to become one of the most influential theologians in Church history.

In 1956, he successfully defended his *Habilitationsschrift* on Bonaventure amid a conflict between his director Söhngen and the second reader, Michael Schmaus (1897–1993), and not without the text being significantly abridged. It would take over half a century before the text would see publication in an unabridged version. Somehow, this conflict has henceforth accompanied Ratzinger for the rest of his life, negatively influencing the reception of his thinking from the start, arguably perhaps even impacting his pontificate (2005–2013).[15]

At Freising Seminary, Ratzinger acquired the reputation of being a gifted theologian with particular competence in Augustinian and Franciscan theology. When the theology department of the *Rheinische-Wil-*

---

12 Romano Guardini, *Vom Sinn der Kirche* (Mainz: Grünewald, 1922).

13 De Gaál, *Theology of Benedict XVI*, 66–72.

14 *Sources Chrétiennes*, ed. Henri de Lubac and Jean Daniélou (Paris: Cerf, 1942–).

15 Ratzinger, *Milestones*, 103–14.

helms-Universität in Bonn announced an opening for the chair in fundamental theology, two candidates were invited to deliver guest (i.e., trial) lectures: Professor Heinrich Dolch from Paderborn and Ratzinger.[16] Already, the previous occupant, Albert Lang (1890–1973), had been known for discarding nineteenth-century apologetics in favor of the then still novel discipline of fundamental theology.[17] In order to appreciate the invitation extended to Ratzinger, one must know of Lang's stature at that time as the leading fundamental theologian in the German-speaking countries. On June 20, 1958, on a Friday evening, Ratzinger delivered a paper titled "Der Weg der religiösen Erkenntnis nach dem Heiligen Augustinus" ("The Way of Religious Insight according to St. Augustine"). Immediately following the presentation, the dean and renowned historian and patristic scholar Theodor Klauser (1894–1984) is reported to have exclaimed enthusiastically: "*He* will be our new professor of fundamental theology."[18] Klauser was then editing the celebrated *Reallexikon für Antike und Christentum*.[19] In all probability, Söhngen had recommended Ratzinger to the department where he had once served as *Privatdozent* for seven years.[20]

At the same time, in 1958, Schmaus had attempted to sidetrack Ratzinger's career by attempting to convince the archbishop of Munich, Cardinal Joseph Wendel (1901–1960), to send Ratzinger from Freising to an insignificant college of education located in Munich-Pasing.[21] Showing a letter from the Bonn theology department, Ratzinger was able to persuade Wendel to keep him at Bonn. In these trying times, as Ratzinger was torn between obedience to his ordinary and the call to teach demanding theology at a respected institution, the famous Bonn Church historian Hubert Jedin (1900–1980) encouraged the young priest not to give in. To-

---

[16] Ironically, Dolch would immediately succeed Ratzinger at this university. The Nordrhein-Westfalen's (a German provincial) ministry of education had placed Ratzinger before Heinrich Moritz Dolch (from the Erzbischöfliche Akademie Paderborn) and Hermann Lais (from the theologate in Dillingen) as the preferred candidate on the list for the chair of fundamental theology at Bonn (Schlögl, *Am Anfang eines grossen Weges*, 19–20).

[17] See Albert Lang, *Fundamentaltheologie* (Munich: Hueber, 1954) [amplified in Lang, *Fundamentaltheologie*, vol. 1, *Die Sendung Christi* (Munich: Hueber, 1957); and *Fundamentaltheologie*, vol. 2, *Der Auftrag der Kirche* (Munich: Hueber, 1958)].

[18] Schlögl, *Am Anfang eines großen Weges*, 19.

[19] *Reallexikon für Christentum und Antike*, ed. Theodor Klauser, Gerhard Schöllgen, Franz Joseph Dölger, multiple vols. (Stuttgart: A. Hiersemann, 1950–).

[20] Ratzinger, *Milestones*, 113.

[21] Läpple, "That New Beginning That Bloomed among the Ruins," 66.

gether with Ratzinger, Jedin would later serve as *peritus* for Cardinal Josef Frings during the Second Vatican Council.[22]

On April 15, 1959, the first day of the summer semester, Ratzinger began lecturing in Bonn on philosophy of religion and theological epistemology, first in lecture hall IX and soon in the larger lecture halls X and XI. The popularity of his courses continued throughout his Bonn years: some students had to make do by sitting on window sills. In the *album professorum* he noted: "With April 1, 1959, . . . I have returned to my field of competence—fundamental theology, henceforth my life's task with God's help."[23] This move also brought geographic distance from the Schmaus school, so dominant in Munich and gaining then in influence throughout the German-speaking countries. Gradually it was to be complemented and finally superseded by the Rahnerian approach.[24]

THE INAUGURAL LECTURE

At 12 p.m. (*cum tempore*) on June 24, 1959, in lecture hall VIII, located in the main building of Bonn University, Ratzinger delivered his inaugural lecture: "The God of Faith and the God of the Philosophers: A Contribution to the Problem of a *theologia naturalis*."[25] In retrospect, Pope Benedict XVI would declare that this much attended lecture contained "the main theme of my thoughts."[26] In this concisely argued *tour d'horizon*, he investigated the relationship between the God of Christian revelation and the range of human cognition. What are the natural bases for religion? In what ways is God different from what philosophers assume to be God? How can God call upon human beings to convert and become disciples of Christ? As Benedict XVI succinctly phrased it later: "Which kind of rationality is appropriate for Christian faith?"[27] Intimately connected with

---

22 Schlögl, *Am Anfang eines großen Weges*, 20.

23 Schlögl, *Am Anfang eines großen Weges*, 25: "Mit der zum 1. April erfolgten Berufung . . . bin ich wieder in mein engeres Fachgebiet—die Fundamentaltheologie—zurückgekehrt, dem meine künftige Lebensarbeit mit Gottes Hilfe gelten soll."

24 Ratzinger, *Milestones*, 115–19.

25 This has been published under its original title: Joseph Ratzinger / Benedikt XVI, *Der Gott des Glaubens und der Gott der Philosophen: Ein Beitrag zum Problem der theologia naturalis*, ed. Heino Sonnemans, 2nd amplified ed. (Leutesdorf: Johannes Verlag, 2005).

26 "Der Leitfaden meines Denkens" (Ratzinger, *Der Gott des Glaubens*, 7).

27 Ratzinger, *Der Gott des Glaubens*, 8. See also de Gaál, *Theology of Benedict XVI*, 73–77. For a brief summary of this lecture, see Hansjürgen Verweyen, *Joseph Ratzinger—Benedikt XVI: Die Entwicklung seines Denkens* (Darmstadt: Wissenschaftliche Buchgesellschaft, 2007), 28–30.

these questions is the relationship between ancient Greek philosophy and biblical faith. Rhetorically, the later pope asks whether Greek rationality belongs to "the essence of Christianity" or is, rather, an alliance founded upon "a disastrous misunderstanding."[28]

These and similar questions would resurface in his classic *Introduction to Christianity* in 1968 and in his lecture "Christianity—the true Religion" delivered in 1999 at the Sorbonne in Paris. On their own, scientific arguments and philosophical reasoning have definite limits. Christian faith defends the priority of reason and of things reasonable without believing in an actual proof of Christian faith, and Ratzinger asks whether human reason can remain reasonable and not arbitrary without recourse to the *Logos*.[29]

In the brief introduction to his 1959 lecture, Ratzinger presents the 1654 *Mémorial* of Blaise Pascal (1623–1662): "Fire. 'God of Abraham, God of Isaac, God of Jacob' not of the philosophers and scholars." Perhaps unlike his early contemporary René Descartes (1596–1650), the mathematician-logician Pascal had encountered the living God of Christian faith—"dem Du Gottes" (the "Thou of God"). Thereby Pascal discovers something philosophy is unable to reach on its own: "the irresolvable intertwinedness of greatness and wretchedness in the immediate encounter with God, who is the living response to the open question of human existence."[30] Pascal concludes that this is no one else than Jesus Christ, the merciful God of Abraham, Isaac, and Jacob. Ratzinger reminds his audience—listening with rapt attention—of the unbridgeable gap between, but also the intrinsic complementarity of, the *esprit de géometrie* and the *esprit de finesse*, the latter penetrating far deeper into the essence of human existence than the grandest mathematical formula. In this context, he notes that only Kant's considerably later dismantling of speculative metaphysics and Friedrich Schleiermacher's (1768–1834) transferring religion into "the extra-rational and extra-metaphysical realm of feeling" helped bring Pascal's much earlier realization to the fore as "a radical aggravation of the problem."[31] Indirectly, Kant and Schleiermacher demonstrate that theoretical reason cannot access a personal God. But now, a singular, infelicitous *caesura* occurs with long-term ramifications: reason vacates the

---

[28] Ratzinger, *Der Gott des Glaubens*, 8.

[29] Joseph Ratzinger, *Truth and Tolerance: Christian Belief and World Religions*, trans. Henry Taylor (San Francisco: Ignatius Press, 2004), 138–209.

[30] Ratzinger, *Der Gott des Glaubens*, 12.

[31] Ratzinger, *Der Gott des Glaubens*, 12–13.

area of religion. Ergo, dogmas are seemingly no longer tenable, as religion is relegated to the realm of subjective experience while philosophy alone is in command of that of objective theory. Fatefully, this now positions faith in a heretofore uncountenanced opposition to knowledge.

Apart from Pascal's fragmentary *Pensées*, in this brief but clear outline of the issue at hand, Ratzinger utilizes primarily Romano Guardini's *Christliches Bewußtsein*, his own *Doktorvater* Söhngen's essay "Die Neubegründung der Metaphysik und die Gotteserkenntnis" ("Reconstituting Metaphysics and Insight into God"), and two texts from then equally young and promising Protestant theologian Wolfhart Pannenberg (1928–2014).[32]

Having stated the problem, he presents two different approaches: that of Thomas Aquinas, and that of the Swiss Protestant dialectical theologian Emil Brunner (1889–1966), a stalwart defender of the *theologia naturalis* who had likewise been influenced by the Jewish thinker Buber.

Ratzinger sees Thomas's view as bringing the God of religion and that of philosophy precariously close to coinciding, whereas he himself maintains that the two are distinct. While there does exist an insoluble relationship between the two, he holds that the God of religion transcends the one of philosophy. Ratzinger points out that, to Thomas's mind, whatever a non-Judeo-Christian religion holds concerning God beyond what philosophy can ascertain must be "Abfall und Verirrung" (decline and aberration).[33] Outside Christianity, philosophy describes the highest point the human mind can reach concerning matters divine.[34] Ratzinger underscores and appropriates for his line of argument the scholastic dictum "gratia non destruit, sed elevat et perfecit naturam" to crystalize his own position. As is well known, Thomas incorporates the Aristotelian God. Yet, Christian faith grasps this God infinitely more deeply and as an entity constituted as person(s). Ratzinger concludes his treatment of Thomas by observing that the Christian faith is related to (natural) philosophical

---

32 Romano Guardini, *Christliches Bewußtsein: Versuche über Pascal* (Munich: Kösel, 1950) [English: *Pascal for our Time*, 2nd ed. (New York: Herder and Herder, 1966)]; Gottlieb Söhngen, "Die Neubegründung der Metaphysik und die Gotteserkenntnis," in *Probleme der Gotteserkenntnis*, ed. Adolf Dyroff, Alberts-Magnus-Akademie II 3 (Münster: Aschendorff, 1928), 1–55; Wolfhart Pannenberg "Gott V," in *Religion in Geschichte und Gegenwart* II, 3rd. ed. (Tübingen: Mohr, 1962), 1729–30; Pannenberg, "Die Aufnahme des philosophischen Gottesbegriffs als dogmatisches Problem der frühchristlichen Theologie," *Zeitschrift für Kirchengeschichte* 70 (1959): 1–45.

33 Ratzinger, *Der Gott des Glaubens*, 15.

34 Ratzinger, *Der Gott des Glaubens*, 15.

insight into God, as man's eschatological vision of God is to his (supernatural) faith. In sum, they constitute but three stages on a single path.[35] For his presentation of Thomas, he relies on *Summa theologiae* II-II, q. 1, a. 1, and q. 2, a. 2, ad 1. In addition, he briefly references the philosopher and sociologist Max Scheler (1874–1928) and Catholic theologian Heinrich Fries (1911–1998), who would later write one of the seminal textbooks in the area of fundamental theology.[36]

In order to bring the *problématique* at hand into better focus, Ratzinger then discusses Brunner's position as an antithesis to this Thomistic harmony of human cognition and the self-revealing God. The Swiss theologian detects in the Old Testament "a double development." While God receives increasingly more names, God also becomes more abstract. These opposing movements notwithstanding, the awareness of God having a name becomes firmly established among the Israelites. This culminates in John 17:6: "I have manifested your name to the men whom you gave me" (see John 17:26; 12:28; and Matt 6:9). Revelation conveys the certainty that God can be addressed while not revealing divine aseity. God alone can establish humankind's close *Mitexistenz* (co-existence) with him.[37] No human effort, however ingenious, can supplant divine initiative in this regard. While admittedly yielding profound metaphysical knowledge, the God of philosophers cannot establish what the searching and inquiring human spirit ultimately desires: community with God. Admittedly, to the philosopher's mind, the term "God's name" must remain unsettling and objectionable. Yet, human cognition cannot reach more than what it is capable of thinking on its own and, therefore, can never imagine a personal and self-communicating God who nevertheless remains utterly transcendent.[38] The God revealing himself becomes, in the very process, the one who veils himself yet more, a *paradoxon* the philosopher must find objectionable. To Ratzinger, Brunner infelicitously develops an irreconcilable contradiction between the God of the philosophers and the one of faith.

Ratzinger notes that this seemingly irreconcilable contradiction is precisely captured by the Old Testament in the Hebrew words of God addressing Moses in the burning fire bush: "aehjaeh ašaer aehjae" (com-

---

35 Ratzinger, *Der Gott des Glaubens*, 16.

36 Max Scheler, *Vom Ewigen im Menschen* (Leipzig: Der neue Geist, 1921), 323ff; Henrich Fries, *Die katholische Religionsphilosophie der Gegenwart* (Heidelberg: F. H. Kerle, 1949), 61–62.

37 Ratzinger, *Der Gott des Glaubens*, 18.

38 Ratzinger, *Der Gott des Glaubens*, 19.

monly transliterated in English as *Ehyeh asher ehyeh*)—"I am who I am"—rendered in the Septuagint into the Greek words "Εγώ ειμι 'ο ων" ("I am the being one"), thereby transforming the divinely sovereign "I am" into the philosophical term "the Being" (Exod 3:14). A surprising agreement and, dare one say, synthesis occurs between biblical faith and Greek philosophy, between divine existence and essence, the consequences of which will be manifested in patristic and scholastic thought. According to the LXX translators, what human metaphysical reflection intends to reach and what Scripture reveals about God coincide. At this point, Ratzinger asks whether the possibility of a conflation of the content of the two had heretofore been sufficiently countenanced.[39]

However, and in notable contradistinction to the Alexandrian translators, Brunner detects an irresolvable material disjunction between the Hebrew Scripture and Greek philosophy and describes what the Greek translation of the Hebrew Old Testament achieved as amounting to "a devastating misunderstanding," thereby condemning also the "hyphen" Augustine accomplished between neo-Platonic ontology and biblical faith.[40] Brunner detects a chasm between the essentially dialogical God of Scripture and the monological or static God of Greek philosophy. Therefore, to Brunner, this translation is nothing short of *the* central distortion of the biblical message. The result is that the Christian authors of the first millennium and of the Middle Ages do not appreciate the radical opposition between Judeo-Christian revelation and human exploits into the area of metaphysics.

Indeed, Ratzinger detects in Brunner's observations a question tangating the very essence of Christianity. If there is no positive connection between (monological) philosophy and (dialogical) revelation, then the *analogia entis* must be considered illegitimate. Closely allied to this is the basic understanding of the nature of Christianity, so much contested between Catholic and Protestant (*evangelische*) theology since the sixteenth century. In this issue, Ratzinger discovers a crucial question Catholic fundamental theology must confront.[41]

As in the introductory section of his address, Ratzinger here again makes use of the *Doctor Angelicus*, along with Söhngen, Pannenberg, and Scheler. In addition, he extensively references not only Brunner but also two other contemporary theologians, Erich Przywara, S.J. (1889–1972),

---

[39] Ratzinger, *Der Gott des Glaubens*, 20.

[40] Ratzinger, *Der Gott des Glaubens*, 21.

[41] Ratzinger, *Der Gott des Glaubens*, 22.

and Hans Urs von Balthasar (1905–1988), thereby engaging the most current contributions to the issue at hand.[42]

In the third and last section of the lecture, Ratzinger attempts a resolution. He alerts his audience that one must consider the intellectual and religious ambience that gave rise to the Greek philosophical *Gottesbegriff* (term of God). The Stoa had differentiated between *theologia mythica*, *theologia civilis*, and *theologia naturalis*.[43] This Stoic tripartite approximation of God is reflected in Marcus Terentius Varro's (116–27 BC) now only partially extant *Antiquitates rerum humanarum et divinarum*. The distinction between *theologia civilis* and *theologia mythica* serves "probably apologetic and reforming" purposes, Ratzinger surmises.[44] While *theologia mythica* belongs to the realm of the poets and *theologia civilis* to that of the average people, the *theologia naturalis* is reserved for the philosophers and *physici*. It is this last *theologia* that attempts to approximate cognitively the problem of divine reality.[45]

He summarizes this section by quoting from his doctoral dissertation: "Civil theology ultimately has no God, but merely 'religion,' 'natural theology has no religion, but merely a deity."[46] Far from mere pointless speculation, to him, philosophy "uncovers the truth of the real and there-

[42] Emil Brunner, *Die christliche Lehre von Gott (Dogmatik I)*, 3rd ed. (Zürich: Zwingli-Verlag, 1953), 121–40; Brunner, *Wahrheit als Begegnung: Sechs Vorlesungen über das christliche Wahrheitsverständnis* (Berlin: Furche Verlag, 1938). He also made use of Ferdinand Ebner; see *Für Ferdinand Ebner*, ed. Hildegard Jone (Regensburg: Pustet, 1935), 12–15. Concerning the then much discussed area of the *analogia entis*, he consulted Gottlieb Söhngen, *Die Einheit der Theologie* (Munich: Zink, 1952), 235–64. See also Hans Urs von Balthasar, *Karl Barth* (Köln: Hegner, 1951); and Erich Przywara, S.J., "Analogia entis und Analogia fidei," in *Lexikon für Theologie und Kirche*, 2nd ed., vol. 1 (Freiburg im Breisgau: Herder, 1959), 470–76.

[43] Θεολογία μυθική, -πολιτική, -φυσική (Ratzinger, *Der Gott des Glaubens*, 24). He cites: Jakob Bilz, "Theologie," in *Lexikon für Theologie und Kirche*, vol. 10 (Freiburg im Breisgau: Herder, 1959), 65–66; Pierre Batiffol, "Theologie, Theologi," *Ephemerides Theologicae Lovaniensis* 5 (1928): 205–20; Josef Stiglmayr, "Mannigfache Bedeutung von 'Theologie' und 'Theologen,'" *Theologie und Glaube* 11 (1919): 296–309.

[44] For these insights, he refers to his doctoral dissertation: Joseph Ratzinger, *Volk und Haus Gottes in Augustins Lehre von der Kirche* (Munich: Zink, 1954), 265–76. He again cites Pannenberg, "Die Aufnahme des philosophischen Gottesbegriffs."

[45] He refers to Augustine, *De civitate Dei* 6.5, cited according to *Sancti Augustini de Civitate Dei, Libri I–X, Ad fidem quartae editionis teubnerianae quam a. MCMXVXVIII–MXMXXIX*, ed. B. Dombart and A. Kalb, in *Corpus Christianorum* 47 (Turnhout, BE: Brepols, 1955), 171. See *De civitate Dei* 4.32 (*Corpus Christianorum*, 47:126).

[46] Ratzinger, *Volk und Haus Gottes*, 270.

by the ontic truth of the divine."[47] In Ratzinger's judgment, there exists a conceptual proximity between monotheism—as subscribed to also by the philosophers' understanding of God—and the *Menschgott* (man-God) of Abraham, Isaac, and Jacob.[48] Ratzinger deduces that it is legitimate for Augustine to perceive the Christian God as the "hyphenated" God, posited between neo-Platonic ontology and Scripture. The abstract God, perceived in philosophical terms, becomes in Jesus Christ the God human beings can address.

This entails far-reaching consequences. Over and against Brunner's position, Ratzinger argues that the synthesis of biblical faith with the Hellenic *Geist* (mind) achieved by the Church Fathers—but which, it is important to note, the Old Testament had anticipated—is legitimate and even "necessary," thereby presupposing the *analogia entis*, which would not be taught explicitly until the Middle Ages. The analogy of being is "a necessary dimension of the Christian reality."[49] The absolute God of monotheism and the biblical God turning to humankind coincide. Ratzinger sees this development as being justified already as early on as Deutero-Isaiah relating the God of Israel as no ethnic or immanent or fertility deity, but rather as "the absolute ground of the world."[50] He substantiates this view by quoting Isaiah 40:12–18: "Who has measured the waters . . . weighed the mountains? . . . Behold, the nations are like a drop from a bucket. . . . All the nations are as nothing before him. . . . To whom then will you liken God or what likeness compare with him?"[51]

Poetically circumscribed by the prophet, the singular God of Israel utterly transcends all empires and human imagination. Paradoxically, in this Israelite perspective, the absolutely ineffable God is presented as the God who simultaneously both is accessible to human beings and retains the character of utter ineffability. He parallels this with passages from Ezra and Daniel. The *Deus otiosus* (God resting in his aseity) becomes close and yet retains the qualities of radical otherness, ruling over all peoples. Herein, Ratzinger

[47] Ratzinger, *Der Gott des Glaubens*, 26.

[48] The text refers to Eduard Zeller, *Philosophie der Griechen*, 4th ed., vol. 3/2 (Leipzig: Reisland, 1903); and Heinrich von Glasenapp, *Die Nichtchristlichen Religionen*, *Fischer-Lexikon*, vol. 1 (Frankfurt am Main: Fischer Bücherei, 1957), 76ff and 156ff.

[49] Ratzinger, *Der Gott des Glaubens*, 30.

[50] Ratzinger, *Der Gott des Glaubens*, 30.

[51] Ratzinger, *Der Gott des Glaubens*, 30. For this section, he consulted Alfons Deißler's article "Gott," in *Bibeltheologisches Wörterbuch*, ed. J. B. Bauer (Graz, AT: Styria, 1959), 352–68; and Walther Eichrodt, *Theologie des Alten Testaments*, vol. 1 (Leipzig: Hinrichsen, 1913).

detects already in late-sixth-century-BC Israel the God of the philosophers and the one of biblical faith becoming close to being synonymous.

At the same time, he cautions against facilely conflating philosophical and biblical terms, such as divine eternity, omnipotence, unity, truth, goodness, and sanctity. Yet there is a remarkable approximation between *theologia naturalis* and the revealed God of Scripture already at a time when philosophical terms had only gradually begun to develop in ancient Greece. Concurrently, Israel apprehends God by virtue of his ontic density as the one God liberated from anthropomorphisms.[52] Significantly, Ratzinger avers, the appropriation of an abstract or philosophical understanding of God by ancient, "less expansive" Israel logically leads to the now essentially missionary and evangelizing form of biblical faith in Christianity. This is the case precisely on account of the fact that the God of biblical revelation can be "translated" into "the common language of human reason."[53] He summarizes: "The true claim of Christian faith in its greatness and earnestness can ever again be rendered visible only through the hyphen towards that which human beings have already earlier grasped [philosophically] in some form as the absolute."[54] Ratzinger asserts that, if Christianity were to surrender the metaphysical dimensions of the Judeo-Christian understanding of God, then invariably it would simultaneously give up on its claim to universality.

He concludes his lecture by discussing the relational unity (*Beziehungseinheit*) of philosophy and faith. He acknowledges there is validity in "the partial system of identity"[55] as developed by Thomas. In a footnote, he concedes, however, referencing his predecessor on the Bonn chair, Albert Lang, that Scheler's reservations are justified, as there can be only a unity of relation between faith and philosophy, as there can never be an identity of *religio naturalis* and *theologia naturalis*. Against Scheler, he detects this being, in fact, also rather close to Thomas's position.[56] Likewise, there must be legitimacy to "the hyphen" between the God of faith and the God of the philosophers. This notwithstanding, he recognizes in Brunner's position a genuine concern one must take seriously.[57] He argues that, precisely by possessing its own methods and approaches, philosophy can be that discipline

[52] Ratzinger, *Der Gott des Glaubens*, 31

[53] Ratzinger, *Der Gott des Glaubens*, 31.

[54] Ratzinger, *Der Gott des Glaubens*, 31–32.

[55] Ratzinger, *Der Gott des Glaubens*, 33.

[56] Ratzinger, *Der Gott des Glaubens*, 64n17. See also Ratzinger's reference to Albert Lang, *Wesen und Wahrheit der Religion* (Munich: Hueber, 1957), 88–89.

[57] Ratzinger, *Der Gott des Glaubens*, 33.

to which faith intends to relate and by which it makes itself understood. By shedding all vestiges of polytheism, he sees philosophy preparing humankind to become the properly prepared addressee of divine revelation.[58] The great achievement of Greek natural theology was being veracious enough not to distill from human thought a god for mythical or religious piety.

Ratzinger admits remaining somewhat critical of this approximation of biblical faith and metaphysics by Christian apologetics and the Church Fathers. Nevertheless, he considers this process as necessary and beneficial for both sides. The nature of the question pleads for maintaining a tension between the two. In relation to each other, both disciplines gain their respective contours, acquire greater depth, and achieve their "requisite critical purification and transformation" ("kritische[n] *Läuterung und Verwandlung*").[59] If God is indeed personal, then, from this insight, philosophical language must be revisited and rethought afresh, a task not performed by first millennium Christianity. He suggests this is a question Catholic and Protestant theologians could now jointly address.

In closing, he reminds his audience of the actual mission of "theo-logy" according to Psalm 104:4, Augustine, and Richard of St. Victor: "*Quaerite faciem eius semper*—seek constantly His face." He remarks: "The task of theology remains in this aeon necessarily incomplete. It is precisely the ever fresh seeking for God's countenance 'until he comes' and is Himself the answer to all questions."[60] Indicative of his own theological proclivities, he quotes from Hans Urs von Balthasar's translation of Augustine's *Ennarrationes in Psalmos* 104.[61]

OBSERVATIONS

In this early stage of his academic life, Ratzinger reveals himself as what will later be known as a *communio* theologian. In addition, he subscribes to a form of dialogical personalism similar to Brunner's position. Unlike

[58] On this point, he refers readers to his article "Ewigkeit II," in *Lexikon für Theologie und Kirche*, vol. 3, 2nd ed. (Freiburg im Breisgau: Herder, 1959), 1268ff. There he had already developed a dialectical relationship between faith and reason.

[59] Ratzinger does not specify what he might mean by *Verwandlung* but, in a footnote, refers the reader to Pannenberg's already cited *Aufnahme*. He also references his own "Ewigkeit II"and *Der Gott des Glaubens*, 64n18. There, transformation is defined as "Gemeinschaft mit dem Gott-Menschen Christus Jesus." This is the *aevum* between *aeternum* and temporality.

[60] Ratzinger, *Der Gott des Glaubens*, 35.

[61] Ratzinger, *Der Gott des Glaubens*, 65n20. There, reference is made to Augustine, *Das Antlitz der Kirche*, ed. Hans Urs von Balthasar (Einsiedeln: Johannes, 1942), 352.

the transcendental Thomist Karl Rahner, Ratzinger sees no need to develop independently a natural theology to which a theology of revelation will then give account.[62]

He is careful to note an insurmountable material difference between what philosophy can yield as regards what/who God might be and what God actually reveals of himself. He registers a material difference, but equally an ontological coincidence, between a philosophical understanding of God and what faith knows God to be. The historical horizon of the philosophical quest for God is ultimately open to the same God as the one proclaimed by Judeo-Christian revelation. The truth of humankind's existential and intellectual search is welcomed and transformed by the true God in his self-communication. This notwithstanding, the God of revelation is radically different from what finite cognition can reach with the resources at its disposal, oftentimes self-constrained by a rigid, closed systematization of the question. However, the merit of such thinking "on the border of reason" is to highlight that the human being is, by his nature, "a surplus" that encounters its fulfillment in revelation, which it cannot reach on its own. Philosophical truth becomes personal, divine-human truth in Jesus Christ as the *Logos*. Truth and charity become synonymous in Christ. Rather apodictically, he states that negating the possibility of a correlation between philosophy and revelation amounts to abolishing humankind, as almost five decades later he and Jürgen Habermas would agree in 2004.[63] The inaugural lecture of 1959 demonstrates the remarkable consistency of positions, insights, and lines of argumentation of the theologian Ratzinger over the decades. Ratzinger also reminds listeners of the abiding relevance of Thomas Aquinas on this point. *Ab initio*, he thereby argues against facile simplifications, as manifested in fideism and rationalism. Both faith and reason stand to gain from relating to one another time and again. Were faith to retreat from rationality into the realm of "mere piety," it would betray the Incarnation of the eternal *Logos*, Jesus Christ, as Ratzinger later demonstrates in his classic *Introduction to Christianity*.[64] In the same vein, one may not deny philosophy its meta-

---

[62] Ratzinger, *Milestones*, 128–29. See also Karl Rahner, *Hörer des Wortes: Zur Grundlegung einer Religionsphilosophie* (Munich: Kösel, 1942) [English: *Hearer of the Word: Laying the Foundation for a Philosophy of Religion*, trans. Joseph Donceel (New York: Continuum, 1994)].

[63] Jürgen Habermas and Joseph Ratzinger, *Dialectics of Secularization: Reason and Religion*, trans. Brian McNeil (San Francisco: Ignatius Press, 2006).

[64] Joseph Ratzinger, *Introduction to Christianity*, trans. J. R. Foster (San Francisco: Ignatius Press, 2004), 184–90.

physical competence, as this would deprive faith of "air to breathe." Faith and reason are not autonomous entities. As he later succinctly phrases the situation: without faith, reason fails to become authentic; however, faith without reason fails to become humane.[65]

Ratzinger's understanding of Christian revelation as divine self-communication will significantly inform the Second Vatican Council's Dogmatic Constitution on Divine Revelation, *Dei Verbum*.

St. John Paul II, in all probability indebted to Ratzinger, succinctly captured this mutually indebted relationship of faith and reason in the *prooemium* to his encyclical *Fides et ratio*: "Faith and reason are like two wings on which the human spirit rises to the contemplation of truth and God has placed in the heart a desire to know the truth—in a word, to know himself—so that, by knowing and loving God, men and women may also come to the fullness of truth about themselves (cf. Ex 33:18; Ps 27:8–9; 63:2–3; Jn 14:8; 1 Jn 3:2)."[66]

A few years later, in his now famous dialogue with Habermas, Ratzinger states that there is a requisite correlationality between reason and faith: they are called to a reciprocal purification and sanctification, and both sides are in need of recognizing this.[67] Then, the words of Our Lord are freeing human rationality from being "amputated reason" and from the fallacies attendant to all ideologies: "I am the way, and the truth, and the life" (John 14:6). This is what Ratzinger means when defining Christianity as the synthesis of faith and reason.

A Course on Fundamental Theology

Professor Ratzinger lectured from notes and keywords he had jotted down in an exercise book commonly used in German schools. Usually, he never prepared university lectures word by word. Only some scripts authored by

---

[65] Joseph Ratzinger, *Glaube—Wahrheit—Vernunft Das Christentum und die Weltreligionen* (Freiburg im Breisgau: Herder, 2003), 110: "Die Vernunft wird ohne den Glauben nicht heil, aber der Glaube wird ohne die Vernunft nicht menschlich."

[66] Pope John Paul II, Encyclical Letter on the Relationship between Faith and Reason *Fides et Ratio* (Vatican City: Libreria Editrice Vaticana, 1998), 3.

[67] "Ich würde . . . von einer notwendigen Korrelationaltät von Vernunft und Glaube, Vernunft und Religion sprechen, die zu gegenseitiger Reinigung und Heilung berufen sind und die sich gegenseitig brauchen und das gegenseitig anerkennen müssen" (Jürgen Habermas and Joseph Ratzinger, "Vorpolitische moralische Grundlagen eines freiheitlichen Staates," *zur debatte: Themen der Katholischen Akademie in Bayern* 34, no. 1 [2004]: 1–7, at 7).

individual students are now extant—but remain unpublished.[68] While it is safe to assume a difference between what Ratzinger actually lectured and how students received his elaborations, one encounters a similar situation already with some of Aristotle's most crucial writings. It was on the basis of such a typed and mimeographed script that students would prepare for the oral examination with Father Ratzinger, usually lasting twenty minutes. The student typing a script would earn a bit on the side by selling copies to his fellow students.

Though by avocation a fundamental theologian, he would read also in the area of dogmatics. In fact, of the forty-four lectures, seminars, and colloquia he held between the winter semester of 1954/1955 and the winter semester of 1962/1963 in Freising and Bonn, only nineteen can be considered as covering aspects of fundamental theology in the strict sense of that discipline.[69] The renaissance, versatile nature of his courses needs to be

---

[68] Schlögl, *Am Anfang eines grossen Weges*, 126.

[69] The following are the courses he taught at Freising Seminary. Winter Semester [WS] 1954/1955: *Die Lehre vom dreieinigen Gott* (lecture); *Colloquium zur Vorlesung* (colloquium). Summer Semester [SS] 1955: *Die Lehre von der Schöpfung* (lecture); *Grundprobleme der Confessiones Augustins* (seminar). WS 1955/1956: *Dogmatik: Die Lehre von unserem Heil in Jesus Christus* (lecture); *Fundamentaltheologie I: Grundlinien der Religionsphänomenologie und Religionsphilosophie* (lecture); *Moderne christologische und mariologische Literatur* (seminar). SS 1956: *Dogmatik: Gnadenlehre* (lecture); *Fundamentaltheologie II: Religion und Offenbarung* (lecture); *Ausgewählte Texte zur Gnadenlehre des Thomas von Aquin* (seminar). WS 1956/1957: *Dogmatik: Sakramentenlehre, I. Teil* (lecture); *Fundamentaltheologie III: Ekklesiologie* (lecture); *Fundamentaltheologie: Übungen zum Kirchenbegriff unter besonderer Berücksichtigung des Petrusproblems* (seminar). SS 1957: *Dogmatik: Sakramentenlehre, 2. Teil/ Eschatologie* (lecture); *Mariologie; Seminar, Die theologischen Probleme der heutigen Mariologie* (lecture). WS 1957/1958: *Dogmatik: Die Lehre vom dreieinigen Gott* (lecture); *Die Lehre von den Letzten Dingen* (lecture); *Fundamentaltheologisches Kolloquium zur Frage des Traditionsbegriffs* (seminar). SS 1958: *Dogmatik: Der Schöpfergott und Sein Werk* (lecture); *Fundamentaltheologie IV: Grundprobleme der theologischen Erkenntnislehre* (lecture); *Die moderne Diskussion über das Verhältnis von Natur und Übernatürlichem* (seminar). WS 1958/1959: *Dogmatik: Die Lehre vom Heil des Menschen in Christus Jesus* (lecture); *Fundamentaltheologie I: Wesen und Wahrheit der Religionen* (lecture); *Kritische Lektüre der Augsburger Konfession* (seminar).

At the Rheinische Friedrich-Wilhelms-Universität in Bonn, he taught the following courses. SS 1959: *Einführung in die Religionsphilosophie* (lecture); *Theologische Erkenntnislehre: Glaube und Theologie* (lecture); *Der Theologiebegriff in Bonaventuras De reductione artium ad theologiam* (major seminar). WS 1959/1960: *Wesen und Wirklichkeit der göttlichen Offenbarung* (lecture); *Gottesbeweise in Geschichte und Gegenwart* (seminar). SS 1960: *Die Lehre von der Kirche* (lecture); *Kirche, Sakrament und Glaube nach der Augsburgischen Konfession* (seminar). WS 1960/1961: *Religionsphilosophie I:*

emphasized. In his courses on religion, he would incorporate the most recent findings from non-biblical religions and peoples or the natural sciences. Oftentimes, a philosophical perspective would be employed to enrich a theological insight. The seminars he held display ecumenical interests, such as Melanchthon and the *Augsburg Confession*. Though his terminal studies had focused on the thought of Augustine and Bonaventure, he displayed a consistent interest in Thomas Aquinas, such as the relationship of grace and nature and the natural and supernatural. In the area of dogmatics, he read tractates on Mariology, ecclesiology, sacraments, soteriology, creation, eschatology, and the Blessed Trinity. In fundamental theology, he addressed the topics of revelation, the nature of religion and philosophy of religion, the Petrine office, the nature of Tradition, religious epistemology, proofs of God's existence, the natural sciences, and the nature of contemporary apologetics.

A *scriptum* titled "Wesen und Wahrheit der Religion—Grundlinien einer Phänomenologie und Philosophie der Religion, Nach einer Vorlesung aus der Fundamentaltheologie" ("The Nature and Truth of Religion—An Outline of a Phenomenology and Philosophy of Religion, according to a Course in Fundamental Theology"), written by the seminarian and future priest Josef Mühlbacher at Freising Seminary during the winter semester of 1958/1959, offers insight into Ratzinger's theological concerns at that time.[70]

In this course, Ratzinger first discusses the possibilities and limits of a *theologia fundamentalis* (§1). This is followed by a presentation of the

Religionsgeschichtliche Grundlegung (lecture); *Probleme der frühchristlichen Kirchenverständnisses* (seminar, jointly with the noted patristic scholar Alfred Stuiber [1912–1981]). SS 1961: *Fundamentaltheologie I: Gottes Offenbarung in Jesus Christus* (lecture); *Grundfragen der Religionsphilosophie* (seminar); *Religionsphilosophische Probleme in den Confessiones Augustins* (seminar). WS 1961/1962: *Religionsphilosophie II: Religion und Offenbarung* (lecture); *Colloquium Für Laientheologen über Probleme einer zeitgemäßen Apologetik* (colloquium); *Gesetz und Gnade nach Thomas von Aquin* (seminar). SS 1962: *Fundamentaltheologie II: Die Lehre von der Kirche* (lecture); *Grenzfragen zwischen Naturwissenschaft und Glaube* (seminar). WS 1962/1963: *Religionsphilosophie I: Religionsgeschichtliche Grundlegung* (lecture); *Melanchtons Tractatus de potestate papae* (seminar).

For these details, see *Joseph Ratzinger / Papst Benedikt XVI, Das Werk: Veröffentlichungen bis zur Papstwahl*, ed. Vinzenz Pfnür (Augsburg: St. Ulrich, 2009), 401–3.

70 Pfnür, *Das Werk*, 402. All quotations of Mühlbacher's *scriptum* for the course will be taken from Pfnür's volume and will be cited simply as "*Scriptum*"; please note that the page numbers given for these citations are an original numbering that is internal to Mühlbacher's *scriptum* and included in Pfnür's presentation of the document's contents, rather than Pfnür's own volume page numbers.

genesis of the terms "philosophy of religion" and "phenomenology of religion" (§2). In continuity with this trajectory, theories regarding the origin of religion are discussed (§3). On these bases, he then discusses the unity and pluriformity of religions (§4). Upon this broad anthropological background, he subsequently presents the "metaphysical type" of insight as exemplified by Thomas Aquinas and the "religious type" as advanced by Augustine (§§5–6). In the final section, he then relates metaphysical and religious insight to "the truth of religion" (§§7–8).

It is interesting to note that Ratzinger had delivered a course on §2 already during the winter semester of 1955/1956, while during the summer semester of 1956, he had devoted a course to §§5–6.[71]

In §1, Ratzinger asserts "the inner right" of fundamental theology to supply a rational basis for faith. He admits, however, that there exists "a double aporia" for fundamental theology. Conventional apologetics seems no longer tenable in light of scientism. A rational penetration of faith is commonly considered not viable. With reference to messianic cries of jubilee in Matthew 11:25–27 and Luke 10:21–22, he sees rationality as unable to access faith. Paul underscores this separation in his *moria* (folly) teaching (1 Cor 1:18–2:5): there is a qualitative difference between insight into revelation and scientific knowledge. As exemplars of this position, he presents Peter Damian, Bernard of Clairvaux, and Francis of Assisi. He regards Martin Luther as indebted to Peter Damian for his anti-intellectual stance, on the basis of which he rejected Scholasticism *in globo*. Indebted to such earlier Lutheran, anthropological decisions, and coming from different perspectives, Kant and Schleiermacher drive yet deeper the wedge between faith and science. Ratzinger observes: "One can state that Kant became the Aristotle of Protestantism (while) Schleiermacher became its Thomas."[72]

Subsequently, he presents the "Catholic solution to this aporia." On the basis of the Johannine Christ as *the Logos*, the rationality of Christianity is laid forth. He mentions that Lutheran theologian and friend Heinrich Schlier (1900–1978) converted to Catholicism when he discovered this form of Christianity doing justice to the intellectual quality of Christian faith, which he found is original to the New Testament.[73] Ratzinger lists a number of "intellectual" theologians: Athanasius, Hil-

---

[71] Pfnür, *Das Werk*, 401.

[72] *Scriptum*, 3.

[73] *Scriptum*, 5.

ary, Augustine, Bonaventure, and Thomas Aquinas.[74] Ergo, Jesus Christ is rational *and* divine self-communication—objective and subjective at the same time—as "Offenbarung ist die Selbsterschließung Gottes an den Menschen" ("revelation is the self-disclosure of God to man"), or phrased differently: "revelation is the [human] 'I' being touched by the 'Thou' of God."[75] Therefore, faith is indeed, as the Council of Trent declares, *virtus supernaturalis*.[76] It follows for Ratzinger that "[göttliche Selbst-] Offenbarung ist inwendiges Hineintauchen in das Herz des je einzelnen Ich, das vor Gott steht" ("[divine self-] revelation is the interior immersion into the heart of the individual 'I,' standing in front of God").[77] Echoing de Lubac's seminal study *Catholicisme*, he observes that such revelation is transmitted in community. While there is an internal inspiration by virtue of the (subjective) *verbum inspiratum*, an equally important second component must be noted: the *doctrina externa*, which is based on the (historical) *verbum incarnatum*—Jesus Christ. Together, these two moments describe revelation. The actual insight into revelation occurs in the personal, interior contact with God ("inwendiger Kontakt mit Gott") and, thus, is beyond the range of scientific investigation. Exactly on account of this personal constitution of revelation, it can be accessed equally by the *näpios* (childlike) and the *moiros* (fortunate).[78] This delineates simultaneously "the grandeur and limits of theology."[79] While reflecting on and expressing the positive content of revelation, theology needs to remain ever mindful of the personal—and thus ultimately unscientific and inexplicable—dimensions of faith, which by its very nature is mystery. This permits Ratzinger to circumscribe fundamental theology as follows: it "kann nicht den Offenbarungsglauben erzeugen oder begründen, das kann nur Gott allein, aber Fundamentaltheologie kann die Sinngemäßheit der mit dem Offenbarungsglauben verbundenen Lehre aufweisen" (it "cannot generate or establish the faith of revelation, this only God can do, but fundamen-

74 *Scriptum*, 5.

75 *Scriptum*, 5.

76 *Scriptum*, 5, refers to a section of Denzinger-Schönmetzer (DS 1789)—Denzinger-Schönmetzer, *Enchiridion Definitionum* add Freiburg i. Br.: Herder, 1958 and Hünermann with UMLAUTS Denzinger-Hünermann, *Enchiridion Definitionum*, Freiburg i. Br.: Herder, 2008—that is not reprinted in the 43rd German edition, edited by Peter Hünermann, and thus does not appear in the 2012 Ignatius Press Latin–English edition edited by Robert Fastiggi and Anne Englund Nash (DH).

77 *Scriptum*, 5.

78 *Scriptum*, 7.

79 *Scriptum*, 7.

tal theology can evidence the inner intellectual coherence of the doctrine connected to the faith of revelation").[80]

Discussing philosophy of religion and phenomenology of religion, he demonstrates how both terms are colored by Deism's reduced vision of religion—and, by extension, of the human being. Limited to sense experience, man can no longer penetrate metaphysical reality. Ratzinger presents the positions of Schleiermacher and Kant, as well those of Albrecht Ritschl, Wilhelm Herrmann, and Karl Barth, as indebted to this epochal context. This presentation is followed by a brief discussion of early-twentieth-century thinkers Edmund Husserl, Max Scheler, Martin Heidegger, Rudolf Bultmann, and Nicolai Hartmann. For Ratzinger, merely descriptive religious phenomenology is philosophically unsatisfactory. Likewise, the logical but scientific *Quinque viae* of Thomas are inaccessible for our age. At the same time, the uncertainty principle discovered by Werner Heisenberg in the field of physics cautions against overconfidence in the positive sciences. The positive sciences cannot always be trusted in producing unambiguous results.[81]

He alerts his students that, according to Pascal, human reason can gain insight and state what is true and false. But it is volition that can achieve bliss or beatitude as it existentially differentiates between salvation and damnation (*Heil und Unheil*).[82] Only human volition can decide the question of God's existence, as there is no completely convincing proof for God's existence by human reason. This Pascalian position best reflects Ratzinger's own position.

In the section on the origin and nature of religion in general (§3), he apprehends history as a valuable aid. He discusses dynamism, fetishism, and animism, all of which ultimately recognize the reality of a soul and of all being as ensouled. He mentions critically the theory of a primordial monotheism preceding the advent of polytheism as propounded by Wilhem Schmidt, S.V.D.[83] The primordially religious orientation of human existence suggests humankind being created, *ab initio*, for God: the

---

[80] *Scriptum*, 7.

[81] *Scriptum*, 13. See also Werner Heisenberg, *Der Teil und das Ganze* (Munich: Piper, 1969). Heisenberg discovered the uncertainty principle already in 1927. This principle takes into account the fact that light may appear as either wave or corpuscle, but never at the same time and under the same consideration.

[82] *Scriptum*, 10.

[83] See Wilhelm Schmidt, *Der Ursprung der Gottesidee: eine historisch-kritische und positive Studie*, 12 vols. (Münster: Aschendorff, 1926–1955).

capacitas infiniti.[84] If this is indeed the case, Ratzinger asks, "What does religious cult intend?" And he responds that it intends "adoration," which is "a radical form of love."[85] This leads Ratzinger to the insight that it is "God who loves and not we human beings. . . . The most sublime parable for religion remains bridal, matrimonial love (OT-NT)."[86] This in turn permits the professor to define religion, notably from a philosophical vantage point, as ". . . based on the fact that man is *capax infiniti*, capable of God, in need of God . . . [and as] the acceptance of one's being, as being loved and of loving in turn the eternal love, called adoration, and which finds concrete form in cult."[87] However, allowing magic to enter the sphere of religion dispenses of love. In this context, he reminds his students of the always valid critique of the Old Testament prophets and King Saul.

In the next section, he discusses first Gotthold Ephraim Lessing's (1729–1781) famous ring parable in the dramatic poem *Nathan the Wise.* He then sees essentially two patterns of religious experience existing, what he circumscribes as the Eastern and Western variants.[88] While Judaism, Christianity, and Islam are unambiguously monotheistic, Eastern religions are essentially polytheistic. For the former, there is an inherent value to this contingent reality, as there (human) persons can address a God perceived as personal. In the latter, no deity can be addressed, as it is not considered personal, and on this point, the East parallels the philosophical positions of Plato and Aristotle. To the Eastern mind, all activities are preliminary (and therefore futile) to a final state that becomes one of negation of anything previous. Whatever is palpable in the here and now is but deception.[89]

Hinduism receives rather extensive treatment. He discusses the concept of *Karma*, which considers the world as "a single wheel without beginning and end." In a similar vein, *samsara* is frighteningly negative, since it holds that "there is no redemption in this world, but only from this world."[90] This world is seen by the Hindu philosopher Shankara (AD

[84] *Scriptum*, 17.

[85] *Scriptum*, 17.

[86] *Scriptum*, 17.

[87] *Scriptum*, 17: "Philosophische Definition: Religion beruht auf der Tatsache, da- der Mensch capax infiniti, gottfähig, gottbedürftig, ist. Sie ist die Annahme des eigenen Seins als Geliebt-sein und jenes wiederlieben der ewigen Liebe, das Anbetung heißt und im Kult konkrete Gestalt findet."

[88] *Scriptum*, 18.

[89] *Scriptum*, 20.

[90] *Scriptum*, 20.

800) as but a dangerously deceptive illusion (*maya*). Ratzinger registers passivity and unity as the outstanding, presumably positive characteristics of the Hindu deity, which one is allowed to enter someday. When speaking of Buddhism, Ratzinger notes that *nirvana* is not merely liberation from *samsara* (change) and the burdensome human "I," but defines entry into a radically different world, shedding one of one's identity. He also notes that Buddhist "love of neighbor" is quite unlike the Christian understanding of this term. In Christianity, this love is due to a worldview of an infinite valuing of one's own personhood and an elevating of every other human being to the same level of esteem. In contrast, he cautions his students, Buddhism practices not love of neighbor, but compassion with everyone and everything animate—including plants. Ergo, "the foreign I [i.e., other person] should be loved as little as my own I."[91]

The Eastern God is thus not one of action, but of negation vis-à-vis the restless activities of the world. The "antinomy" between Western and Eastern religions can be resolved only in the unity of the divine and human natures of Jesus Christ as defined by the Council of Chalcedon: united, unconfused, unchanging, indivisible, and inseparable,[92] who alone reconciles "immanence and transcendence." The normativity of Jesus Christ notwithstanding, he cautions his listeners: "We should assimilate the positive aspects of all religions, integrating them into the salvific Christ [*Christusheil*]."[93]

For this section, Ratzinger consulted books authored by the French scholar Jacques A. Cuttat and Franz König, later cardinal and archbishop of Vienna.[94]

In the next two sections, he differentiates between two principle modes of insight into divine existence: "metaphysical insight" as developed by Thomas Aquinas and "religious insight" (distinguishing terms he adopts from Scheler) as represented by Augustine. In §5, he presents and discusses "metaphysical insight." While Augustine had stated that "Deum esse est verum indubitabile" ("divine being is truly indubitable"), Thomas believed that "Deum esse est demonstrabile" ("divine being is demonstra-

---

[91] *Scriptum*, 21: "das fremde Ich soll so wenig geliebt werden, wie das eigene."

[92] DH 302.

[93] *Scriptum*, 22.

[94] *Scriptum*, 23. See also: Jacques A. Cuttat, *Begegnung der Religionen* (Einsiedeln: Johannes, 1956); Franz König, *Christus und die Religionen der Erde*, 3 vols. (Freiburg im Breisgau: Herder, 1951); König, *Religionswissenschaftliches Wörterbuch* (Freiburg im Breisgau: Herder, 1956).

ble").[95] These "analytical" statements define the respective thinkers' positions as regards the question of God. With Thomas's approach, Ratzinger argues, one is able to reach "*Deus per se*, but not *quoad nos*," while Augustine's position yields "Deus esse per se quoad nos" (divine being insofar as for us). To Thomas's mind, there exists in humans a yearning for beatitude that is "a dark preliminary knowledge of God."[96] Any knowledge of God presupposes something noetic and anthropological. The latter, however, Thomas "barely indicates."[97] It is on this crucial point that Ratzinger critiques him. While admitting the need to prove the sentence "God exists," Thomas actually "does not go beyond" a rational distillation.[98] Though Thomas admits that Augustine is right to assert God is presupposed in every true statement, as he is the *prima veritas*, the great Dominican theologian tragically and subcutaneously constricts God to being per se and implicitly excludes his being for us.[99]

After these preliminary remarks, Ratzinger discusses *in extenso* the *Quinque viae*.[100] Being loyal to the Aristotelian philosophical self-limitation to sense perception, Ratzinger sees evidenced in the Thomistic proof of God's existence not a creator God, but merely a first mover. He considers Thomas's conclusion of "et hoc omnes nominant Deum" ("and this all call God") to be illegitimate, as here, *sub rosa*, metaphysics and religion are conflated: "Thomas raises a question he does not provide an answer for."[101] He merely demonstrates the final or first member of a physical chain. Hence, on the basis of a Christian perspective, Thomas's approach must nowadays be disregarded. Rather, in discourse with contemporaries, reference should be made to "the objective spirit" one encounters on a daily basis in the world (*objektiven Geist*).[102] Is this meant with a nod to Rahner's much discussed *Geist in der Welt*?[103] On a purely scientific

---

95 *Scriptum*, 23 (as quoted).

96 *Scriptum*, 24.

97 *Scriptum*, 24.

98 *Scriptum*, 24.

99 *Scriptum*, 25.

100 *Scriptum*, 25–29. See also Thomas Aquinas, *Summa Theologiae* I, q. 2, a. 1, and *Summa Contra Gentiles* I, ch. 13.

101 *Scriptum*, 27: "Unter der Hand wird Metaphysik und Religion identifiziert. Dieser Schritt vom ‚Erstbeweger' zum Gott der Religion ist keine Selbstverständlichkeit. Bei Aristoteles hat das ‚protokinum' nichts mit Religion zu tun. Thomas wirft eine Frage auf, die bei ihm nicht beantwortet ist; von dieser Frage hängt aber der Wert des Gottesbeweises ab."

102 *Scriptum*, 28.

103 An endnote reference is made to Rahner, *Hörer des Wortes*, 141; see *Scriptum*, 14.

basis, one should readily admit the aporetic nature of the quest for proving God's existence. He envisions four possible theoretical responses: materialism, idealism, Christian theism, or dualism. The first two he considers "Identitätssysteme."[104] The incontrovertible fact of objective spirit existing in the world eliminates materialism as a viable option for resolving the problem of God. On the other hand, idealism cannot explain the individual human person. It is in Christianity that both the objectivity of God and the unique individuality of the human person are safeguarded and come to the fore and that the human being is dignified beyond imagination (the latter seems to be implied in the script).[105] Reference is made to the writings of Eugen Rolfes, A. Dondeyne, and J. Allan in this section.[106]

Counterintuitively, only now does Ratzinger discuss the "religious type" as represented by Augustine. Here the *cor mundum* (the cleansed heart) is the singular locus of insight into God. Ever confident of the epistemological import of the senses, Thomas states, "Et hoc omnes intelligent Deum" ("and this all recognize as God"). Diametrically opposed to this approach, Augustine argues (in Ratzinger's inimitable words): "God stands behind man. When I intend recognizing God, I need to turn around."[107] The interiority of the human mind is central. Beyond the *videre corpore sensibus* (seeing bodily via the senses), there is for him the *videre corde mentis intuite interior homine* (beholding the heart of the mind intuitively by the interior man). Truth is present to the human spirit, but sin alienates from the attendant interior eyesight. It is regained via an ascetical *purgatio cordis*.[108] Without any preceding academic problematization on his part, Augustine had recognized this.

In his presentation, Ratzinger genetically traces Augustine's thoughts on this matter from his time at Cassiacum, to his ministry as priest, and finally to his ministry as bishop. A key insight is offered to Augustine by Acts 15:9: "He had purified their hearts through faith." The *homo exterior* becomes, through Christ, the *homo interior*. Later, for Augustine, the Petrine motif is enriched by the Pauline (Eph 3:18) and Johannine (John 14:9) motifs. Conformity to *both* beams of the Cross of Christ permits

---

[104] *Scriptum*, 28.

[105] *Scriptum*, 29.

[106] *Scriptum*, 29. See also: Eugen Rolfes, *Der Gottesbeweis bei Thomas und Aristoteles* (Limburg: Steffen, 1927); Albert Dondeyne, "Die Existenz Gottes und der zeitgenössische Materialismus," in *Gott, Mensch, Universum* (Graz, AT: Styria, 1957), 25ff; Donald James Allan, *Die Philosophie des Aristoteles* (Hamburg: F. Meiner, 1955).

[107] *Scriptum*, 29.

[108] *Scriptum*, 29.

one to gain heuristic progress: "love so that you may behold" ("ama, ut videas"). On this point, Ratzinger observes that Augustine is considerably clearer than Scheler. It is in this *Mystik des Dienstes* (mysticism of service), drawing its inspiration from the horizontal beam of the Cross, that ever greater knowledge can be reached—which explains Augustine as the great "pastor of souls" ("als Seelsorger").[109] As God is essentially invisible, any insight into God depends on God revealing himself. Ratzinger seconds this Augustinian position by way of recourse to Blessed John Henry Newman, when the latter states that God is recognized by one's conscience.[110] While Augustine does see humankind seeking beatitude, Ratzinger points out that this does not serve for the African Church Father as a proof of God's existence.[111]

With a diagram, Ratzinger summarizes Augustine's theology. While philosophy may entail purgation and humility, which lead to love and beatitude, theology is underpinned by faith and the Incarnation, as unfolded in the Old and New Testaments and Christian doctrine. This leads to charity and to Christ as God, which are sustained by cult, importantly bifurcated into Eucharist and love of one's neighbor. Ratzinger apprehends a grand unity in this Augustinian thought.[112]

This is followed by brief but penetrating summaries of the views of Pascal, Newman, and Scheler. He sees Pascal arguing that a metaphysical proof of God, while legitimate, remains but an abstract insight, void of religious relevance.[113] Regarding Newman, he presents this Englishman's distinction between notional and real assent and discusses his famous statement that "many a man will live and die upon a dogma, no man will be a martyr for a conclusion."[114] It is of great import for Christianity that at her beginning stood the testimony of simple believers and not a learned lecture.[115] Scheler's position is discussed at greater length. On the basis of a distinction between "being" and "value" (*Sein* and *Wert*), Scheler illustrates that a saint can exist only as a *Personwert* (person of value).[116] Far from being something emotional, for Scheler, "to feel" is object-ori-

---

[109] *Scriptum*, 31.

[110] John Henry Newman, *A Grammar of Assent* (Notre Dame, IN: Notre Dame, 2001), 98ff.

[111] *Scriptum*, 32.

[112] *Scriptum*, 33.

[113] *Scriptum*, 33.

[114] *Scriptum*, 34. See also Newman, *A Grammar of Assent*, 89.

[115] *Scriptum*, 34.

[116] *Scriptum*, 34.

ented and culminates in a *Wertfühlen* (being sensitized for values), which can inform both hatred and charity. Ratzinger also critiques Scheler. For instance, Scheler incorrectly simplified the issue by claiming that, for Augustine, charity enjoys primacy while, for Thomas, pure insight rules supreme, thus burying charity. Ratzinger points out that Augustine expressly denies granting charity undisputed primacy.[117] He does, however, agree with Scheler's defining the human person as a unity of acts of charity. This means that one can apprehend the highest person, God, only if one perceives him also as the highest good by way of imitating divine charity. From this follows that authentic recognition of God requires "Mitlieben mit seiner ewigen Liebe" ("loving along with God's eternal charity").[118]

Ratzinger concludes this section by stating that God is never representationally (*gegenständlich*) recognizable or an object of human reason. As God is person, God could also conceal himself. It follows that any human, personal apprehension of God is grounded in divine condescension to reveal himself "naturally."[119] Such historical communication, however, may not be misunderstood as rendering God objectifiable, as Scholasticism had erroneously tried to demonstrate that he is. Anyone attempting to apprehend God merely rationally or metaphysically is unable to grasp divine personhood.[120]

This obvious advantage of religious insight notwithstanding, in §7, Ratzinger advocates for a relational unity (*Beziehungseinheit*) between metaphysical and religious insight. In the *ductus* of Scheler—and, to a lesser degree, of Söhngen—he distinguishes between systems of identity, of duality, and of conformity.[121]

He associates the Enlightenment, and especially Kant, with the first system. When religious and metaphysical insights are identical, then this is, to Ratzinger, gnostic. This also applies when religious insight is generated from metaphysical insight: it is subsumed under the system of identity.[122]

The system of duality, where religion and metaphysics are unrelated, is perceived as ultimately one of agnosticism and irrationalism. This con-

[117] *Scriptum*, 35.

[118] *Scriptum*, 35.

[119] In all probability "naturally" is intended to mean "historically."

[120] "Jede personale Gotterfassung gründet dann auch auf einer Herablassung Gottes, einer natürlichen Offenbarung Gottes. Das darf aber nicht im objektivistischen Sinne (wie in der Scholastik) aufgefaßt werden. Wer Gott nur ‚natürlich' (rational, metaphysisch) erkennt, der kann die Personalität Gottes nie erfassen" (*Scriptum*, 36).

[121] *Scriptum*, 36.

[122] *Scriptum*, 36.

cept of duality does not allow for any rational access to faith. He identifies Schleiermacher as the main representative of this current.

As the *via media*, the system of conformity is in principle the correct solution for him. Metaphysical and religious insight are different but not separate, as they are intimately related to one another, thereby allowing order to come about. Certitude exists only in faith, whereas philosophy can provide probability. It is in this context that sainthood is achieved: by permitting God to work wondrous things with people.[123] Such perspective allows human insight and human marveling to coexist in harmony. This model vouches for God's utter transcendence remaining intact and yet dignifies the human person beyond compare. Crucially, he notes, the object is "intentionally identical, but materially different."[124] He even ventures to say: "The status of a religion depends on its ability to see this unity of the God of the philosophers and the God of faith. Thus, only jointly can religion and metaphysics recognize the true image of God."[125] This insight leads to the following concluding observation: religion enjoys primacy of insight, as religion supplies its own justification. Religion implies possessing something and being possessed by something greater than one can imagine on one's own—and which remains at the same time always unfathomable, a mystery.[126]

Upon this background, Ratzinger cogently argues that it is religion that grounds and irradiates philosophical metaphysics and allows for it to be pursued in the first place. But now an equally powerful complementary argument emerges, justifying the afore-stated: metaphysics becomes the external condition for religion. Proofs of God's existence legitimize religion. They remain indispensable as they anchor religion in human existence. The relationship of religion to metaphysics corresponds roughly to that of faith to theology.[127]

In §8, he concludes his course by addressing "the truth of religion." By way of introduction, he discusses Gustav Mensching's position of a plurality of religious truths.[128] His *point d'appui* is that were one to

[123] "Der Heilige ist ein Mensch, an dem Gott Wunderbares tut, das bis zum Wunderlichen gehen kann" (*Scriptum*, 37; this is a quotation from Söhngen).

[124] *Scriptum*, 37.

[125] *Scriptum*, 37.

[126] *Scriptum*, 37.

[127] *Scriptum*, 37.

[128] Gustav Mensching, *Die Religionen und die Welt: Typen religiöser Weltanschauung* (Bonn: Ludwig Röhrscheid, 1947). Influenced by Rudolf Otto, Mensching (1901–1978) had been a Protestant German theologian who developed his understanding over

comprehend religious statements as rational, firm knowledge, à la Mensching, thereby exposing these to criticism from rational sciences, one would counterfeit religion's purpose and nature. To Mensching, intolerance becomes impossible, provided one accepts a plurality of symbols. While this concern is *prima vista* laudable, intriguing, and perhaps even captivating, it does not do justice to the very essence of religion, Ratzinger responds. Every religiously inclined human being assumes receiving a truth answerable to reason ("eine rational verantwortbare Wahrheit").[129] Quite artificially, Mensching positions *veritas ontologica* and *gnoseologica* in opposition to one another. However, every religion not only believes God to be true, but ultimately even that God is *the* truth per se. In fact, God is the highest form of insight. Every kind of religious truth intends being plausible and reasonable. He concludes that were this not the case, then Christians could not be held responsible for the way the world evolves and "the Protestant withdrawal from the world" would be the only viable alternative.[130]

This does not, however, occasion Ratzinger to take up cudgels on behalf of a total intelligibility of faith. Referring to Aristotle's characterization of our eyes as stupid like the eyes of owls vis-à-vis what is most luminous, he posits a twofold delimitation vis-à-vis a rationalization of religious truth: (1) objective intelligibility does not correspond to subjective visibility, and (2) God is not an objectively intelligible entity in such a manner that human beings can take possession of him at random (i.e., God is not any kind of object, such as a wine glass, plant, or elephant, but is *sui generis*). This consideration shows that the Scholastic distinction between ontological truth and gnoseological truth is insufficient. To Ratzinger's mind, one needs to introduce also a *veritas mere rationalis* and a *veritas personalis vel veritas integraliter humana* (a personal truth or a truth integral to human nature).[131] This *veritas personalis*—to which religion first and foremost relates—is characterized by it being inseparable from the totality of the human person. Ratzinger observes almost apodictically: "Person muß auf Person antworten, mit der ratio allein geht es nicht" ("person needs to respond to person, reason alone is inadequate"), and this is all the more on account of the object's ontological superiori-

and against theology and the Protestant creeds. He had been a member of the Nazi party (NSDAP) and had taught at Bonn University.

[129] *Scriptum*, 39.

[130] *Scriptum*, 39. This remark is not clarified in the script.

[131] *Scriptum*, 40. In this regard, there is a helpful diagram on *Scriptum*, 42.

ty.[132] Religious truth is rational and much more. At this point, he cannot help observing that the error of St. Thomas and of medieval philosophy of religion in general was to define "so-called natural religion in purely rational terms."[133] Yet, religion is "a truth one cannot fully rationalize."[134] This applies to all religions. Religious truth encompasses the totality of human existence and includes divine reality, "which is not a passive partner of insight."[135] Insight into divine existence constitutively involves a personal and dynamic dimension.

Every religion can be true in two regards: objectively, if it is divine self-communication, and subjectively, when it becomes true for the human person insofar as the human being must posit "himself into openness to God."[136] While Christianity always remains objectively the true religion, it may be that a Christian lives less in the true religion than "a Buddhist or Muslim, . . . [as] it requires the addition of a subjective moment, in which truth fulfills itself."[137]

Placing Augustine and Thomas on a scale, he suggests that every human being can progress from *ratio pura* to *ratio purgata*. Insight into God is not a path of simple, intellectual demonstration, but rather first of existential and personal *purgatio cordis*, which then *a posteriori* opens the path to a rational demonstration of faith. For this journey, human beings should cast away all preconceived assumptions. The only permissible assumption is the human being himself. It would miss the level on which religion operates were it to be *a priori* rationally verifiable. Nevertheless, its rational coherence is *a posteriori* recognizable and demonstrable.[138]

The twofold delimitation Ratzinger introduced earlier in this section enables him to state in conclusion a parallel twofold extension of rational statements concerning religious truth: (1) a more intensive opening of human beings to God and (2) a more intensive opening of God to human beings than is humanly imaginable. "From this perspective one can render rationally visible the superiority and absoluteness of Christianity."[139] By this he means that the Chalcedonian formula of Christ being, equally, fully human and fully God states the most monumental thing that any

[132] *Scriptum*, 40.
[133] *Scriptum*, 41.
[134] *Scriptum*, 41.
[135] "Der göttlichen Wirklichkeit, die nicht passiver Erkenntnispartner ist" (*Scriptum*, 41).
[136] *Scriptum*, 41.
[137] *Scriptum*, 41.
[138] *Scriptum*, 42.
[139] *Scriptum*, 43.

religion can possibly define rationally. At the same time, the greatest possibility is stated concerning human beings: "radical openness to God."[140] Both God and human beings are thought in the highest radicalness possible. Heretofore, God had been the faceless *Deus absconditus*, the concealed God. In Christ Jesus, God becomes "the open God," and human beings need do nothing else but enter into this divine openness. Human beings cannot create such openness for the divine on their own. One clearly recognizes now what Christian revelation truly means. It means that God exists in a form that is accessible for all, irrespective of a person's rational sophistication. By teaching reciprocal and total openness, Christianity represents the highest conceivable "religious idea." From this incarnational perspective, any religion left to its own devices appears as "a hopeless endeavor" if divine openness is missing.[141]

A Speech at the Eve of Vatican II

In his Bonn years, Ratzinger contributed in many ways to fundamental theology and he was a much-valued interlocutor. For instance, when the nuncio to West Germany, Archbishop Corrado Bafile, had prepared a talk for an ecumenical gathering, he first consulted Ratzinger in his Bonn apartment before delivering the paper.[142] Little wonder that Joseph Ratzinger became the theological *peritus* to the most influential German bishop during Vatican II.

In sum, while in the Rhineland, Ratzinger had written three smaller books, thirty-three articles/essays, twenty book reviews, and twenty-two dictionary entries.[143] He had planned to publish a textbook on Catholic dogmatic theology during his Bonn years. Though Maria Ratzinger, the theologian's sister, had put several hundred pages to paper and the Munich *Wewel Verlag* had anticipated printing it, the project never materialized.[144] This is regrettable, as it would have not only displayed Ratzinger's superior synthetic powers but may also have positively influenced the reception of Vatican II.

---

[140] *Scriptum*, 43.

[141] *Scriptum*, 43.

[142] "Esequie dell'Em.mo Card. Corrado Bafile. Omelia del Card. Joseph Ratzinger," February 3, 2005, accessed December 4, 2017, http://www.vatican.va/news_services/liturgy/2005/documents/ns_lit_doc_20050205_notification_it.html.

[143] Pfnür, *Das Werk*, 14–15, 115–30.

[144] Ratzinger, *Milestones*, 150.

In an entry under the heading "Katholische Theologie" for the Protestant encyclopedia *Religion in Geschichte und Gegenwart,* he defines fundamental theology thus:

> Fundamental theology is positioned vis-à-vis dogmatic theology as a kind of basic science, which is to justify the claim of the [theological] science presupposing faith and [therein] specifically the right of dogmatic theology of applying a [specific] method. The fact that this foundational science predicates itself as theology demonstrates that the concern is not one of a rational construction of faith, but rather of uncovering that faith is answerable to reason.[145]

The age-old principle of *fides quaerens intellectum* is utilized by Ratzinger in order to localize in the twentieth century the specific charism of the new discipline of fundamental theology.[146] Uncovering and defending the intelligible bases for faith is a recurring leitmotif in his vast *œuvre,* for instance, in *Introduction to Christianity, Principles of Catholic Theology,* and volume 1 of *Jesus of Nazareth.*[147] At the 2004 sixtieth commemoration of the allied landing in Normandy, he famously warned of a pathology of faith and a pathology of reason.[148]

This is an urgent task for him, as he argued in 1961. In a talk he had prepared for Cardinal Josef Frings titled "The Council and Modern Intellectual Life," he states that the inexorable process of globalization entails imposing a technical perspective upon all aspects of life, compelling people *nolens volens* to believe exclusively in the positive sciences as being

---

[145] To dogmatics, "ist . . . die . . . Fundamentaltheologie als eine Art theologischer Grundwissenschaft vorgebaut, welche das Recht einer den Glauben voraussetzenden Wissenschaft und so speziell das Recht der in der Dogmatik angewendeten Methode rechtfertigen soll. Daß diese Grundlegungswissenschaft selbst Theologie heißt, zeigt, daß es nicht um eine rationale Konstruktion des Glaubens geht, sondern darum, die rationale Verantwortbarkeit dieses Glaubens aufzudecken" (Joseph Ratzinger, "Katholische Theologie," in *Religion in Geschichte und Gegenwart,* ed. Kurt Galling and Hans von Campenhausen, 3rd ed., vol. 6 [Tübingen: Mohr, 1962], 775–79, at 776).

[146] Insightful also is Joseph Ratzinger, "Theologia perennis? Über Zeitgemäßheit und Zeitlosigkeit in der Theologie," *Weisheit und Wissenschaft* 15 (1960): 179–88.

[147] Ratzinger, *Introduction to Christianity,* 74–79; Joseph Ratzinger, *Principles of Catholic Theology,* trans. Sr. Mary Frances McCarthy, S.N.D. (San Francisco: Ignatius Press, 1989), 315–31. Joseph Ratzinger, *Jesus of Nazareth,* vol. 1, *From the Baptism in the Jordan to the Transfiguration* (New York: Doubleday, 2007), xi–8.

[148] Joseph Ratzinger, *Values in a Time of Upheaval,* trans. Brian McNeil (San Francisco: Ignatius Press, 2006), 160ff.

capable of offering solutions to questions human beings raise. A unified global culture (*Einheitskultur*) will evolve that will relativize the achievements of every culture, and Christianity will no longer be able to present itself to a globalized community in its European variant. Nevertheless, relativizing a particular manifestation of Christian faith need not, in and of itself, be viewed negatively. By extension, he argues, it is important to preserve the core of Christian faith—revelation—and to employ the principles of rationality as developed by Greek philosophy to enunciate the Gospel to the new, global community.

In the epochal process of globalization, however, he presciently asserts a vainglorious "self-divinization of humankind" as occurring, clad in the guise of atheism. Two ideologies serve to promote this epochal development: neoliberalism and communism. It is the task of Christians to uncover the genuinely Christian attitudes hidden in seemingly profane and un-Christian modernity and to demonstrate convincingly to the world how precious and livable our faith is. In this process, Christian faith need not fear the sciences, nor fear itself being transformed into new forms that might counterfeit it, "as she feels safe [*geborgen*] in God's truth."[149]

Conclusion

Automatically, at numerous points in the *scriptum* on fundamental theology, the reader would like to raise a question or two, but alas, this is not possible. The intention of the present article has been to share the main lines of thought of the early fundamental theologian Joseph Ratzinger. There is undeniably, from the very beginning, "a modern turn to the subject" in his thoughts that will spiritually underpin all his subsequent theological writings. This notwithstanding, as it is grounded in the historical objectivity of the God of Israel and Christianity, his position never becomes subjectivist.

Ratzinger's course on fundamental theology refreshes an important Augustinian insight: the quest for God is, by its nature, radically different from any other human investigation. It requires both an intellectual and an ethical effort on the part of the human being embarking on a search

---

[149] Josef Frings, "Das Konzil und die moderne Gedankenwelt," *Herder Korrespondenz* 16 (1961–1962): 168–74, at 174. See also Emery de Gaál, "The Theologian Joseph Ratzinger at Vatican II: His Theological Vision and Role," *Lateranum* 78, no. 3 (2012): 515–48, at 519–24. Also quite illuminative is Manuel Schlögl, "'Ich durfte den Weg des Konzils von innen her mitgehen': Anmerkungen zum Konzilstheologen Joseph Ratzinger," *Klerusblatt* 93 (2013): 146–49.

for God, since human reason also remains inextricably post-lapsarian. In a scientific probe, the human being can assume a neutral position. Yet, when it comes to the problem of God, the human being is already existentially involved and neutrality is impossible. In all probability, this entails the following consequence for Ratzinger: negating outright the possibility of divine existence is a morally bad option. If not subscribing *expressis verbis* to God's existence, the only morally permissible position would be of a form of agnosticism sympathetic to the hypothesis of God. While intellectual veracity is certainly required for any inquiry to succeed, both intellectual veracity *and* virtue must decidedly inform the outcome in order to arrive at an answer concerning God's existence. Ratzinger perceptively offers the contemporary discussion on God a helpful, and indeed redemptive, corrective: both God and the human person are greater than the range of positive, scientific investigation.

The problem of God stands under two differences: the alternatives between right and wrong *and* between good and bad. And then it still retains the quality of personal donation, of gift, in order to become religious truth: the mystery of grace, and thus human gratitude vis-à-vis the grantor, transforms mere insight into *Mitexistenz*.

There is a profound, indeed unfathomable, relationship between the God of philosophers and the God of faith, but the two do not collapse into identity. To Ratzinger, something not unlike Heisenberg's uncertainty principle also applies to the relationship between faith and reason, as the ontological difference between God and human being is in principle insurmountable. And, most importantly, it is God who first loves.

CHAPTER 4

Pope Benedict XVI, Fátima, and the Church

The Immaculate Heart of Mary Giving Confidence to the Catholic Creative Minorities[1]

It is most telling. In September 2011, Pope Benedict XVI visited Germany for four days. Most of the crowds were small. In large cities, it was difficult to fill the venues with practicing Catholics. However, the Holy Father also visited a small, almost unknown Marian shrine: Etzelsbach (formerly part of East Germany). It has poor infrastructure and had been suppressed by the Nazis and again by the communists. Under pain of persecution, Catholics would walk and hike to this place in lonesome, much-forested Thuringia during these reigns of terror. Not even in passing does a Mariological dictionary or encyclopedia mention this place of Catholic hope and strength. It is precisely in this inconspicuous location that the most Catholics gathered to pray and celebrate with Pope Benedict. We witness how the genius of Mary works throughout history. She also brought about the almost completely nonviolent collapse of the atheist Soviet Union and of atheist Eastern Europe. Repeatedly, Our Lady proves victorious in the course of human history.

Since Our Lady appeared to three poor shepherd children in the fields of Fátima, the *Cova da Iria*, in the year 1917, her message plays a signifi-

[1] This essay was originally published as "Pope Benedict XVI, Fátima, and the Church: Giving Confidence to the Catholic Creative Minorities" in *Chicago Studies* 51, no. 2 (Summer 2012): 238–251; copyright: Civitas Dei Foundation. Used by permission.

cant and vigorous role in the Catholic Church, revealing both her nature and her mission.

Pope Benedict XVI in Fátima in 2010

During his visit on the occasion of the tenth anniversary of the beatification of Jacinta and Francesco Marto in 2010, Pope Benedict XVI affirmed that the third secret of Fátima is of permanent "and ongoing significance" for the Church.[2] Its relevance did not cease with the failed assassination attempt on St. John Paul II (1920–2005) in St. Peter's Square in 1981. He said to the estimated 500,000 people gathered in front of the shrine that it would be a "mistake" to assume that "Fátima's prophetic mission is complete." It continues to be relevant as it continually invites men and women of faith "to save the city of man." Joining the sentiments of the shepherd children, he had come to pray for the human family and to entrust to Our Lady the intimate confession that "'I love' Jesus, [and] that the Church and priests 'love' him." For, it is Mary who introduced the children of Fátima "to a deep knowledge of the Love of the Blessed Trinity and led them to savour God himself as the most beautiful reality of human existence." Benedict continued by observing: "Blessed Jacinta, in particular, proved tireless in sharing with the needy and in making sacrifices for the conversion of sinners. Only with this fraternal and generous love will we succeed in building a civilization of love and peace." With these words, Pope Benedict XVI describes the essence of the message of Fátima and the essence of what it means to be Church. He recounted that in a dire time in history, Mary came from heaven offering to implant in the hearts of all those who trust in her the love of God that is burning in her own heart. With these words, the Pope describes also our vocation: "We must cultivate an interior watchfulness of the heart . . . [since] God can come to us, and show himself to the eyes of our heart."

Fátima in the Life and Thoughts of Pope Benedict XVI

Pope Benedict is no stranger to the messages of Our Lady at Fátima. As a child, he would pray the Rosary with his parents and two siblings, adding

[2] Pope Benedict XVI, Homily at the Shrine of Our Lady of Fatima on the Tenth Anniversary of the Beatification of Jacinta and Francisco Marto (May 13, 2010), available from http://www.vatican.va.

after the *Gloria Patri*, "O my Jesus, forgive us our sins, save us from the fires of hell, lead all souls to heaven, especially those most in need (of thy mercy)."[3] Between World War I and World War II, Catholics considered Fátima a powerful fulcrum expressing their concerns regarding Communism, which at the time was gaining influence. And, more importantly, it offered them a means to overcome this menace of almost apocalyptic proportions. Never before in the history of humankind had a nation declared itself atheistic and firmly expressed its resolve to subject the whole world to its Marxist brand of atheism.

As a young and promising theologian at the University of Bonn, in 1961, the future pope wrote an insightful book review for the Munich theological journal on a significant study dealing with the theology underlying the apparitions of Our Lady at Fátima, Portugal.[4] The book goes beyond a superficial description of Fátima and attempts to penetrate its spiritual and theological essence. After supplying the reader with the book's content, Ratzinger faults the author for not going beyond generalities and developing the theological necessity of Fátima devotion.[5] It was this weakness that Ratzinger, in his various roles as professor, prefect, and pope, would try to fill. Interiority and the apostolic dimension of our Christian existence, Mary, Jesus Christ, and the Church require correlation. This illustrates, in Ratzinger's estimation, the greatness of the three children-visionaries: "Smallness possesses its own greatness."[6]

In the year 2000, as prefect of the Congregation for the Doctrine of the Faith, Ratzinger addressed the message of Fátima in a lengthy and thorough commentary, printed in the respected German monthly journal *Bote von Fátima*.[7] In 1996, he visited Fátima and met the surviving visionary, Sister Lúcia, in the Portuguese city of Coimbra on October 14. Following the *Catechism of the Catholic Church*, he reminds the reader of revelation being closed with the Incarnation of the second Person of the

---

3 William Thomas Walsh, *Our Lady of Fátima* (New York: Doubleday, 1990), 220.

4 Joseph Ratzinger, "Eine Theologie über Fátima: zu Virgil Marions gleichnamigen Buch," *Münchener Theologische Zeitschrift* 12 (1961): 305–7. He reviewed Virgil Marion, *Eine Theologie über Fátima: Versuch einer Sinndeutung der Sühneforderung Marias* (Innsbruck: Rauch, 1960).

5 "Ich kann nicht finden, daß aus Marions Ausführungen die Notwendigkeit der Fátima-Frömmigkeit hervorleuchtet, die zu beweisen doch offenbar sein Anliegen ist" (Ratzinger, "Eine Theologie über Fátima," 306).

6 "Das Kleine seine eigene Größe hat" (Ratzinger, "Eine Theologie über Fátima," 307).

7 Joseph Kardinal Ratzinger, "Kommentar zum Geheimnis von Fátima 1. und 2. Teil," *Bote von Fátima* (October–November 2000): 130–133 and 147–50, respectively.

Blessed Trinity, but "not exhausted."[8] We must always be mindful of the profound words of Pope Gregory the Great (ca. 540–604): "The divine words grow with the readers [Gregory the Great, *Homilae in Hiezechielem* 1.7.8]" (CCC 94). Private revelations do not serve the task of perfecting the definitive revelation in Jesus Christ. Rather, they intend to draw believers more deeply into its meaning in a particular age.[9] Much earlier, the respected Flemish theologian Édouard Dhanis (1902–1978) had listed the essential criteria for an ecclesial approbation of a private revelation: (1) the message contains nothing contrary to faith and good morals; (2) it is permitted to publicize the message; and (3) the faithful are authorized to grant it their prudent assent.[10] After summarizing his position, Ratzinger emphasizes that Fátima is ordered towards Christ and promotes the supernatural virtues of faith, hope, and charity as the lasting path to salvation. This flows into lived liturgy. Popular piety in turn becomes the mode of enculturating the faith.

In every age, the Church is given the gift of prophecy. In the Acts of the Apostles, one reads of the persecution of the Apostles, but also of how wondrously the Lord protects them: "But at night an angel of the Lord opened the prison doors and brought them out and said, 'Go and stand in the temple and speak to the people all the words of this Life.' And when they heard this, they entered the temple at daybreak and taught" (Acts 5:19–21). This allows us, the believers, to apprehend the presence of Christ in our midst. Cardinal Ratzinger organizes private revelation in the traditional manner as sensible, imaginative, or intellectual visions (*visio sensibilis, imaginativa, intellectualis*). For the third secret of Fátima, he uses the second category. It is an interior perception granted exclusively to the visionaries. It calls for an alertness of the heart. Such interior beholding of a content is not, Ratzinger insists, a pious fantasy, but a genuine and proper way of percep-

---

8 Ratzinger, "Kommentar," 130. See *Catechism of the Catholic Church* [CCC], 2nd edition (New York: Doubleday, 2003), 66: "Yet even if Revelation is already complete; it remains for Christian faith gradually to grasp its full significance over the course of the centuries."

9 Ratzinger, "Kommentar," 131. See also CCC 67: "Throughout the ages, there have been so-called 'private' revelations, some of which have been recognized by the authority of the Church. They do not belong, however, to the deposit of faith. It is not their role to improve or complete Christ's definitive Revelation, but to help live more fully by it in a certain period of history. Guided by the Magisterium of the Church, the *sensus fidelium* knows how to discern and welcome in these revelations whatever constitutes an authentic call of Christ or his saints to the Church."

10 The official Vatican publication is found as Édouard Dhanis, "Sguardo su Fátima e Bilancio di una Discussione," *La Civiltà Cattolica* 104, no. 2 (1953): 392–406, at 397.

tion. It is the outcome, the fruit, of "a real perception from above and below."[11] The children of Fátima have actually seen the terrors of hell, "the souls of the poor sinners." This frightening reality must inspire us to labor to save people by venerating the Immaculate Heart of Mary. As one reads in 1 Peter 1:9: "As the outcome of your faith you obtain the salvation of your souls." Devotion to the Immaculate Heart of Mary leads the believer to the very center of human existence. The heart is the fulcrum for human reason, volition, and sentiments. The human being finds "his unity and his inner direction" in the encounter with the Immaculate Heart of Mary. In Matthew 5:8, one hears Our Lord say, "Blessed are the pure in heart, for they shall see God." This promotes the supernatural virtues of faith, hope, and charity. At this point of his commentary, Ratzinger underlines that by no means is the future of human history irreversibly determined. With Mary, we are able to contribute to a more humane and Christ-filled future.

The nonfatal outcome of the assassination attempt on Pope John Paul II at the hands of a deranged Turk was not predetermined. It was the *mano materna*, the maternal hand of Mary, that diverted the otherwise mortal bullet. This fact contains, for Cardinal Ratzinger, a clear message for us as to what the nature of the Church is. The conclusion of the secret reminds one of images of the early Church, of angels gathering the blood of martyrs and using it to water the souls of those who set off to meet God. "Now I rejoice in my sufferings for your sake, and in my flesh I complete what is lacking in Christ's afflictions for the sake of his body, that is, the church." Ratzinger quotes Colossians 1:24 in order to stress the ecclesial dimension of Fátima. Their lives have become Eucharist, entering the mystery of the dying grain of wheat (John 12:24). The African Church Father Tertullian (ca. 160–ca. 225) famously said: "The blood of the martyrs is the seed of Christians."[12] In this vein, Ratzinger observes: "No life is in vain, and especially a suffering Church, a Church of the martyrs, becomes a signpost for humankind's search for God."[13] In God's good hands, not only those who suffer find rest. Lazarus also found consolation (John 11–12). "From the suffering of the martyrs issues forth a power of purification and renewal, as it renders present Christ's own suffering and hands on His saving works'

[11] "Die von ihnen (den Kindern) aufgezeichneten Bilder sind keineswegs bloß Ausdruck ihrer Fantasie, sondern Frucht einer wirklichen Wahrnehmung von oben und unten her . . ." (Ratzinger, "Kommentar," 132).

[12] Tertullian, *Apologeticum* 50.13 (*Corpus Christianorum Series Latina*, 1:171).

[13] "Kein Leben ist umsonst, und gerade eine leidende Kirche, eine Kirche der Märtyrer, wird zum Wegzeichen auf der Suche der Menschen nach Gott" (Ratzinger, "Kommentar," 149).

efficaciousness to the present age,"[14] thus renewing ever again the face of the earth (Ps 104:30).

Ratzinger, Mary, the Church, and Vatican II

A cursory survey of average parish life nowadays indicates a loss of Marian devotions. Homilies make less reference to the *Theotokos*. Yet, paradoxically, reading the documents of the Second Vatican Council reveals how central the Council Fathers perceived Mary to be in the salvation plan of God and to the nature of the Church.

As a young theologian and *peritus* to Cardinal Josef Frings (1887–1978) during the Council, Ratzinger played a significant role in drafting conciliar documents.

The question occupying the Council Fathers in 1963 was that of whether, on the one hand, to draft a separate text on Mary or, on the other, to integrate her into the dogmatic constitution *Lumen gentium*, the Church as "Light to the Nations."[15] The cardinal-archbishop of Vienna, Franz König (1905–2004), suggested incorporating Mary in the text on the Church, while the cardinal-archbishop of Manila, Rufino Santos (1908–1978), "made the case for the independence of the Marian element."[16] In a close vote, 1114 bishops expressed support for Cardinal König's proposal and 1071 for Cardinal Santos's suggestion. Prior to the Council, numerous significant theologians had developed, on biblical and liturgical grounds, the close connection between Mary and the Church. Particularly such theological luminaries as Hugo Rahner (1900–1968), René Laurentin (1917–2017), and Otto Semmelroth (1912–1979) had established in the 1950s the intrinsic and inseparable relationship between Mary and the Church.[17] Later Ratzinger will observe, however: "[As] facts

[14] "Vom Leiden der Zeugen kommt eine Kraft der Reinigung und der Erneuerung, weil es Vergegenwärtigung von Christi eigenem Leiden ist und seine heilende Wirkung an die Gegenwart weiterreicht" (Ratzinger, "Kommentar," 149).

[15] Second Vatican Council, Dogmatic Constitution on the Church *Lumen Gentium* (November 21, 1964), available from http://www.vatican.va (hereafter cited in text as LG).

[16] Joseph Ratzinger, "Thoughts on the Place of Marian Doctrine and Piety in Faith and Theology as a Whole," *Communio* 30 (Spring 2003): 147–60, at 149; printed also in Hans Urs von Balthasar and Joseph Cardinal Ratzinger, *Mary: The Church at the Source*, trans. Adrian Walker (San Francisco: Ignatius Press, 1997), 13–95.

[17] Ratzinger, "Thoughts on the Place of Marian Doctrine and Piety," 150. See also Hugo Rahner, *Our Lady and the Church*, trans. Sebastian Bullough (Bethesda, MD: Zaccheus Press, 2004); Rahner, *Mater Ecclesia: Lobpreis der Kirche aus dem ersten Jahrtausend* (Einsiedeln: Benzinger, 1944); Alois Müller, *Ecclesia-Maria: Die Einheit Marias und*

stand, . . . the Marian chapter of *Lumen gentium* was only partly successful in persuasively and vigorously fleshing out the proposals these authors had outlined."[18] A lack of appreciation for the theological category of Tradition and a one-sided reading of the Council favoring the sufficiency of Scripture à la the Tübingen theologian Josef Rupert Geiselmann (1890–1970)[19] prevented some in the post-conciliar period from properly appreciating the central role the figure of Mary plays in the life of the Church. At the end of the Council, Pope Paul VI (1897–1978) wisely introduced the title "Mother of the Church" in order to underline the Council's teaching on Mary. This notwithstanding, Ratzinger writes, far from the intentions of the Council Fathers, "the immediate outcome of the victory of (an) ecclesiocentric Mariology was the collapse of Mariology altogether."[20] Thus, we now encounter difficulties on the part of some in accessing the mystery and reality that the Church is by her very nature.

Vatican II's Close Linkage between Mary and the Church

In the eighth chapter of *Lumen gentium*, the Dogmatic Constitution on the Church, we read of the indispensable position Mary occupies in the Church. While the woman of Nazareth is also an essential member of the Church and the first redeemed, she is at the same time the type of the Church and its primordial image. On the same account, she transcends the Church, as she is the Mother of God, and therefore is intimately connected with the Church coming into being in the first place. As a fellow *peritus* of Ratzinger, Semmelroth explained that Mary is so connected with the person and work of Christ that the significance of both is underscored by their relationship to one another.[21] The Marian portion of the document opens: "Wishing in his supreme goodness and wisdom to effect the re-

der Kirche (Fribourg, CH: Universitätsverlag Fribourg, 1955); Karl Delahaye, *Erneuerung der Seelsorgsformen aus der Sicht der frühen Patristik* (Freiburg im Breisgau: Herder, 1958); René Laurentin, *Court traité de la théologie mariale* (Paris: P. Lethielleux, 1953); Otto Semmelroth, S.J., *Urbild der Kirche: Organischer Aufbau des Mariengeheimnisses* (Würzburg: Echter, 1950).

18 Ratzinger, "Thoughts on the Place of Marian Doctrine and Piety," 150.

19 Josef Rupert Geiselmann, *Die Heilige Schrift und die Tradition* (Freiburg im Breisgau: Herder, 1962).

20 Ratzinger, "Thoughts on the Place of Marian Doctrine and Piety," 151.

21 Otto Semmelroth, S.J., "Maria im Geheimnis Christi und der Kirche," in *Das neue Volk Gottes: Eine Einführung in die dogmatische Konstitution "Über die Kirche,"* ed. Wilhelm Sandfuchs (Würzburg: Arena, 1967), 102–14, at 108.

demption of the world, 'when the fullness of the time came, God sent his Son, born of a woman . . . that we might receive the adoption of sons' (Gal 4:4)" (LG 52). This accesses an additional dimension: Mary as the personal, primal image of the Church. The two are not only related, Ratzinger argues, but Mary is the beginning of the Church: at the Annunciation, at the Crucifixion, and at Pentecost. While the direct composition of the text has numerous authors, there is no doubt regarding Ratzinger's influence and approval of this section of *Lumen gentium*. We read in this document:

> Because of this gift of sublime grace she far surpasses all creatures, both in heaven and on earth. At the same time, however, because she belongs to the offspring of Adam she is one with all those who are to be saved. She is "the mother of the members of Christ . . . having cooperated by charity that faithful might be born in the Church, who are members of that Head." Wherefore she is hailed as a pre-eminent and singular member of the Church, and as its type and excellent exemplar in faith and charity. The Catholic Church, taught by the Holy Spirit, honors her with filial affection and piety as a most beloved mother (LG 53).

The Greek term for Mary as the *typos*, or "type," conveys in its original meaning something like Mary being the "origin," "prototype," "template," and "the lasting presence of the origin" of the Church.

In this section, the Council quotes St. Augustine, Ratzinger's favorite theologian.[22] Perhaps it was inserted upon his suggestion? Through catechesis and Baptism, the Church, like the Mother of God, becomes ever anew the mother of her members through the power of the Holy Spirit (LG 64). The council warns against an exaggerated and one-sided veneration of Our Lady, but equally also against scant regard for her (LG 67). Thus, while being ecumenically sensitive, the Council Fathers at the same time vigorously affirm the old spiritual principle *per Mariam ad Jesum*—through Mary to Jesus.

The Future of the Church Is Essentially Marian

Mary enriches our understanding of the Church in two ways, Pope Benedict argues. (1) As both Mary and the Church are feminine in both Greek and Latin, they point to a mystery beyond "structure and action." This view

[22] St. Augustine, *De Sancta Virginitate* 6 (PL, 40:399).

liberates the Church from a merely sociological perception. On this point, Ratzinger is also indebted to the nuptial theology of the Swiss theologian Hans Urs von Balthasar (1905–1988).[23] This enables the believer to apprehend in the Church a second, equally important reality. (2) The Church is not an organization, but first and foremost the Body of Christ. It is Mary who gives us Christ, the Savior. Thus, we in turn become "people of God." In this fashion, the Church is seen as a dynamic and personal reality; "a dialogical reciprocity" comes about.[24] As the Church is guarded from being reduced to an impersonal structure, Pope Benedict sees Mary as the true "vanquisher of all heresies." The Church is far more than a mere gathering of like-minded people. The incarnate *Logos* born of Mary lives on in the Church, enabling *ex toto corde*—"from the depth of the heart"—ever anew a personal relationship of believers to the living God and to Mary. This permits Christians to call the Church "virgin Church" (*virgo ecclesia*), "Mother Church" (*mater ecclesia*), and "assumed Church" (*ecclesia assumpta*). The figure of the woman of Nazareth, the *Theotokos*, vouches for and guarantees the close link between Jesus Christ and his Church. Therefore, in Pope Benedict's estimation, one cannot ignore Mary and yet do justice to either Christ in the world or the Catholic Church. There exists an intrinsic interwovenness of these three mysteries—Mary, Jesus Christ, and the Church—that must be celebrated in worship, taught in catechesis, and preached in homilies over and again, lest every single one of these mysteries suffer. This leads the Christian to appreciate his or her true destiny: divinization.

Mary's singular heroism lies in her *fiat* spoken to the Angel Gabriel at the Annunciation. It enabled this *nexus mysteriorum*, this close interdependence of Mary, Jesus Christ, and the Church, to come about in the first place. Pope Benedict states categorically: "At the moment when she pronounces her Yes, Mary is Israel in person; she is the Church in person and as a person."[25] In his twentieth-century classic *Introduction to Christianity*, published shortly after the Council, Ratzinger wrote: "With her begins, according to St. Luke's text, the new Israel; indeed, it does not just begin with her; she *is* it, the holy 'daughter of Zion' in whom God sets the new beginning."[26]

[23] See Hans Urs von Balthasar, *Sponsa Verbi* (Einsiedeln: Johannes, 1960), esp. 148–202.

[24] Ratzinger, "Thoughts on the Place of Marian Doctrine and Piety," 153.

[25] Ratzinger, "Thoughts on the Place of Marian Doctrine and Piety," 155.

[26] Joseph Ratzinger, *Introduction to Christianity*, trans. J. R. Foster (San Francisco: Ignatius Press, 2004), 272 (more broadly, see 271–80). See also Ratzinger, *Daughter Zion: Meditations on the Church's Marian Belief*, trans. John M. McDermott, S.J. (San Francisco: Ignatius Press, 1983).

Therefore, in his judgment, Marian piety is not a superfluous addition to worship, but central to understanding and celebrating the fullness of our Catholic faith and forming an integral faith community. We must deliberately assume a Marian mind frame when celebrating Advent, Christmas, Candlemas, Easter, Pentecost, her Annunciation, and her Assumption. This means becoming constantly again "Church." Thus, ever anew, faith in Jesus Christ becomes personal and incarnational. Along with the Protestant theologian Ulrich Wickert (1927–), Ratzinger reminds us that the evangelist Luke portrays Mary twice as heralding Advent: at the beginning of the Gospel when awaiting the birth of the Savior of the world and at the beginning of the Acts of the Apostles when she awaits the birth of the Church.[27]

The Vision of Pope Benedict XVI?

Pope Benedict XVI would probably appreciate the way religious freedom is practiced in America. The multicultural situation in the United States allows for the free exercise of religion. In part, this is the case because it is not bogged down by a fateful history of Caesaropapism, as many European countries are. In addition, he believes that "one can undoubtedly learn from the United States" a "process by which the state makes room for religion, which is not imposed, but which, thanks to the state, lives, exists and has a public creative force."[28] Inspired by the noted British historian Arnold J. Toynbee (1889–1975), he sees Catholics being "a creative minority." For Toynbee, civilizations break down if the motivating power of a creative minority fails. Via mimesis on the part of the majority, creative minorities provide unity for the whole of society.[29] Christian minorities can—so Pope Benedict argues repeatedly and passionately—live a prayerful life, live the sacraments, and joyfully bear witness for Jesus Christ with Mary and engage the larger culture.[30]

The theologian Joseph Ratzinger reminds us already shortly after the

---

[27] Ratzinger, "Thoughts on the Place of Marian Doctrine and Piety," 159. See also Ulrich Wickert, "Maria und die Kirche," *Theologie und Glaube* 68 (1978): 384–407, at 402.

[28] "Cardinal Ratzinger Commends U.S. Model of Laicism," *Zenit*, November 25, 2004, accessed December 11, 2017, https://zenit.org/articles/cardinal-ratzinger-commends-u-s-model-of-laicism/.

[29] Arnold J. Toynbee, *A Study of History*, vol. 1 (Oxford: Oxford University Press, 1947), 578.

[30] John L. Allen, Jr., "Benedict Hopes to Tap the 'Creative Minority' of French Catholics," *National Catholic Reporter*, September 5, 2008, accessed December 11, 2017, https://www.ncronline.org/blogs/all-things-catholic/benedict-hopes-tap-creative-minority-french-catholics.

Second Vatican Council that, as seen in the opening words of the Dogmatic Constitution on the Church—*Lumen gentium*—the Church as the "light to the nations" is a sacrament bringing about communion between God and us, and thereby between us and our fellow human beings. By rekindling Marian devotions in parishes, we can be, with Mary, mindful of the Church as the divine wellspring expressing and living ever anew the vital powers of God and the divine-human saving acts of Jesus Christ.[31] The intrinsic relationship between Church, liturgy, and faith is restored. With Mary's generosity, we appreciate afresh that the Church does not offer individualistic sacraments, but enables us to be a community of joy-filled people grounded in liturgical life and the redeeming charity of Jesus Christ. In this sense, Mary "co-redeems" us from secular loneliness by leading us to the overflowing abundance of the triune God.[32]

It is in Mary that we see the relationship of the human person with God restored. As the one with the Immaculate Heart, Mary is full of grace. Total Marian devotion leads unfailingly to a greater commitment to follow Jesus Christ. Devotion to the Immaculate Heart of Mary unfailingly leads to the Heart of her divine Son Jesus Christ, whose Sacred Heart is always in tune with God the Father's will and intent on saving humankind. Knowing her, we strive to imitate her virtues. Our Lady of Fátima asks us to make reparation for sins committed against her Immaculate Heart on the first Saturday of five consecutive months.

When we live in this knowledge of Mary as the archetype of the Church, as the loving mother of all, then we do not succumb to the temptations of numbing consumerism, uninspiring skepticism, arid rationalism, or sad resignation, but we confidently rejuvenate the Church. This is achieved also by rekindling Marian devotions in parishes and in homes, by gently reminding priests and deacons to preach on Mary, or by alerting homilists that to end frequently a sermon with Mary means to present Mary as *the* unsurpassable example of a grateful and joyful faith, of a faith that is not defined primarily by institutional structures, its rational penetration, or ecclesiastical titles, but first and foremost by reverent worship of the triune God and magnanimous service to one another.

Our Lady of Fátima, pray for us!

---

[31] See Joseph Ratzinger, "Kirche und Liturgie" [originally 1958], in *Joseph Ratzinger, Gesammelte Schriften*, vol. 8.1, ed. Gerhard Ludwig Müller (Freiburg im Breisgau: Herder, 2010), 157–77, at 165.

[32] See "Die Kirche als Heilssakrament" [originally 1977], in *Gesammelte Schriften*, 8.1:244–57, at 251–52.

CHAPTER 5

Professor Joseph Ratzinger's Only Mariology Course[1]

> Faith means surrendering oneself and being pure openness to God. . . . [Mary] is not contrasted to us. Rather, she appears as the exemplary realization of what ultimately . . . must occur with all of us; she is the primordial representation of Christian faith par excellence.
>
> —Joseph Ratzinger 1957

DURING THE SUMMER SEMESTER of 1957, at barely thirty years of age, Joseph Ratzinger held his only Mariology course in his twenty-two-year career as theology professor (winter semester 1954/1955 until winter semester 1976/1977). He held this course, which met twice a week, at the Freising Seminary, more precisely at the *Philosophisch-Theologische Hochschule Freising*—its official title. In addition, during politically churned up times, he conducted a seminar titled "Probleme der Mariologie" in the winter semester of 1967/1968 at the Eberhard Karls University in Tübingen.[2]

---

1 This essay was originally published as "Pope Benedict's First Christology Course–Winter Semester 1955/56" in *Opera Theologiae Systematicae*, vol. 4, *Współczesne Kontrowersje Chrystologiczne* (Wrocław: Papieski Wydział Teologiczny we Wrocławiu, 2016), 145–174. Used by permission.

2 *Joseph Ratzinger / Papst Benedikt XVI, Das Werk: Veröffentlichungen bis zur Papstwahl*, ed. Vinzenz Pfnür [this text was pre-edited by Ratzinger's Schülerkreis] (Augsburg: St. Ulrich, 2009), 401 and 404. This lecture course is listed in the concordance as "L15–F VL: Mariologie (2std)" and detailed as meeting twice per week (see p. 401). In the present paper, this course is referred to as *Scriptum* and the page numbers given for these citations are an original numbering that is internal to this *scriptum* and preserved

Graciously, the *Papst Benedikt XVI Institut* in Regensburg provided the present author with a copy of a student's unpublished script. This text must be considered *cum grano salis,* as it is a secondary source. However, Aristotle's *De anima*, for example, is also preserved for posterity exclusively by way of student scripts, but in its present form, it permits us to important conclusions regarding this Greek philosopher's teaching on the soul.

This transcript has been produced as a manuscript in clear and regular shorthand in a DIN A 3 booklet and contains supplementary or summarizing notes on the margins in normal, cursive handwriting. It is fifty-six pages long and is divided into:

Considerations[3]

Part 1. Mariology as Christology

- §1 Mary, the Mother of God
  - I. The Testimony of the Fathers
  - II. The Testimony of Scripture in the Light of the Fathers' Witness
  - III. Speculative Considerations
- §2 Virgin and Mother

in Pfnür's presentation of the document's contents, rather than Pfnür's own volume page numbers. All translations from the German original of this *scriptum* is the work of the present author. In general, concerning Ratzinger's Mariology, see: Michele Giulio Masciarelli, *Il segno della donna: Maria nella teologia di Joseph Ratzinger* (Milan, IT: Cinisello Balsamo, 2007); Masciarelli, "Maria 'figlia di Sion' e 'Chiesa nascente' nella riflessione di Ratzinger," *Marianum* 68, nos. 169–170 (2006): 321–415; Franz Courth, "Mariens leibliche Verherrlichung: zu einem Entwurf von Joseph Ratzinger," *Trierer Theologische Zeitschrift* 88, no. 1 (1979): 34–42; Antonio Staglianò, *Madre di Dio: la mariologia personalista di Ratzinger* (Milan, IT: San Paolo, 2010); Emery de Gaál, *The Theology of Pope Benedict XVI: The Christocentric Shift* (New York: Palgrave Macmillan, 2010), 287–96; de Gaál, "The Theologian Joseph Ratzinger at Vatican II," *Lateranum* 78, no. 3 (2012): 515–48, at 536–38; Denis Robert Lemieux, *She Is Our Response: The Virgin Mary and the Church's Encounter in the Writings of Ratzinger* (New Bedford, MA: Academy of the Immaculata, 2011); Matthew Levering, "Mary in the Theology of Joseph Ratzinger," in *Explorations in the Theology of Benedict XVI*, ed. John C. Cavadini (Notre Dame, IN: Notre Dame Press, 2012), 279–97; Rainer Hangler, *Juble, Tochter Zion: Zur Mariologie von Joseph Ratzinger/Benedikt XVI*, Ratzinger Studien 9 (Regensburg: Pustet, 2016), 61–71 (here Hangler refers to a shorter version of the Mariology course); Imre v. Gaál, "Die einzige Mariologie Vorlesung Professor Joseph Ratzingers," *Sedes Sapientiae* 22, no. 1 (2016): 33–55.

[3] We have included this outline from Ratzinger, although there is inconsistency with the corresponding subheadings that treat the subject matter immediately following the outline—Editor.

Chapter 1: The Question of the Marian Basic Principle (Grundprinzip)
- I. The Testimony of Scripture
- II. The Testimony of Tradition

Part 2. Mariology as Ecclesiology
- §3 Mariological Points of Departure in Holy Scripture
  - I. Delimitation of the Theological Significance of the Bodily
  - II. Mary and Israel; The Marian Approach of the Lucan Childhood Narrative
  - III. Mariological Starting Points in the Johannine Gospel
  - IV. The Problem of Rev 12
- §4 The Main Principles of Patristic Mariology
  - I. Eve and Mary
  - II. Mary and *Ecclesia*

Appendix: Mary, the Soil of the Church
- §5 The Result

Chapter 2: The Individual Mariological Statements
- §6 The Immaculate Conception
- §7 Assumed into Heaven
- §8 Mary's Mediation of Grace
- §9 The Question Regarding the Involvement of Mary in the Work of Redemption
- §10 The Kingdom [*sic*] of Mary
- §11 The Ecclesiological Ramification of Mary's Holiness
- §12 The Veneration of Mary

Although the organization of the outline is not quite uniform, one clearly detects a logical structure with biblical and patristic emphases and the vision of an organically unfolding, systematic whole. From about the middle of the semester onward, the individual sections become noticeably shorter and less subdivided. Whether this is due to the professor, to unexpected time delays, or to the student who wrote the *scriptum* cannot be ascertained.

Introductory Considerations

From the perspective of the 1950s, Ratzinger's prolegomena identifies two seemingly opposing currents: on the one hand, there is the "Marian century," with rather numerous Marian apparitions and the solemn definitions of two Marian dogmas as its climaxes; on the other hand, there is the liturgical movement. He reminds his students that theology strives to reject "sentimentality" and "baroque exuberance." In a "simple theocentrism," the young professor makes out a salutary "theological anti-baroque."[4] The positive and the valuable in both movements is expressed in "the patristic statement" that "Mary is the primordial image of the Church." In the process, he underscores that "Mariology is ecclesiology," and thus "the Mariological dogmas are . . . ecclesiological dogmas."[5] "The *Theotokos* statement stands apart, [for] it states a fact that is indicated in the Scriptures with full clarity; but not only as a fact; she [Mary] *continues* to be the Christ-bearer"[6] in heaven and on earth.

Part 1: Mariology as Christology

Under §1, the councils of Ephesus, Chalcedon, and Constantinople II are treated. In order to grasp the proper valence of Mariology, one must note that the Christological disputes also come to a resolution with the clarification of the question concerning the nature and role of Mary. In this historical process of illumination, the dogma of the *Theotokos* figures prominently and is decisive for the subsequent verbalization of the Christian faith. This development is paralleled by a corresponding patristic theology: the testimonies of Origen, Hippolytus, and Gregory of Nazianzen are cited. Interestingly, he emphasizes that the Roman Synod of 430 had anticipated the dogmatic definition of Mary as *Theotokos / Dei Genetrix* at Ephesus in 431. In Mary, nothing less than "the axis of salvation history, of Christian existence, is pronounced."[7] One recognizes in the history of dogma "Mary as the vanquisher of all heresies."[8] Henceforth, this insight is decisive for the Church's self-understanding. Tellingly, it is only on this historical background that Ratzinger turns to scriptural evidence. Already, the childhood narrative presents Jesus as the Son of God, born of Mary. 2 Corinthians 8:9, 1 Corinthians 10:4 and 8:6, Philippians 2:6–7, Colossians 1:16–17, "and perhaps Luke 1:35f" teach the pre-existence of Jesus. With a speculative reflection, he concludes this

---

4 *Scriptum*, 1.

5 *Scriptum*, 1.

6 *Scriptum*, 1 (present author's emphasis). Here Ratzinger references Michael Schmaus, *Katholische Dogmatik*, vol. 5, *Mariologie* (Munich: Hueber, 1955) and Paul Sträter, *Katholische Marienkunde*, 2nd. ed. [?] (Paderborn: Schöningh, 1952).

7 *Scriptum*, 4.

8 *Scriptum*, 4.

section: only the concept of the hypostatic union allows one to speak of a *Theotokos* instead of a "mythical" figure such as the one advocated by Nestorius. "One thing is true: from the statement of the Mother of God follows an unusual nobility for this woman (*gratia plena*)—but to derive from this a pure [probably in the sense of an independent, self-standing] theology would be an abuse," Ratzinger states almost apodictically.[9]

In the next paragraph, §2, the terms "virgin" and "Mother of God" are extensively related to one another. With fifteen pages, this section is the longest in the script. First, the evidence of Scripture is treated. This presents Christ to the reader as the final "Counter Adam" (*Gegenadam*).[10] The speculation of Gregory of Nyssa and Augustine that Mary, as a child, had made a vow of virginity is not met in principle with skepticism on Ratzinger's part, though he admits this is not supported by evidence from the canonical Scripture. He reminds his students that the Essenes had been familiar with such vows and that Mary had been related to Elizabeth, the wife of the priest Zachary. "We know almost nothing about popular piety" of that time, Ratzinger cautions.[11] Along with Luke 1:27 and 2:5 and the corresponding exegesis of the celebrated French Mariologist René Laurentin (1917–2017), Ratzinger considers Mary as publicly betrothed: in fact, she lives in a virginal marriage.[12]

To Ratzinger's mind, the fact that the birth of Jesus Christ from the Holy Spirit is not conceived as generation, but as creation, now becomes understandable (Luke 1:35). The Adam–Christ parallel makes it clear that God had opened in Christ's birth a new chapter in his covenantal relationship with humankind, but it should be noted well that this does not require a radical new beginning: one encounters in the history of salvation "continuity in discontinuity." This is the paradigmatic basis for every Christian's "existence as eschatological virginity."[13] Mary's objective virginity is a statement concerning the orientation that should be a part of every Christian. With reference to the Protestant theologian Gerhard Delling (1905–1986),[14] thoughts about the extra-Christian figures of

---

9 *Scriptum*, 5.

10 *Scriptum*, 6.

11 *Scriptum*, 7.

12 See René Laurentin, *Maria, Ecclesia, Sacerdotium* (Paris: Nouvelles éditions latines, 1952–1953); Laurentin, *Structure et théologie de Luc I-II* (Paris: J. Gabalda, 1957); Laurentin, *Court traité de théologie mariale* (Paris: Lethielleux, 1954). In all probability Ratzinger had consulted these books.

13 *Scriptum*, 9.

14 Gerhard Delling, *Paulus' Stellung zur Frau und Ehe* (Stuttgart: Kohlhammer, 1931), or the first edition of Delling, *Antike Wundertexte*, re-organized 2nd ed. (Berlin: de

Aphrodite, Hera, Artemis, Plato, and Apis are entertained. Are, for instance, the pagan ideas of *parthenos* ("virgin") perhaps a *praeparatio evangelica*, an inchoate yearning for the virginal incarnation of a god? Ratzinger asks whether these figures might be premonitions and archetypes that Christianity "takes up, purifies and ennobles."[15]

Turning to the religious world of Israel, the singularity of the birth of Jesus comes into even greater focus when considering that the possibility of procreation has never been attributed exclusively to the *ruah/pneuma* in the Palestinian realm.

Indicative of his foundational view on the figure of Mary, Ratzinger states: "The Virgin Mother has embodied the salvific figure of creation. She embodies not God, but the creature in the order of God."[16] In this salvation-historical context, he already apprehends Mary as *the* primordial image of the Church anticipated. The Old Testament "agrees" with this salvation-historical *ductus*, as evidenced by Isaiah 7:14, Micah 1:3, and Judges 13. The hopes of the world as a whole, and especially Israel's expectations for redemption, are crystallized in the form of the one woman who is already prophetically anticipated in Isaiah 7:14. "The virginal birth, . . . the line beginning with Sara and leading to its fulfillment in the utmost of purity [is found in the woman from Nazareth]. This intends to express the totally grace-filled state; she is the *signum gratiae*."[17] The testimony of Ephrem the Syrian intends to teach us: "Mary has received the Son of God through the ear; she received him in hearing the faith; in obedience . . . [analogous to Mary, also,] our relationship to God . . . [is one of a] hearing faith."[18] The doctrine of the supernatural birth of Jesus is supported and buttressed by the *Tomus Leonis*,[19] by canon 3 of the Lateran Synod of 649,[20]

Gruyter, 1960). These are, in all probability, the texts he had consulted in preparation for this course. Bibliographical information for the first edition of the last title cannot be established.

15 *Scriptum*, 13.

16 *Scriptum*, 13.

17 *Scriptum*, 15.

18 *Scriptum*, 15.

19 With reference to Denzinger [henceforth, the edition of Denzinger to which Ratzinger refers in the *scriptum* will be simply "Denz."; he lists no specific edition of Denzinger, though—Denzinger/Umberg perhaps?] 144 [Denz. section number matching Heinrich Denzinger, *Enchiridion Symbolorum: Compendium of Creeds, Definitions, and Declarations on Matters of Faith and Morals*, ed. Peter Hünermann, 43rd ed., English edition, ed. Robert Fastiggi and Anne Englund Nash (San Francisco: Ignatius Press, 2012), 294] [henceforth, DH].

20 Denz. 256 (DH 503).

and by the testimonies of Tertullian, Ambrose, Gregory of Nyssa, Zeno of Verona, Proclus of Constantinople (fifth century), and Pseudo-Epiphanius. This insight is gained—is "struggled for" (*errungen*), as Ratzinger circumscribes this process—in the controversies surrounding the heresy of Docetism. This historical development also sharpens our understanding of the ongoing reality of original sin, Ratzinger remarks to his seminarians.

With references to the *Tomus ad Flavian*, as well as Tertullian, Victorinus of Pettau, Helvidius, and the apocryphal Gospel according to the Ebionites, Ratzinger now discusses the perpetual virginity of Mary. The term "firstborn" does not initially refer to a person who was the first child born into the world to particular parents, but rather predicates someone who is reserved to God in the integrity of his person.[21] Mark 15:40 is interpreted as a reference to a mother other than Mary for the Lord's "brothers." "Why does Jesus, on the Cross, entrust his mother to John, when siblings are still there?" Ratzinger asks. The siblings are "cousins," the theology professor deduces, by analyzing the Septuagint version of Genesis 12:5, 13:8, and 29:10.[22]

Part 2: Mariology as Ecclesiology

The dogma of the *Theotokos* is defined as the "basic principle" (*Grundprinzip*) of Mariology. Holy Scripture alone cannot provide the arguments for this concept, the professor observes. Nevertheless, Mark 3:31–35 and its parallels illustrate the singularity of Jesus's spiritual relationship with and commitment to the Father—to the detriment of all natural relations of kinship. "Blessed rather are those who hear the word, and keep it"—Luke 11:27–26, together with Luke 2:49ff, shows that Jesus lives from his heavenly Father. The marriage at Cana (John 2:4) confirms this insight: Jesus's pneumatic nature, as well as his messianicity, stand in the foreground.[23] In the Pauline opposition of earthly and spiritual knowledge

---

[21] *Scriptum*, 20.

[22] For this section, Ratzinger points to: Gerhard Delling, "Parthenos," in *Theologisches Wörterbuch zum Neuen Testament*, ed. Gerhard Kittel, vol. 5 (Stuttgart: Kohlhammer, 1932), 824–35; *Regensburger Neues Testament*, ed. Alfred Wikenhauser, Otto Kuss, Joseph Freundorfer, 3rd revised ed., vols. 1–3 [Matt, Mark, Luke] (Regensburg: Pustet, 1956–1957); (most probably) Mircea Eliade *Die Religionen und das Heilige: Elemente der Religionsgeschichte* (Salzburg: O. Müller, 1954); Albert Mitterer, *Dogma und Biologie der Heiligen Familie: nach dem Weltbild des Hl. Thomas von Aquin und dem der Gegenwart* (Vienna, AT: Herder, 1952).

[23] *Scriptum*, 22.

concerning the identity of Jesus in 2 Corinthians 5:16, Ratzinger sees this view affirmed (see John 7:3–6 and Gal 4:4). The parallel texts of Mark 3:34, 10:30, and 13:12 ("the rift through the family is an eschatological sign, a sign of the impending end time in Christ," says Ratzinger) confirm the priority of the supernaturality and messiahship of Christ. Here we are confronted with the remark that "we must admit that the New Testament does not recognize the fact of bodily birth as a *locus theologicus*."[24] At this point, Ratzinger emphasizes the faith of Mary and does not advocate a flat biologism: "The entire childhood narrative presents Mary as the great believer," he states immediately—she brings forth "from her faith" the Son of God. For this reason, she is named "*Regina Patriarchorum*, . . . *Regina Christianorum*, [and] Mother of all believers" in elongation of Scripture, analogous to Abraham, who is called "the father of all believers" (see Heb 11 and Rom 4).[25] Ratzinger concludes:

> Faith means to give up on oneself [the original *aufgeben* is stronger than simply "self-surrender"] and be pure openness to God. . . . She [Mary] is not contrasted to us, rather she appears as the exemplar realization of what ultimately . . . must happen to us all; she is the primordial [i.e., prototypical] representation of the Christian faith par excellence.[26]

In the second section, Mary is contrasted with the people of Israel, and the personal figure of *Theotokos* is made out as the new Israel in which "God dwells."[27] This is the result of a nuanced comparison between Wisdom 3:14–17 and Luke 1:28–33. In a joint salutation—χαιρε and the promises βασιλεις . . . κυριος (Wisdom) / ὁ κυριος μετα σοῦ (Luke)—Old Testament *topoi* are carried forward and concretized in the New Testament. What is promised to the corporate community of Israel is applied "in a condensed [form] to Mary."[28] This insight is confirmed by the parallels of 2 Samuel 2:12–16 with Luke 1:32f and 2 Samuel 6:9 with Luke 1:43. The promise to Daniel and the image of the covenantal ark are transferred to Mary. In Luke 1:42, "blessed are you among women" is an "exact

---

24 *Scriptum*, 23.

25 *Scriptum*, 24.

26 *Scriptum*, 25.

27 *Scriptum*, 26.

28 *Scriptum*, 26. See also Regina Agnes Willi, "Die marianische Deutung der alttestamentlichen 'Weisheit' bei Joseph Ratzinger und Leo Scheffczyk," *Forum Katholische Theologie* 29, no. 2 (2013): 110–25.

contrast" to Judith 13:18. He notes, "[The] Lucan childhood narrative has taken over 60 of the 102 Old Testament words."[29] Luke 1:46–48a replicates "almost verbatim" the *Canticum Animae* from 1 Samuel 2:1ff. To Ratzinger's mind, it is decisive that "Mary exceeds the self-praise of all generations of Israel." In fact, no one but "Mary is putting herself in the place of Israel!"[30] This bold statement of a simple woman from among the common people defies all reasonable measures of both Israelites and pagan people alike. It is confidently claimed. One need give the unheard of, revolutionary quality of this statement particular attention.

In John's Gospel, for example in Jesus's "curt dismissal" of Mary as "woman," but also in the *sic et non* vis-à-vis Mary's request for her son to perform a miracle in the Cana pericope, Ratzinger sees this interpretation confirmed. The *restrictio mentalis* of Our Lord, which the German theologian Karl Adam (1876–1966) had pointed out, is expressly not shared by Ratzinger.[31] The Gospel according to John is treated by him in astonishing detail. "The problem of the hour" is interpreted eschatologically as an "anticipation," as a *Vorgriff*, a term Karl Rahner had coined. Ratzinger says: "The hour of Jesus is also the hour of Mary; under the cross!"[32] The marriage in Cana is "a symbolic sign of the mystical wedding of Christ with the Church": "Wherever there is talk of the Church, there one must also speak of Mary."[33]

Ratzinger asks rhetorically about the mother of Jesus under the Cross (John 19:25–27): "Does this place have a theological valence, or is it merely the fulfillment of a duty to piety [towards a mother]?"[34] He notes *en passant*: "Loisy and Bultmann opine John had not intended to relate a historical event, but rather a historically twisted symbolism."[35] Ratzinger counters resolutely:

> John undoubtedly wants to report history. But John is equally anxious not merely to provide a [one-dimensional] narrative, but

---

29 *Scriptum*, 26.

30 *Scriptum*, 27.

31 *Scriptum*, 28. No bibliographical information is supplied on this point. Likely Ratzinger has in mind an earlier edition of Karl Adam, *Christus, unser Bruder*, 9th ed. (Regensburg: Pustet, 1960).

32 *Scriptum*, 29.

33 *Scriptum*, 29. For this section, Ratzinger lists two authors: Brown (work not given) and Johann Michl, *Bemerkungen zu Joh. 2,4* (Rome: Pontificio Istituto Biblico, 1955).

34 *Scriptum*, 30.

35 *Scriptum*, 32.

> to make history transparent to its meaning. Here John understands the concrete form of history as σημειον. *Factum audivimus mysterium requiramus*![36]

"Mary may from this point be designated as *causa exemplaris*, as the prototype [and primordial image] of the Church."[37] Thus, the distancing, impersonal "address 'woman' antithetically becomes the new woman par excellence," and "in the γυνη [female] in Gen 3," Ratzinger recognizes "a leitmotiv": "Here again this woman, who is standing at the tree of life; it recalls that time. It is interesting that the Eve–Mary parallel comes from the circle around John (Justin, Irenaeus)."[38]

He treats the problem of Revelation 12 under section IV. Along with Tradition, the reference to the twelve stars is interpreted as an allusion to the twelve tribes of Israel. The apocalyptic woman personifies this new people, which appears as the center of the cosmos. Ratzinger perceives, despite all the textual indeterminateness, "an all-encompassing unity of being" that is called the true Israel and is interpreted as the Church.[39] The professor reminds his students that the corporate thinking of Israel as the *qahal* of YHWH must be considered here:

> [Together with] Matthew and Luke, we know that Mary is the woman in whom this has been fulfilled. In this knowledge we can say, that . . . in Mary the essence of the apocalyptic woman is realized in the densest way; that she pulls the meaning of the collective [of all human beings] into one point.[40]

In this connection, he notes the dogmatician's right to believe in the unity of Scripture. This assumption is confirmed in the statement that "*Ecclesia* and Mary are closely related to one another in this text."[41]

---

36 *Scriptum*, 31. Quoting Augustine, *In Ioannem* 50.6, and citing Karl Wennemer, *Die Aufnahme Mariens in den Himmel und die Heilige Schrift* (Frankfurt am Main: Knecht, 1950).

37 *Scriptum*, 32.

38 *Scriptum*, 32–33.

39 *Scriptum*, 34.

40 *Scriptum*, 34.

41 *Scriptum*, 35. For this section, the following titles are mentioned: Wikenhauser et al., *Regensburger Neues Testament*, vols. 1 and 3; Eugen Walter, *Maria: Mutter der Glaubenden* (Freiburg im Breisgau: Herder, 1956); Josef Weiser, *Maria von Nazareth* (Munich: Schnell & Steiner, 1954); Schmaus, *Mariologie*, 211–17; Paul Gächter, *Maria in Kana (Jo 2,1–11)* (Innsbruck: Felizian Rauch, 1931); Johann Michl, "Gen 3,15," *Biblica* 33

These exegetical explanations now allow Ratzinger to treat the foundational, basic principle of patristic Mariology under §4. He first discusses the Eve–Mary parallel. It is also the doctrine of recapitulation championed by Irenaeus of Lyon that makes it possible to recognize the *antitypus* of Eve in Mary, analogous to the Adam–Christ parallel. This task of salvation history Mary accomplishes by being heroically obedient. "Eve believes the serpent, Mary believes God," Ratzinger succinctly summarizes.[42] He strictly rejects Matthias Joseph Scheeben's (1835–1888) designation of Mary as the "bride of Christ." The term "bride of Christ" was unknown to the entire Patristic era, as the Mother of God was most highly esteemed for her exemplary obedience. "The . . . new Eve was for them [the Church Fathers] the Church. . . . Prior to any theological knowledge about the individual figure of Mary [*Mariengestalt*], there is the recognition of the Church as the new woman."[43] *Ab initio*, for Christianity, this interpretation is foundational to Paul and the Synoptics. In order to secure this biblically, reference is made to 2 Corinthians 11:2, Ephesians 5:25–33, and Mark 2:18–22. Thus, the Shepherd of Hermas and the Second Letter of Clement interpret Genesis 1:27. This is attested to in the "uninterrupted" Tradition from Irenaeus, via Ambrose and Ephrem, to the Venerable Bede: Mary is perceived as the incomparable *Dei genetrix ecclesia*.[44] With reference to Cyril of Alexandria, he concludes: "The theological rank of the term *Theotokos* [*Theotokosbegriff*] is that it does not stand alone, but is the concrete representation of the new Eve, the Church."[45] He notes that, "at the end of antiquity, there is a radical change in piety." The result is a "personal piety, which is now being applied personally [to the individual believer], and is now centered on the historical Jesus and no longer on the exalted Lord."[46] Along with this development, the figure of Mary as *the* typos of *Ecclesia* recedes around the twelfth and thirteenth centuries.

In the appendix to this section, Ratzinger places the rare and notable picture of "Mary, the earth of the Church" into the center of his thoughts

(1952): [no page range given]. Michl taught the seminarian Ratzinger while the latter was still studying in Freising.

42 *Scriptum*, 36.

43 *Scriptum*, 37.

44 At this point, one invariably thinks of Hugo Rahner, *Mater Ecclesia: Lobpreis der Kirche aus dem ersten Jahrtausend* (Einsiedeln: Benziger, 1944). However, this title is not explicitly mentioned.

45 *Scriptum*, 38.

46 *Scriptum*, 38.

in order to reaffirm the previous insight. "Mary's religious position is not on the side of God over and against us, but it is on the side of man as an image of what we should be and can be ourselves."[47] Here—perhaps with a point against the then-virulent existentialism of French philosopher Jean-Paul Sartre (1905–80)—he emphasizes that "man is not active, as it were, a self-organizer of his destiny; his being is openness" to God with Mary.[48] At this point, Ratzinger asks the students why the Holy Scripture presents God exclusively as a father, and he provides the following answer: the image of a God as Father "expresses a function—namely, that of shaping—while the typos of the woman signalizes the willingness to hear God's Word."[49]

What has been said in chapter 1 is summarized in §5. Referencing Romans 4, Ratzinger notes that the New Testament speaks essentially of Christ and his Church, while every human being becomes secondary: "The *totus* of Christ is the purpose of Scripture. Everything else is a shadow [prefigurement and purpose] of this *sacramentum futuri*." [50] By means of the figure of the Church as both virgin and mother, the believer is able to recognize and live the perduring reality of the Incarnation of Christ in the here and now. "This fact leads to the ever-paler fact that Mary is the simple representation of the Church par excellence, in fact, she is the *summula Ecclesiae* [small summit of the Church]."[51] This insight into the mystery of the Church as essentially Marian is the decisive *point d'appui* for all subsequent knowledge. Therefore, Ratzinger argues: "Mariology as insight and doctrine cannot be deduced from the fact of the historical figure of Mary herself, but can be deduced only from the understanding of this fact [the ecclesiastical life of the real Church]. Mariology is never a pure Mariology [as a discipline in unrelated isolation], but an application of ecclesiology."[52] This becomes all the more comprehensible when one considers

---

[47] *Scriptum*, 39.

[48] *Scriptum*, 39.

[49] *Scriptum*, 39. For this section, following bibliographical information is provided: Hugo Rahner, S.J., *Maria und die Kirche* (Innsbruck: Marianischer, 1951) [English: *Our Lady and the Church*, trans. Sebastian Bullough (Bethesda, MD: Zaccheus Press, 2004); Alois Müller, *Ecclesia-Maria: die Einheit Marias und der Kirche* (Fribourg, CH: Universitätsverlag Fribourg, 1955); Karl *Delahaye, "Maria: Typus der Kirche," Wissenschaft und Weisheit* 12 (1949): 79–92; Otto Semmelroth, *Urbild der Kirche: organischer Aufbau des Mariengeheimnisses* (Würzburg: Echter, 1950); Henri de Lubac, *Méditation sur l'Eglise* (Paris: Aubier, 1954).

[50] *Scriptum*, 40.

[51] *Scriptum*, 40.

[52] *Scriptum*, 41.

that "Mariology is indebted to being a piece of typological interpretation of the Holy Scriptures"[53] found already in this corpus (see John 5:46 and Luke 24:25ff). On the one hand, it is wrong to "try to demonstrate the individual dogmas from individual writings or to find them in the finished form among the Fathers."[54] On the other hand, however, Ratzinger also reminds his seminarians that there must necessarily be an organic development of doctrine. The earliest verbalized stage is not necessarily the best form. Many things remain, for the time being, preserved only in the oral tradition. As an organic continuity, Tradition is essential for faith. It is crucial that there is no change in the principles within which the truth of faith can ever afresh and anew manifest itself more deeply. It is precisely in this situation that it becomes clear that "not theology, but the Church as the supreme interpreter of Scripture"[55] vouches for the correctness of doctrine. As an ecclesiastically enradicated science, theology is an important, yet secondary, reality vis-à-vis the considerably more comprehensive reality of the Church, which enables theology—within its vital sacramental space—to make its most highly legitimate existence possible in the first place. Thus practiced, "theology [again] must show that the scriptural interpretation of the Church is possible and in principle justified."[56]

Chapter 2: The Individual Mariological Statements

Under §6, the Immaculate Conception is treated. This belief is presented with reference to the bull *Ineffabilis Deus*[57] as *de fide*, but as anticipated

[53] *Scriptum*, 41.

[54] *Scriptum*, 41. It cannot be established whether, at this point, indirect criticism is aired concerning the two most recent Marian dogmatic definitions. This is likely due to Gottlieb Söhngen's—Ratzinger's dissertation and *Habilitationschrift* director—guarded criticism of the dogma of 1950. See: Joseph Ratzinger, *Aus meinem Leben: Erinnerungen* (Stuttgart: Deutsche Verlags-Anstalt, 1998), 65–67; Ratzinger, *Milestones: Memoirs, 1927–1977*, trans. Erasmo Leiva-Merikakis (San Francisco: Ignatius Press, 1998), 58–60. Surprisingly, at no point in the course is the then-standard dogmatic textbook mentioned: Ludwig Ott, *Grundriß der Dogmatik* (Freiburg im Breisgau: Herder, 1952). Certainly, this circumstance attests to Ratzinger's general reservations regarding the propositional presentation of creedal truths.

[55] *Scriptum*, 42.

[56] *Scriptum*, 42.

[57] Denz. 1641 (DH 2800–2804). See also *Der Glaube der Kirche in den Urkunden der Lehrverkündigung*, ed. Josef Neuner and Heinrich Roos (Regensburg: Pustet, 1954), 325, and the more recent English edition, *The Christian Faith in the Doctrinal Docu-*

long before in the liturgical life and piety of the Church: for example, by Sixtus IV in the apostolic constitution *Grave nimis*,[58] and by the Council of Florence in 1439. Here Ratzinger discusses the relationship between nature and grace with references to the decree on original sin from the Council of Trent,[59] the bull *Ex omnibus afflictionibus* issued by Pius V in reaction to the theses of Michael Baius in 1567,[60] and Clement XI's constitution *Unigenitus Dei Filius* responding to the errors of Pasquier Quesnels in 1713.[61]

This is followed by an analysis of evidence from Scripture. The exegesis of Genesis 3:15 leads to the realization that there is "no definite victory over the serpent": "[The] theological valence is: a lasting struggle of mankind with the power of the demons is prophesied."[62] At this point, Ratzinger compares the text variants in the *Vetus Latina*, the Septuagint, and the Vulgate. Finally, with Ephesians 5:27, the *Ecclesia sine macula et virgo* is confirmed. "The [miraculous] birth of Mary is the rebirth of Israel, of humankind to *Ecclesia*,"[63] as Ratzinger formulates. This can be detected in Tradition by the third and fourth centuries. Ambrose and Augustine in particular are convinced of the sinlessness of Mary and that of the Church. In this context, the contributions of the Cappadocians, Bernard of Clairvaux, Duns Scotus, and Roman Lull are particularly mentioned: "We speak of pre-redemption."[64] Here he states: "[The] grace of Mary is not identical with the paradisiacal state! Her grace is a saving grace. The result is: she knows pain, illness, and death." In this connection, he explicitly refers to Karl Rahner, who claimed that the "temporal difference between liberation of the sins for us and Mary is not the content of dogma!"[65] Ratzinger poses the hypothetical question of whether all of humankind could refuse salvation and comes to the conclusion that this cannot be true of Mary.

> Why precisely the mother? Because office and grace do not disintegrate, fall apart at the decisive points in the history of salvation. Messiah-motherhood is such an office. Christ's salvific

ments of the Catholic Church, ed. Josef Neuner and Jacques Dupuis (New York: Alba House, 2001), 479.

58 Sixtus IV, Apostolic Constitution *Grave Nimis*, from 1483 (DH 1425).

59 In particular, Denz. 792 (DH 1515–16).

60 Denz. 1073 (DH 1901–1980).

61 DH 2400ff. Here the manuscript errs when indicating Denz. 1110.

62 *Scriptum*, 43.

63 *Scriptum*, 45.

64 *Scriptum*, 46.

65 *Scriptum*, 47. This claim occurs rather unexpectedly.

> work cannot remain fruitless. According to Rahner's thesis, the dogma [of 1854] would state that office and grace are ultimately not separable.[66]

Subsequently, Ratzinger inquires about the holiness of Mary. Certainly Mary has been free from all sin, and yet she matured as Mother of God and her merits increased until her death. That is why, in the logic of her earthly existence, she is found worthy to be crowned in heaven.[67]

The assumption of Mary into heaven is treated in §7. He mentions that, for the Tübingen theologian Josef Rupert Geiselmann (1890–1970), the *Assumptio* was not "a date" of salvation history, comparable to the Crucifixion or Resurrection. At this section, Ratzinger points out that the Assumption of Mary, though not in and of itself a necessary fact for the person Mary, is nevertheless a decisive factor for the proper understanding of salvation. Thus, also in the pre-born Mary, God had acted in hiddenness as a "pure act of grace,"[68] even though the common scriptural proofs are, of course, "meaningless."[69] Here Ratzinger implicitly applies the critical distinction between primary truth of faith (Christ) and secondary truth (Mary), but without cancelling out the latter, as occurs occasionally. Following the inner logic of salvation history, Ratzinger mentions the apocryphal *Transitus Mariae* from the fourth or fifth century. Timothy of Jerusalem seconded this in the following period: it is *transitus* for Mary, not death. There are texts now known as fabrications that Jerome or Augustine use to buttress the doctrine of the *Dormitio* of the Mother of God. Astonishingly, for Ratzinger, Modestos of Jerusalem († 630) allegedly mentions a feast celebrating the Dormition of Mary (Modestos is mentioned both in the East and in the West at the same time—this is suspicious). "It was only in the eighth century that the idea of Mary's Assumption into heaven was expressly stated. John of Damascus [states]: Mary, as the new Eve, could not herself have fallen prey to death."[70] From the tenth century onward, this became a commonly held doctrine.

The doctrinal teaching on Mary's Assumption reminds the faithful of the fact that, beyond a *theologia crucis*, and as it were, exalting it, there is also a *theologia gloriae*. Already, Matthew 27:2 teaches that the human

---

[66] *Scriptum*, 47–48. Also mentioned is Karl Rahner, *Schriften zur Theologie*, vol. 1 (Zürich/Köln: Einseideln/Benziger, 1954), 123–237.

[67] *Scriptum*, 48.

[68] *Scriptum*, 48.

[69] *Scriptum*, 49.

[70] *Scriptum*, 49.

person is being perfected in Christ. Based on this insight, the Church is already partially living in eschatological perfection, proving Mary's bodily incorruptibility. As infallible dogmatic definitions, both the *Immaculata* and *Assumptio* are thus also statements about the nature of the Church.[71]

If one were ever to speak of a death of Mary, this must be conceived of as radically different from all other mortal human beings. "Mary's death is not the answer to sin, but the self-giving away of love, or the overwhelming power of love, which broke the outer shell and prepared the way for the true form [*Gestalt*]."[72]

In the thesis of the mediation of grace by Mary, in §8, the statement is contained that no man receives salvation "that is not mediated by special intercession by Mary."[73] Even though this is not already unfolded in Scripture, this thought is nascently present in the biblical Eve–Mary parallel. Bernard of Clairvaux touches on this, and Louis de Montfort and Alphonsus Liguori are the great promoters of this veneration. Also Leo XIII, Pius X, Pius XI, and Pius XII are mentioned in this regard.

Ratzinger defines the role of Mary as:

> Moral mediation by intercession . . . [and] . . . physical [by motherhood]: Mary is ontologically the place of passage of all graces and is therefore supra-sacrament [*Übersakrament*]. . . . Between the function of Mary and all other Christians, there is no essential difference, but only a gradual one, which can also be great! . . . Every Christian is a mediator of all grace! Especially Mary.[74]

This charism places Ratzinger in the Eucharistic context of the *communio sanctorum*, wherein Mary is both the supra-temporal and temporal image of the Church. This is all the more evident by the following Pauline delimitation: "For there is one God, and there is one mediator between God and men, the man Christ Jesus" (1 Tim 2:5).[75]

---

71 *Scriptum*, 50.

72 "Marias Tod ist nicht Antwort auf die Sünde, sondern das Sichverschenken der Liebe, oder das Übermächtigwerden der Liebe, die das äußere Gehäuse zerbrach und der wahren Gestalt den Weg bereitete." This line from *Scriptum*, 51, is a good example of Ratzinger's poetic style when teaching. This section refers to Rahner, *Schriften zur Theologie*, 1:139–252, as well as Josef Rupert Geiselmann, *Jesus der Christus: Die Urform des apostolischen Kerygmas als Norm unserer Verkündigung und Theologie von Jesus Christus* (Stuttgart: Katholisches Bibelwerk, 1951), 101–3.

73 *Scriptum*, 51.

74 *Scriptum*, 51.

75 *Scriptum*, 52.

This is followed, in section §9, by a reflection on the participation of Mary in Jesus Christ's work of salvation. As regards the term *Coredemptrix* and its possible ecclesial recognition, this would have the following consequence, argues the dogmatician Ratzinger:

"On the Cross with Christ, Mary, had been atoning and earning graces during the objective event of redemption, and she has also earned the same grace that Christ earned through his death for humankind. Mary . . . [is logically] a con-principle of redemption [if the title *Coredemptrix* were ever actually conferred on her]." In this context, Ratzinger refers to the already differentiating statement of Pius X: "Mary earned *de congruo* what Christ *condigno* earned."[76] This statement is "a harmless version," but "it is dangerous, as Christ had earned grace by *modum causae finalis*, while Mary has earned grace morally by *modum causa efficiens*."[77] At this point, the young professor rhetorically asks the priesthood candidates whether one may speak of Mary as "a priestess." This had already been prohibited by the "Holy Office," and Scheeben had also spoken out against implied speech of "two priests." Scheeben especially disliked the transferal of the hierarchical grace to a woman. With recourse to the biblically and patristically well-based Eve–Mary parallel, one should rather speak of Mary as "a companion of Jesus at the cross-sacrifice."[78]

The title *Coredemptrix* can be best understood in the sense of the dictum of Augustine: "Who created you, does not redeem you without you."[79] All salvation demands free acceptance by man. In this qualifying sense, there is, in fact, a cooperation on the part of people at the sacrifice on the Cross. But here, too, Ratzinger emphasizes the absolute priority of divine grace, "which, however, is a transforming power."[80] Here again, the Church as a whole moves to the center of the reflection as "whole, actively con-suffering and sympathetic [under the Cross] as a body of Christ": "In her, Christ's suffering is first brought into history. Col 1:24! . . . Mary has preceded in the purest fashion on the path of the *Ecclesia* as a whole; one of humble acceptance of grace."[81] Here he points to the position of the noted Mariologist Heinrich Maria Köster, who makes out in Mary's *fiat* at the time of the Annunciation the *specificum* of the co-redeemer as "rep-

[76] *Scriptum*, 53.

[77] *Scriptum*, 53.

[78] *Scriptum*, 53.

[79] See Augustine, *Sermon* 169, 11.13.

[80] *Scriptum*, 54.

[81] *Scriptum*, 54.

resentative of humankind."[82] Against Köster, however, Ratzinger insists that the acceptance of salvific grace lies in the irreplaceable responsibility of the individual.[83] Moreover, Ratzinger argues against Köster's arguments in favor of the title *Coredemptrix* because such a position subscribes to a "one wrong ontologization."[84] It is not through her existence that humanity is redeemed by Christ, but through the actualization of her personal freedom. Mary's "*fiat* was not *causa*, but only a *conditio* of our salvation,"[85] since man can never be himself the cause for his salvation. "A representation of humankind in Mary is to be admitted insofar as she brings to full representation, in the ultimate and fulfilled manner, the believing 'Yes' of all believing people."[86]

In seven lines, the "kingship [*sic*]" of Mary is considered under §10. Starting from 1 Peter 2:2–20 and Revelation 1:6 and 5:10, the active dimension of this kingdom is distilled. "The Kingdom of God is essentially active because it fulfills the innermost essence of human being."[87] In Mary, the true essence of divine rule is revealed as service. He makes a precise statement: "*Ancilla* is *Regina*"—the queen is servant.[88]

Nothing is noted under §11, which regards the ecclesiastic meaning of Mary's holiness (the point is left blank in the *scriptum* except for the heading). A special chapter is dedicated to the veneration of Mary. However, this is presented in brevity, only on a half-page under §12. Here he emphasizes that Mary deserves a form of veneration that goes far beyond those that angels and saints enjoy: *cultus hyperdulia*. He concludes the lecture with a consideration on the oldest prayer to the Virgin Mary—*Sub Tuum Praesidium*—which he still situates in the fourth century, and quotes "show us your Son" in order to complete the lecture with the words "Christ is the Omega of Mariology as he is also the alpha of Mariology."[89]

---

82 *Scriptum*, 54–55.

83 See Heinrich Maria Köster, S.A.C., *Unus Mediator: Gedanken zur marianischen Frage* (Limburg: Lahn, 1950).

84 *Scriptum*, 55.

85 *Scriptum*, 55.

86 *Scriptum*, 55.

87 *Scriptum*, 55.

88 *Scriptum*, 56.

89 *Scriptum*, 56.

Final Assessment

The summary of a one-semester lecture written in staccato style is *nolens volens* more an outline of headwords. This notwithstanding, the core points of Ratzinger's Mariology can be distilled from this course. They recur later in his writings, impact his drafting of chapter 8 of *Lumen gentium* (52–69), and characterize his statements as Supreme Pontiff.

The first chapter of the course follows the well-known outlines established by Matthias Premm, Ludwig Ott, and Michael Schmaus. The *Ephesinum*—namely, Mary as Mother of God—is apprehended as primarily a Christological statement.[90] However, while these theologians emphasize the conventional perspective of Mary's privileges,[91] Ratzinger begs to differ. His new *Mariologisches Grundprinzip* argues from Mary's faith. Mary is the first believer and the origin of the ecclesial reality. This explains the contrast between Christ and the Church/Mary in the *scriptum*, a distinguishing feature of this text. This personalist perspective is subsequently further developed in *Daughter Zion* and *Mary: Church at its Origin*.[92] Mary is the personification and concretion of the Church, of the *ecclesia* as the holy earth, Daughter of Zion, and sign of eschatological perfection. The *scriptum* stresses that Christian existence is grounded in encounter.[93] In Mary, the ideal of divine call and human hearing and response is realized (DCE 42). This Marian understanding of the Church prevents her members from falling prey to the temptation to "make" the Church. Many years later, reflecting on the Second Vatican Council, Ratzinger observes:

---

90 Matthias Premm, *Katholische Glaubenskunde: Lehrbuch der Dogmatik*, vol. 2, *Christus, Maria, Kirche* (Vienna, AT: Herder, 1952), 300–422. Note Premm's sequence: Christ, Mary, and Church. See also: Ott, *Grundriss der katholischen Dogmatik*, 10th ed. (Freiburg im Breisgau: Herder, 1981), 236–61; Schmaus, *Mariologie*.

91 Premm, *Glaubenskunde* 2:301–2; Ott, *Grundriss der Dogmatik*, 23; Schmaus, *Mariologie*, 181.

92 Joseph Ratzinger, *Daughter Zion: Meditations on the Church's Marian Beliefs*, trans. John M. McDermott, S.J. (San Francisco: Ignatius Press, 1983); Hans Urs von Balthasar and Joseph Ratzinger, *Mary: The Church at the Source*, trans. Adrian Walker (San Francisco: Ignatius Press, 2005), 25 and 30 [originally *Maria: Kirche im Ursprung* (Einsiedeln: Johannes, 1997)].

93 The encyclical *Deus caritas est* reiterates: "Being Christian is not the result of an ethical choice or a lofty idea, but the encounter with an event, a person, which gives life a new horizon and a decisive direction" (Pope Benedict XVI, Encyclical Letter on Christian Love *Deus Caritas Est* [December 25, 2005], 1, available from http://www.vatican.va, [hereafter cited in text as DCE]).

> Church is not a contrivance or an apparatus, not merely an institution or one of the usual sociological entities—she is a person. She is a woman; she is a mother. She is alive. The Marian understanding of the Church is the most categorical antithesis to a merely organizational or bureaucratic concept of Church. We cannot make Church; we must be Church. And we *are* Church, and Church is in us only insofar as faith shapes our being, above and beyond anything we do. Only in Marian being do we become Church. At the origins, too, Church was not made but born. She was born when the *fiat* was awakened in Mary's soul. That is the most profound desire of the Council: that the Church might awaken in our souls. Mary shows us the way.[94]

For this reason, he calls the incorporation of Mariology into the Dogmatic Constitution on the Church, *Lumen gentium*, "a spiritual watershed."[95]

His Mariology is decidedly Christocentric, and the figure of Mary is essentially ecclesio-typical. For the theologian Ratzinger, all the other Marian titles emerge from the fifth-century dogmatic definition of the *Theotokos*, which dogmatically undergirds and enables all subsequent statements concerning Mary. Although "canonical exegesis" will only later be a *topos* with Ratzinger, the concept is already implicitly evident in his Mariology course in the sense of Augustine's dictum: "Novum in Vetere latet, Vetus in Novo patet." Pope Benedict XVI has always read Scripture with the canonical nature of the text in mind. It has only more recently become known as the "canonical" approach, thus coined by the American theologian Brevard Childs. It is an essential dimension of his interpretation of Scripture. "It does not contradict the historical-critical interpretation, but carries it forward in an organic way toward becoming theology in the proper sense," as he explains in the first volume of *Jesus of Nazareth*.[96]

The orientation provided by the Gospel of John and by the Book of Revelation is unmistakable. Also, the Johannine emphasis remains a recurring *cantus firmus* in the entire theological œuvre of Ratzinger. Fur-

---

[94] Joseph Ratzinger, *Church, Ecumenism and Politics: New Endeavors in Ecclesiology*, trans. Michael J. Miller (San Francisco: Ignatius Press, 2008), 28.

[95] Balthasar and Ratzinger, *Maria: Kirche im Ursprung*, 16.

[96] Joseph Ratzinger / Pope Benedict XVI, *Jesus of Nazareth*, vol. 1, *From the Baptism in the Jordan to the Transfiguration*, trans. Adrian J. Walker (San Francisco: Ignatius, 2007), xviiiff. See also Joseph Ratzinger, "Ein Versuch zur Frage des Traditionsbegriffs," in Joseph Ratzinger and Karl Rahner, *Offenbarung und Überlieferung*, Quaestiones Disputatae 25 (Freiburg im Breisgau: Herder, 1965), 25–69.

thermore, he recognizes as binding both the scriptural evidence and the *consensus Patrum*. The Church and its testimony are perceived as ultimately beyond the range of investigation, which is the case, last but not least, because they are the very constituents of the Church's own self-reflection.

In many instances, Ratzinger perceives the connection of Mary with the individual Christian as somewhat individualistic, and with the benefit of hindsight, he might revise this view. But even in this point, one can attest to Ratzinger's keen awareness of the problems of the times. He interprets the extra-biblical, cultural-historical findings as preparations for the Incarnation, and this interpretation is based on analogical reasoning: the *analogia entis*, in which the basic congruence of human hope for salvation and its fulfillment in Jesus Christ, is presupposed.

He considers the term *Coredemptrix* infelicitous. This term is not biblically supported, and it is unintentionally dangerous, as it relativizes the salvific work of Jesus Christ. His skepticism against the title of *Coredemptrix* can go back to his Munich teacher/s Gottlieb Söhngen and/or Michael Schmaus. Hugo Rahner and René Laurentin were especially resolute advocates of a recovery of the ecclesial-typological understanding of Mary, and in this Mary–Church typology, Ratzinger was *d'accord* with many well-known theologians of his time. Accordingly, during the Second Vatican Council, the *peritus* Ratzinger took up the cudgels in favor of the title of the eighth chapter of *Lumen gentium*: "The Blessed Virgin Mary, Mother of God in the Mystery of Christ and the Church" (LG 52–69).[97]

Every now and then, one encounters determinations such as *de fide* or *sententia certa*, and he repeatedly refers to the Denzinger.[98] The important scholarly contributions of that era are introduced. He explores Hebrew, Greek, and Latin terms and passages at decisive points in order to clarify the meaning of a dogmatic thought and to undergird or buttress the faith of the Church in this respect.

---

97 Thus, Ratzinger seems to concur with Otto Semmelroth's position: Mary's role in the salvific work of Christ is limited to an exclusively "receptive co-redeemer" ("rezeptiven Miterlöserin"). Reference is made to the well-known Augustine quotation: "der Dich geschaffen hat, erlöst Dich nicht ohne Dich" (Sermon 169, 11.13: "Who created you, does not redeem you without you"). See: Otto Semmelroth, *Maria oder Christus? Christus als Ziel der Marienverehrung* (Frankfurt am Main: Josef Knecht, 1954); Semmelroth, *Urbild der Kirche*. Under all accounts, Gabriele Maria Roschini's "maximalistic position" is vehemently rejected ("maximalistische Position"), and all the more Roschini's thesis of "a redemptive couple" (see Roschini, *Mariologia*, 2nd ed. [Rome: Belardetti, 1947]).

98 Again, a specific edition of the Denzinger is never mentioned.

The figures "Daughter Zion," "Mother of the Church," and "Mother of the Eucharist" are not mentioned in the *scriptum* itself, nor the spiritual Motherhood of Mary, nor the prophetic dimension of Marian apparitions.[99] The relationship between the veneration of the Virgin Mary and the liturgy remains untreated. "Mariology as a concrete doctrine of grace" resurfaces in the *Introduction to Christianity*.[100] With good reasons, he rejects the notion of Mary as a "bride of Christ," famously introduced by Matthias Scheeben into speculative theology.

By establishing a *Mariologisches Grundprinzip* around the *Theotokos* definition of 431 at Ephesus, Ratzinger prioritizes that council vis-à-vis later dogmatic definitions concerning the Mother of God. This may be one reason for him to expect Orthodoxy to accept nothing more than had already been accepted as the *depositum fidei* before 1054:[101] subsequent doctrinal developments are but organic outgrowths of the first Christian millennium.

One already experiences in this course a nuanced, promising *communio* theologian. *Cum grano salis*, this direction is synonymous with the concerns of the *ressourcement* movement. In particular, this current will emphasize the following: (1) the Christian faith as personal and dialogical; (2) the totality of the Church and her witnesses (such as Scripture, liturgy, councils, synods, saints, and theologians); and (3) all the epochs' comprehensive faith as thought from the Eucharistic Lord: "the Eucharist makes the Church and the Church makes the Eucharist"—as Henri de Lubac's (1896–1991) celebrated line reads. As Ratzinger elaborates in his lecture, Mary has lived these three dimensions paradigmatically and fundamentally: (1) she is in dialogue with the archangel Gabriel and praises

---

99 This is being supplied later in Joseph Ratzinger, *Tochter Zion: Betrachtungen über den Marienglauben in der Kirche* (Einsiedeln: Johannes Verlag, 1977).

100 Joseph Ratzinger, *Einführung in das Christentum* (Munich: Deutsche Verlags-Anstalt, 1968), 263; see English translation: *Introduction to Christianity*, trans. J. R. Foster (San Francisco: Ignatius, 2004), 354–55.

101 "Rome must not require more from the East with respect to the doctrine of primacy than what had been formulated and was lived in the first millennium. . . . Rome need not ask for more. Reunion could take place in this context if, on the one hand, the East would cease to oppose as heretical the developments that took place in the West in the second millennium and would accept the Catholic Church as legitimate and orthodox in the form she had acquired in the course of that development, while, on the other hand, the West would recognize the Church of the East as orthodox and legitimate in the form she has always had" (Joseph Ratzinger, *Principles of Catholic Theology: Building Stones for a Fundamental Theology*, trans. Sr. Mary Frances McCarthy, S.N.D. [San Francisco: Ignatius, 1987], 199).

God in the Magnificat; (2) she stands at the beginning and is both parable and sum of the Church; and (3) she is most prominently present at the wedding at Cana, the proleptic anticipation of the Eucharist. Thus, in the tangible figure of Mary, the believing Church and (by way of inclusion) the believing Christian are made visible.

Even in this early period, Ratzinger was a master of the most current research and took clear positions on debated topics. His Mariology course demonstrates the early theological maturity and balanced judgment of the thirty-year-old dogmatician. The typology of Mary as "the Church in its origin" presented by him with verve in his Mariology lecture will prevail *cum grano salis* a few years later during the Second Vatican Council.

In his now classic *Introduction to Christianity*, Ratzinger writes:

> If one wanted to indicate a theological treatise to which Mariology belonged as its concrete illustration, it would probably be the doctrine of grace, which of course goes to form a whole with ecclesiology and anthropology. As the true "daughter of Zion," Mary is the image of the Church, the image of believing man, who can come to salvation and to himself only through the gift of love—through grace. The saying with which Bernanos ends his *Diary of a Country Priest*—"Everything is grace"—a saying in which a life that seemed to be only weakness and futility can see itself as full of riches and fulfillment—truly becomes in Mary, "full of grace" (Lk 1:28), a concrete reality.[102]

[102] Ratzinger, *Introduction to Christianity*, 280.

CHAPTER 6

Pope Benedict XVI's *Jesus of Nazareth: The Infancy Narratives*[1]

Introduction

WITH CHARACTERISTIC MODESTY, Pope Benedict opens his third book on Jesus of Nazareth by remarking that it is not really a third volume, but rather only "an antechamber" to his two previous volumes on the Savior. It hopes to provide theological orientation on the reader's way to Jesus. He underlines the indispensable hermeneutics of this enterprise: both the universal and the personal importance of the truth of Christmas can be unlocked only via the biblical texts because their final and deepest originator is God Himself.[2]

Significantly, the brilliant theologian and eloquent successor to the Apostle Peter reminds the reader that his intention had been all along to introduce one to the "figure and the message of Jesus of Nazareth." Here the author could remind the reader that *figura* is an Augustinian category—akin to Goethe and von Balthasar's *Gestalt*—that conveys the notion of beholding the essence of a person in his totality. Benedict's whole papacy was but one single effort to invite all people to behold in the historical Jesus of Nazareth the eternal Son of God, thereby inaugurating a Christocentric shift, the consequences of which shall probably be felt in scholarship and Christian consciousness only after some time.

1 Pope Benedict XVI, *Jesus of Nazareth*, vol. 3, *The Infancy Narratives* (New York: Random House, 2012). For ease, the work will simply be cited in text parenthetically by page number, unlabeled.

2 This observation is in keeping with the *Doctor Communis*, Thomas Aquinas, in *Summa Theologiae* I, q. 1, a. 10.

This means that the book intends to access an appreciation for the essence of the person Jesus Christ. Benedict is not concerned about accidental features: the Messiah, the eternally begotten second Person of the Blessed Trinity, is the theme of his pontificate. Though shorter than the previous volumes, and even shorter in English (128 pages) than the original German text (170 pages), the book is theologically ambitious and spiritually rich.

That being said, Ratzinger does not want to add to the centuries-old but quite futile quest for the historical Jesus,[3] distilling who Jesus was apart from Scripture and the Church's faith. Without stating it, the Pope is supremely aware of Rudolf Bultmann's famous observation that "all one knows of the historical Jesus fits on the back of one postcard." What he does write about the biblical Jesus Christ can be accepted (*cum grano salis*) by the overwhelming majority of Christians the world over.

This begs a question: "How does one know something about Jesus Christ?" As the Second Vatican Council teaches, it is in the tension between Scripture and Tradition[4] (in the full sense of the latter term) that one beholds Jesus Christ as "the mediator and the fullness of all revelation" (*Dei Verbum* 2 and, more broadly, 2–10).[5] When reading Pope Benedict's *Jesus of Nazareth* trilogy, it is helpful to bear in mind that the young theologian and *peritus* to Cardinal Josef Frings (1887–1978), Joseph Ratzinger, was one of the most significant contributors to the Dogmatic Constitution on Divine Revelation, *Dei Verbum*, insisting that neither Scripture nor Tradition are revelation, but that both attest to Jesus Christ as the full revealer of God: unlike Hermes or Mercury in pagan religions, Jesus Christ is messenger and message at one and the same time.

His Method

Reading the text and the references, one discovers the author making use of a number of sources to pen his own book: Scripture, exegetical studies, the Church Fathers, the saints, and theologians. Under his leadership, the Pontifical Biblical Commission had issued in 1993 a lengthy, in-depth document on biblical scholarship titled *The Interpretation of the Bible in*

---

3 William Baird, *History of New Testament Research*, vol. 1 (Minneapolis, MN: Fortress, 1992), 165–95, 201–8, 246–58, and 333–38.

4 See Karl Rahner and Joseph Ratzinger, *Revelation and Tradition*, trans. W. J. O'Hara, Quaestiones Disputatae 17 (New York: Herder and Herder, 1966).

5 Second Vatican Council, Dogmatic Constitution on Divine Revelation *Dei Verbum* (November 18, 1965), available from http://www.vatican.va (hereafter cited in text as DV).

the Church.[6] There, the historical-critical method is described as an "indispensable method for the scientific study of the meaning of ancient texts."[7] He firmly believes in the need for the historical-critical method, but understanding the meaning of a biblical text requires a multitude of approaches. One cannot exclude one method in favor of another. This is stated clearly in 2002 in his preface to the Pontifical Biblical Commission's document *The Jewish People and Their Sacred Scriptures in the Christian Bible*.[8] In other words, faith cannot be limited to the parameters Immanuel Kant (1724–1804) famously established in his book *Religion within the Boundaries of Mere Reason*.[9] As both the Reformed theologian Karl Barth (1886–1968) and the Catholic Ratzinger insist, *Deus semper maior* (God is always more) than the horizon of human expectations. The solution, for Benedict, is a correlation of faith and reason and a spiritual reading of the biblical texts. Closer to the point, in *Behold the Pierced One*, he argues that the historical-critical method's success depends on the philosophical context in which it is applied: the "hermeneutic of faith."[10] This calls for the integration also of a patristic reading of texts within the *memoria ecclesiae* as the living voice of the *Logos*. In addition, it is crucial to take into account the fact that Scripture and its canon arose within the ambience of sacramental liturgy,[11] a state of affairs that Benedict describes as the "interwoven relationship between Church and Bible, between the people of God and the Word of God."[12] The organic unity of Scripture, sacrament, the Church's faith, and Tradition are *unhintergehbar*—irreducible. He be-

---

6 http://www.vatican.va/roman_curia/congregations/cfaith/pcb_doc_index.htm, accessed March 16, 2018.

7 In his first volume of the *Jesus of Nazareth* trilogy, he had written: "The historical critical method—let me repeat—is an indispensable tool"; see Pope Benedict XVI, *Jesus of Nazareth*, vol. 1, *From the Baptism in the Jordan to the Transfiguration* [New York: Doubleday, 2007], xvi).

8 Pontifical Biblical Commission, *The Jewish People and Their Sacred Scriptures in the Christian Bible* (Vatican City: Libreria Editrice Vaticana, 2002).

9 Immanuel Kant, *Religion within the Boundaries of Mere Reason* (Cambridge: Cambridge University Press, 1998), esp. 6:168–202 (marginal German edition numbering).

10 Joseph Ratzinger, "Appendix II: Afterword to the English Edition," in John Auer and Joseph Ratzinger, *Dogmatic Theology*, vol. 9, *Death: Eshatology: Death and Eternal Life*, trans. Michael Waldstein, ed. Aidan Nichols, O.P. (Washington, DC: Catholic University of America, 1988), 261–74, at 271–72.

11 Joseph Ratzinger, *Principles of Catholic Theology: Building Stones for a Fundamental Theology*, trans. Sr. Mary Frances McCarthy, S.N.D. (San Francisco: Ignatius Press, 1987), 148–50 (see also 133–34).

12 Joseph Ratzinger, *Pilgrim Fellowship of Faith: The Church as Communion*, trans. Henry Taylor (San Francisco: Ignatius Press, 2005), 32–33.

lieves faith to be symphonic: one cannot divorce the historical Jesus from the Christ of faith.

Ergo, the desire to seek with faith and in reverence the face of Christ in the *Jesus of Nazareth* project is not one that cancels out reason, but rather one that makes full use of the modern historical- and text-critical instruments.[13]

The Theological Background to the Pope's Insistence on a Need for a Christocentric Shift

It should be noted well that Benedict XVI never uses the term "Christocentric shift" (*christozentrische Wende*). Coming back from World War II, the young, 18-year-old seminarian at the Freising Domberg found the intellectualistic and propositional presentations of neo-Scholasticism wanting. However, reading Romano Guardini's book *The Lord* and Martin Buber's classic *I and Thou*, he discovered in Jesus Christ a relational God. It was this tripersonal God that sustained him as a military helper on the battlefields. In addition, Henri de Lubac taught him in *Corpus Mysticum* that "the Eucharist makes the Church, and the Church makes the Eucharist." Joseph Ratzinger realized that neither knowledge of Christ nor an encounter with him is possible apart from the living Church. It is Pope Benedict's hope that his *Jesus of Nazareth* trilogy, which is rooted deeply in the Church's faith, will allow his readers to encounter the living Lord more deeply on a personal level.[14]

Brief Exposition of the Pope's Recent Book

The first chapter opens with the Johannine Christ being asked by Pontius Pilate, "Where are you from?" (John 19:9). While this betrays the author as sympathetic to the Fourth Gospel, one soon discovers that Benedict integrates equally the other evangelists, and, in fact, a vast array of biblical, historical, literary, and theological sources. The response is found in Scripture: "My kingship is not of this world" (John 18:36). His origins are

---

13 Joseph Ratzinger, "On the Question of the Foundations and Approaches of Exegesis Today," in *Biblical Interpretation in Crisis: The Ratzinger Conference on Bible and Church*, ed. R. J. Neuhaus (Grand Rapids, MI: Eerdmans, 1989), 6.

14 As the Supreme Pontiff wrote in 2007 in the introduction to *Jesus of Nazareth: From the Baptism in the Jordan to the Transfiguration*, xxiv: "It struck me as the most urgent priority to present the figure and message of Jesus in his public ministry, and so help foster the growth of a living relationship with him."

decidedly mysterious. This is contrasted to the provincial ordinariness of Jesus: his early life as the son of a carpenter in the inconspicuous town of Nazareth. Ratzinger considers the genealogies of Jesus as decisive to solve this riddle: "Only God is truly his 'Father'" (8), and Mary is his actual mother. While placing different accents, both genealogies state something true: for Matthew, Jesus is of Davidic origin, whereas Luke traces his origins back to Adam. This leads Benedict to conclude (and this is crucial to understanding the whole project): "Jesus takes upon himself the whole of humanity, the whole history of man, and he gives it a decisive re-orientation toward a new manner of human existence" (11). The solemn Johannine *Logos*-prologue (John 1:1–18) reveals that Jesus is *the* answer to humanity's search for meaning, as Jesus is the Word. The *Logos* is the true origin of humankind. Using the terms "tent" and "temple," Scripture holds that Jesus is indeed of divine origin. If this is the case, the virginal origin follows rather logically. Those sharing in Mary's belief in the birth of Jesus through the Holy Spirit are thereby spiritually reborn. Christ is their true genealogy: "From Christ, through faith in him, they are now born of God" (11). This is Benedict's brief definition of the term "Christian."

In agreement with the renowned German Catholic exegete Fr. Joachim Gnilka (coincidentally, the Munich thesis director of the present author), Benedict is convinced that Mary is a significant source for the Lucan narrative (16). Not mentioning Mary by name is simply in keeping with her epoch's respect for privacy. It should be noted, however, that Ratzinger does not mention the possibility that Jesus's brother/cousin James, executed AD 62, could also have supplied material for the infancy narratives.

Ratzinger interprets the figure of St. John the Baptist via reference to his priestly (Aaron and Levi) origins: "In John the whole Old Covenant priesthood becomes a prophecy of Jesus" (18). This permits the author to parallel the announcements of the coming birth of John the Baptist and that of Jesus: one in a temple in the context of a liturgy and the other in probably a very humble room in the insignificant town of Nazareth, a place never mentioned by the Old Testament—these circumstances suggest "the sign of the mustard seed" (21). Drawing on the grand seigneur of Catholic Mariology, Fr. René Laurentin, Ratzinger alerts the reader to the fact of 490 days separating the annunciation to Zechariah in the temple from Jesus's presentation in the temple, suggesting nothing short of a divine choreography—though leaving the question open as to whether Luke consciously had this in mind (24–25).

Ever the humanistically trained (at a *humanistisches Gymnasium*) former student, Ratzinger draws attention to the common etymological origin of the Greek words *chaire* (rejoice) and *kecharitōmenē* (blessed/graced) the Angel Gabriel uses when greeting "Hail, full of grace" (Luke 1:28). There is a material connection between joy (*chará*) and grace (*charis*). This connection could have been elaborated much more by Ratzinger, but he does note that Christ becomes *the* source par excellence of our joy and grace (28).

Admitting that, to mere humans, Mary's betrothal to Joseph and staying nevertheless a virgin remains a "riddle," as this notion is unknown to the Judaism of Jesus's time (35), Ratzinger shares the opinion advanced by Gnilka that Mary continued living in her parental home for a year after the betrothal ceremony had taken place. This allows one to apprehend in Joseph a just (*zaddik*) man in the tradition of the Old Testament prophets who "maintains living contact with the word of God" (39). In no way does Joseph live a legalistic understanding of Old Testament faith. Such magnanimity prepares him for the radically different God of Jesus Christ. This is confirmed by the angel revealing to Joseph that Jesus will save his people and forgive sins. To the Jewish mind, the latter is possible only for God. This compels Joseph to allow God to redefine for him who the Messiah is and what task Jesus comes to fulfill: saving people, but not restoring a Davidic royal national kingdom.

The divinity of Christ shines forth in the words to the paralytic: "My son, your sins are forgiven" (Mark 2:5). It is apparent that Jesus is utterly other than what people expected: forgiving the sick man's sins is diametrically opposed to what the audience had expected. Benedict observes, "I consider this whole scene to be of key significance for the question of Jesus' mission." It is Jesus of Nazareth who restores human beings to what they are called from all eternity to be—a healthy "relational being" (44)—by allowing them participation in divine life. Thus the essence of Jesus is revealed to Joseph in the name the child is to receive: Jeshua (Jesus), or "YHWH is salvation" (42).

Ratzinger ponders at length the validity of combining Isaiah 7:14 with the words of the angel in Matthew 1:20–21, as Matthew 1:22 does: "'Behold, a virgin shall conceive and bear a son, and his name shall be called Emmanuel,' which means God with us" (46). With the Catholic Scripture scholar Rudolf Kilian, he regards these words of Isaiah as mysterious. Even the prophet Isaiah himself could probably not provide a satisfactory answer. Along with the Protestant exegete Marius Reiser, he shares the opinion that "the prophet's prediction is like a miraculously formed keyhole, into which the key of Jesus fits perfectly" (50). He is confident that God had given us a sign spanning from the days of the Assyrian ruler

Tiglath-Pileser III (r. 745–727 BC) to Jesus: roughly 700 years. Only Jesus Christ can answer the riddle.

For Pope Benedict, discounting or relativizing the virginal birth of Jesus is tantamount to reducing God to human scale and denying him the ability to be original. Thus, he agrees with Gnilka that the mystery must be assumed as a historical fact giving rise *a posteriori* to its deliberate insertion into the Gospel. This fulfills also the ancient hope in a new beginning *ab integra*, as given poetic expression in Virgil's *Bucolics* between thirty and forty years (probably closer to thirty) prior to Jesus's birth. In this regard, he is of one mind with the great Swiss Reformed theologian Karl Barth (1968): there exists a close connection between Jesus's virginal birth and his Resurrection from the empty tomb. Only the sovereign Creator-God can be humanity's redeemer. "Hence the conception and birth of Jesus from the Virgin Mary is a fundamental element of our faith and a radiant sign of our hope" (57).

As human history is always and inextricably salvation history, Benedict is confident the conjunction of Jesus's birth with the reign of the Roman emperor Augustus is not accidental. A stone in the ancient, now uninhabited Greek harbor town Priene on the western shores of Asia Minor announces in the year 9 BC this earthly emperor as the *soter* (redeemer) bringing an *euangelion* ("good news" / "gospel") of peace. He claims to be *augustus*: worthy to be worshipped as a god. This self-image of a contingent, mortal man is one of unquestioned universality ("the whole *ecumene*"—actually "*oikoumenē*") (63). However dubitable the claim, it illustrates that the ancient world genuinely yearned for a redeemer, who turns out to be indeed the Child in the manger at Bethlehem. Concerning the question of whether, in fact, a tax collection occurred at the time of Jesus's birth, Benedict does not provide a clear answer. However, in agreement with Alois Stöger, he assumes as probable that there had been an ongoing census spanning maybe a few years. As regards the actual date, birth place, and childhood town of Jesus, Benedict agrees with the consensus of current scholarship.

Ratzinger also alerts the reader to a little known fact. In a futile attempt to destroy any traces of Jesus's birth, the Romans turned the birth cave of Christ into the pagan shrine to Tammuz-Adonis. He suggests that, *ex negativo*, the Romans in fact confirm Bethlehem as the town of Jesus's nativity (67–68). While the Gospels mention no animals at the manger, "prayerful reflection" has led people to assume the presence of animals, sensing resonances with the prophetic Isaiah 1:3: "The ox knows its owner, and the ass its master's crib; but Israel does not know, my people does not understand" (69). Mindful of the Pauline words that Christ is "the first-born of all creation" (Col 1:15), Ratzinger sees an inner logic to the image of ox and ass looking on the Redeemer: "Christ, the incarnate Son, is—so to speak—God's first thought, preceding all creation, which is ordered toward him and proceeds from him. He is both the beginning and the goal of the new creation that was initiated with the resurrection" (71).

In the presence of the simple shepherds at the manger, Ratzinger makes out a parallel between the shepherd king David and Jesus: "Jesus is born among shepherds. He is the great Shepherd of mankind (cf. 1 Pet 2:25 and Heb 13:20)" (73). The angelic song "Glory to God" is faulted as a mistranslation, as men are incapable of bringing about God's glory (although, Ratzinger does not offer an alternative, at least in English) (74). In addition, Ratzinger takes exception to the reading "men of good will" and suggests instead "men with whom he is pleased." This leads to a surprising parallel between Christ's birth and his baptism, where a voice says: "You are my beloved Son; with you I am well pleased" (Luke 3:22). This enables him to apprehend the potential of humankind for Christification—"those who are conformed to Christ" (75).

Prior to this time, Pope Benedict had written little on the crucial relationship between nature and grace that had been so characteristic of Western theological discourse since the Middle Ages. However, here he observes how "Grace and freedom are thoroughly interwoven": "It remains true that we could not love if we were not first loved by God" (76). On these pages, Christianity appears as the anti-narrative to the French Revolution of 1789, which left the individual with the burdensome task of defining freedom on his own. It usually means something like a Kantian self-legislating autonomy. Christ Jesus in the manger liberates us moderns from such puerile, emancipatory sentiment, Benedict implies. The triune God is charity par excellence. Yet, "this liberation comes at a cost: the anguish of the Cross" (86). Freedom receives in the figure of Christ its authentic meaning. Demarcated from solipsistic self-determination, freedom receives in Christ Jesus a face dignifying every human being with personhood as he or she is now divinely called freely into a relationship with God through Jesus, one that manifests itself in Christ's uncompromising and utterly relational commitment to the Father (120).

This is confirmed *a fortiori* by the Child knowing the need to stay in the temple with the scribes. The Greek word *dei* (must) is used by the Gospels whenever Jesus's loyalty to His Father is thematized. (124)

How the two natures, divine and human, relate in the one person Jesus Christ, how he can grow in wisdom and yet be the eternal Son of the eternal Father, is a paradox one can only live in the Church's faith. He implies that the teaching of Chalcedon (AD 451)[15] is a sure point of orientation but does not supply us with an answer (127).

Thus, charity, freedom, and peace infinitely outshine anything the public square can ever invent in this area (77). For the Church Fathers and Benedict, pagan societies are marked by insensitivity. Here one hears subcutaneous hints of a critique of secularism and relativism (87).

Another issue the Pope addresses it that of the magi. In the fourth century BC, Aristotle equates magi with philosophers. Matthew informs us they were "wise"—thus they were the "successors of Socrates" (96). They represent all the continents known at the time and, thereby, the universe. Representing the whole cosmos, the magi perform a *proskynesis* (a display of reverence due to a ruler alone). As regards these enigmatic magi, he admits, in agreement with the great patristic scholar Jean Daniélou (1905–1974), that their origin is not dogmatically relevant, but he asserts that anyone who doubts their value must demonstrate their unhistoricity—with a nod to the noted contemporary Heidelberg exegete Klaus Berger.

Along with Johannes Kepler (1571–1630) and other astronomers, he assumes Christ was born in 7 or 6 BC. On this point, he advances the contemporary Viennese astronomer Ferrari d'Occhieppo's theory of a conjunction of the planets Jupiter and Saturn (and dismisses in passing the theory that a supernova occurred simultaneously). "This implies," for Benedict and already the Church Fathers, "that the cosmos speaks of Christ, even though its language is not fully intelligible to man in his present state" (100). In fact, the stars do not guide the fate of Christ, but vice-versa: Christ guides the stars and planets!

Conclusion

Pope Benedict is not concerned with authoring a forced harmony of the four Gospels. He does justice to the respective idiosyncrasies of the various

[15] From the *Chalcedonense*: ". . . our Lord Jesus Christ, the same perfect in divinity and perfect in humanity, the same truly God and truly man composed of rational soul and body, the same one in being [*homoousios*] with the Father as to the divinity and one in being with us as to the humanity, like unto us in all things but sin [cf. Heb 4:15]" (*The Christian Faith in the Doctrinal Documents of the Catholic Church*, ed. Josef Neuner and Jacques Dupuis [New York: Alba House, 2001], 614; Heinrich Denzinger, *Enchiridion Symbolorum: Compendium of Creeds, Definitions, and Declarations on Matters of Faith and Morals*, ed. Peter Hünermann, 43rd ed., English edition ed. Robert Fastiggi and Anne Englund Nash [San Francisco: Ignatius Press, 2012], 301).

testimonies. With the aid of modern day exegetical insights, he uses obviously differing traditions, sources, and perspectives to distil theological insights and subtle commonalities. He is fully loyal to the actual texts, seeing the patristic witness as significant, and is confident both in the Church's faith and in the narratives' historicity. In this ever fruitful tension, he demonstrates that Scripture is open to meaning without reducing meaning to the written words alone.

Jesus being Jewish is not an accident, but a theological necessity. It is not a challenge, but shows the common point of departure for a joint Jewish–Christian dialogue: Bethlehem.

Probably no other living theologian could combine erudition and faith—on the one hand, knowledge of the various theological disciplines and insights into the infancy narratives, and, on the other, a spiritual perspective—as Joseph Ratzinger so ably does. This piece of papal writing is far more than a highly readable and scholarly explication of Christ's infancy narratives, and it is far more than simply a display of this renowned theologian's remarkable synthetic powers. It allows us to see the child Jesus with the eyes of the shepherds and magi and to understand the "figure" of Christ with the post-Easter faith of the apostles. It is nothing short of a fascinating book about a world interpreted coherently by Christian faith. By avoiding simple answers, not evading difficulties, and admitting that he is not able to answer every question, this book speaks the language of a credible, humble believer and a careful scholar. The Pope does not hide behind an immunizing, magisterial façade, but presents his personal belief for critical review.

CHAPTER 7

Revelation as the Thou of Jesus Christ

Joseph Ratzinger's / Pope Benedict XVI's Contribution to a Deeper Understanding of Revelation[1]

Introduction

The rise of deism and positivism in the eighteenth century led the Church to expound on the nature of divine revelation at the First and Second Vatican Councils. In the period between the councils, and at Vatican II itself, Joseph Ratzinger played a pivotal role.

Revelation and the Early Ratzinger

Bonaventure's Foundational Influence

Though Ratzinger's post-doctoral *Habilitationsschrift*,[2] entitled *The Theology of History in St. Bonaventure*, was directed to examining such concepts as history, metaphysics, and eschatology, it also highlights his understanding of revelation. Ratzinger's theology of revelation begins with his study of Bonaventure's (ca. 1217–1274) "spiritual understanding of the Scripture."[3]

---

1 This essay was originally published in *Poznańskie Studia Teologiczne* 30 (2016), 7–56. Used by permission.

2 Joseph Ratzinger, *Milestones: Memoirs, 1927–1977*, trans. Erasmo Leiva-Merikakis (San Francisco: Ignatius Press, 1998), 103.

3 For Bonaventure, a "Spiritual understanding of scripture involved 'manifold divine wisdom' which consists in grasping the three-fold spiritual sense of Scripture—the allegorical, the anagogical and the tropological" (Joseph Ratzinger, *The Theology of History in St. Bonaventure*, trans. Zachary Hayes, O.F.M. [Chicago: Franciscan Herald Press, 1971], 62).

For Ratzinger, the point of departure to understanding Bonaventure's concept of revelation requires[4] penetrating the *Collationes in hexaëmeron*.[5] Indeed, prominent Bonaventure scholar Colt Anderson has stated that reading the *Collationes* "is akin to entering another world drawn along entirely different premises than our own."[6]

Collationes, or lectures, on the *Hexaëmeron* were presented by Bonaventure to his fellow Franciscan brothers in the University of Paris during summer of 1273. Previously withdrawn into solitude, Bonaventure had experienced the spiritual world of Francis of Assisi. Ratzinger says of Bonaventure that, again entering the University of Paris as a professor to lecture, "he came back as an outsider to point out the limits of science from the perspective of faith."[7]

Interpreting the *Hexaëmeron* is difficult: during the thirteenth century, the term *collatio* referred to an afternoon sermon, but Bonaventure delivered them at the university in an academic style. In addition, the original manuscript of Bonaventure's *Hexaëmeron* is not available; only notes of the listeners are extant. Another difficulty was the official *reportatio*: "This text would have been read and approved by Bonaventure; however there was also another recension, published by Ferdinand Delorme, which often varies significantly from the official text."[8] At the time, Bonaventure had not mentioned the names of those who were connected to different problems, but expressed them symbolically.[9] These reasons make it difficult for those interpreting Bonaventure's *Collationes*.

---

4 Zachary Hayes, "Hexaëmeron," in *The New Catholic Encyclopedia* (Washington, DC: Catholic University of America, 2003). The term *hexaëmeron* derives from two Greek words, the numeral "six" and the noun "day," and refers to and interprets the completion of God's creative work in six days in Genesis, followed by the seventh day of the Sabbath rest, connecting this to the six stages of salvation history.

5 Ratzinger, *Theology of History in St. Bonaventure*, 1–3. Bonaventure, after serving as a professor at Paris, was called to replace John of Parma as the seventh successor of St. Francis as the General of the order. After he withdrew to solitude on Mount Alverna in 1259, he allowed himself to be drawn more deeply into the spiritual world of Francis, in whose place he stood. From then on, he called Francis a "Christ-image of the Middle Ages." After ten years, he returned to the same university to teach, but now as an altogether transformed person who pointed out the limits of science from the perspective of faith. It is in this context that we need to understand his *Collationes in Hexaëmeron*, written in 1273.

6 Colt Anderson, *A Call to Piety: St. Bonaventure's Collations on the Six Days* (Quincy, IL: Franciscan Press, 2002), vi.

7 Ratzinger, *Theology of History in St. Bonaventure*, 3.

8 Anderson, *Call to Piety*, vi.

9 Anderson, *Call to Piety*, vii.

The *Hexaëmeron* involved internal and external struggles related to its mission and preaching. Moreover, Bonaventure also prepared his Franciscan brothers for the Second Council of Lyons (1274) by exhorting them to obedience to the bishops and to upholding unity and Christian truth among themselves.[10] While Ratzinger's thesis does not treat every issue the *Hexaëmeron* addressed, it treats the themes directly connected to his understanding of revelation.

Bonaventure preached the *Collationes in hexaëmeron* to his Franciscan brothers to preserve and hold to true Christian wisdom amidst the intellectual "aberrations" of his time.[11] For the Franciscan theologian, the attainment of Christian wisdom was never unrelated to the concrete historical situation. Therefore, Ratzinger noted, "the development of the ideal of wisdom naturally grows into a treatment of the theology of history."[12] In the treatment of theology of history, Bonaventure offered a new theory of scriptural exegesis that gave more importance to the historical character of the scriptural statements—how very "modern."[13]

In his study *The Theology of History in St. Bonaventure*, Ratzinger observes that Bonaventure's scriptural exegesis is multilayered. The first layer consists of the *spiritualis intelligentia*, which understands Scripture in its allegorical or tropological meaning; secondly, there are the *figurae sacramentales* that focus on Christ as the key to understanding Scripture; third, the *multiformes theoriae* give rise to many theories that emerge from Scripture, the fullness of which God alone can grasp in his knowledge. Bonaventure applied the analogy of the "seed" to illustrate the manifold theory:

> From one single seed, entire forests grow up; and they in turn bring forth innumerable seeds, so it happens that innumerable theories can rise from Scripture which only God can grasp in His

10 Anderson, *Call to Piety*, xv.

11 "Bonaventure was involved in at least three identifiable controversies in the late 1260s and early 1270s. The first controversy had to do with the Latin Averroists and centered upon their claims for the legitimacy of an independent philosophy. . . . The second controversy was over the status of the mendicant orders in the universities and over the value of the principle of poverty. The third controversy involved the Franciscan Order internally and externally and was tied to the polemics of the Mendicant and Averroist Controversies" (Anderson, *Call to Piety*, vii).

12 Bonaventure's work "distinguishes six levels of knowledge which are interpreted allegorically in relation to the six days of the creation account. At the same time, the six periods of salvation history are related to the six days of creation" (Ratzinger, *Theology of History in St. Bonaventure*, 6).

13 Ratzinger, *Theology of History in St. Bonaventure*, 7.

> knowledge. As new seeds come from plants, so also new theories and new meaning come from Scripture.[14]

Ratzinger did not find the complete meaning of "theories" in Bonaventure's work. However, Ratzinger interprets: "[Theories] are intimations about future times found in Scripture. Scripture points to the future. . . . The whole of history develops in the broken line of meaning in which, that which is to come may be grasped in the present on the basis of the past."[15] Ratzinger understood theories as prophecies about the future; in other words, the knowledge of the history of salvation enlightens our understanding of the future.

Bonaventure believed in the progress of the understanding of meaning in Scripture as comprising the mysteries of God. For him, "Scripture is closed objectively,"[16] but the seed of understanding grows in every age. What the Fathers of the Church could not have known because of the indefinite future is known to the next generation due to the access they have to history. Future generations, in the same way, will disclose the ideas of the present age, which are unknown now, because the present time turns into history for future generations. In that sense, it can be said we have a more enlightened understanding of Scripture due to historical events. Therefore, because of the progress in understanding the Scripture, new knowledge is obtained. For Bonaventure, theology is the interpretation of Scripture in the Augustinian light of the past, present, and future. Thus, the exegesis of Scripture becomes the theology of history.[17]

Bonaventure observed continuity and progress in the history of salvation. He believed in "inner-worldly and inner-historical messianic hope."[18] He was convinced that through Christ everything that was said in the Old Testament is fulfilled. He cites a prophecy from Isaiah 2:4 to affirm his stance: "Nation shall not lift up sword against nation, neither shall they learn war any more." He did not witness this Scripture passage being fulfilled fully in his lifetime.[19] Hence, Bonaventure believed in inner-historical messianic hope. Nevertheless, Ratzinger foresaw a theological problem in believing in a new salvation history within the limits of the present era:

---

[14] Ratzinger, *Theology of History in St. Bonaventure*, 7.

[15] Ratzinger, *Theology of History in St. Bonaventure*, 8.

[16] Ratzinger, *Theology of History in St. Bonaventure*, 9.

[17] Ratzinger, *Theology of History in St. Bonaventure*, 9.

[18] Ratzinger, *Theology of History in St. Bonaventure*, 13.

[19] Ratzinger, *Theology of History in St. Bonaventure*, 13.

> Bonaventure raises a new, inner-worldly, inner-historical messianic hope. He rejects the view that with Christ the highest degree of inner-historical fulfillment is already realized so that there is nothing left but an eschatological hope for that which lies beyond all history. Bonaventure believes in a new salvation in history, within the limits of this time. This is a very significant shift in the understanding of history, and must be seen as the central historico-theological problem of *Hexaemeron*.[20]

According to Bonaventure, even after the coming of Christ into this world, not everything is perfected. Evil things continue to occur in the world. Ratzinger noted that the "inner-worldly, inner-messianic hope of Bonaventure became clearer in the further reading of *Hexaëmeron*. However, Ratzinger understood Bonaventure's inner-messianic hope in terms of the mission of the Church. The Church carries out Christ's mission until the end of time, fulfilling the prophecies contained in Scripture.[21]

From his reading of the *Hexaëmeron*, Ratzinger sketched the mean of revelation as "the unveiling of the hidden or mystical meaning of the scriptures."[22] Bonaventure analyzed the three directions of the unveiling of the hidden mysteries in particular. The first direction of revelation "unveils the future," the second direction of revelation "unveils the hidden mystical meaning" of Scripture, and the third direction "unveils the imageless divine reality."[23]

Ratzinger detects a tension between the historical and theological understanding of the concept of revelation and the unveiling of the hidden mysteries contained in Scripture. He notes:

> As far as I can see, at no time does Bonaventure refer to the Scriptures themselves as "revelation." He speaks of *revelare* and *revelata* primarily when a particular understanding of Scripture is involved, namely that "manifold divine wisdom" which consists in grasping the three-fold spiritual sense of Scripture, the allegorical, the anagogical and the tropological.[24]

20 Ratzinger, *Theology of History in St. Bonaventure*, 14.
21 Ratzinger, *Theology of History in St. Bonaventure*, 14.
22 Ratzinger, *Theology of History in St. Bonaventure*, 14.
23 Ratzinger, *Theology of History in St. Bonaventure*, 58–59.
24 Ratzinger, *Theology of History in St. Bonaventure*, 62.

One needs the "manifold divine wisdom" in order to understand what God has revealed in Scripture. It involves allegorical, anagogical, and tropological understandings of Scripture.[25] Scripture is purely a book if it is not understood in a dynamic, spiritual sense that grows with the reader. For Bonaventure, "manifold divine wisdom" is considered to be the spiritual understating of Scripture.

Bonaventure used the analogy of Jesus's changing water into wine at Cana (John 2:1–12) to explain how mere words in Scripture are changed into the *words of life*. Scripture is like water that is to be changed into wine through its *in concreto* spiritual understanding. Without the aid of the Holy Spirit, biblical books could be understood merely from a literary point of view. But Scripture is not just a set of documents or books, but rather must become life-giving words through faith: a personal transformation on the part of the addressee that comes about by the work of the Holy Spirit.[26]

In order to understand Scripture spiritually, Bonaventure encouraged his Franciscan brothers to seek the wisdom that comes through divine help. The aim of Christian learning is wisdom, which is obtained solely through Christ-like holiness, not through learning alone. Such divine–human encounter Bonaventure presents as four stages of wisdom in his *Hexaëmeron*: *sapientia uniformis*, *sapientia multiformis*, *sapientia omniformis*, and *sapientia nulliformis*.[27]

Sapientia uniformis is concerned with the knowledge of the laws: the Supreme Soul must be worshipped, Truth must be believed, and the Supreme Good must be loved and accepted. These laws are inscribed in the first tablet of the Ten Commandments, and they guide the human intellect. Knowledge of these laws is connected to philosophy. They enable a person to march toward God, yet God is never fully comprehended with this kind of wisdom. Divine light is not accessible to such wisdom.[28]

The second type of knowledge is *multiformis*, which takes over *sapientia uniformis*. The multiform face of wisdom is manifested in the mysteries of Scripture. It enables a person to unveil Scripture's deeper meaning. Paul considered himself a teacher of such wisdom, which was revealed by the Holy Spirit (Eph 3:8–10): "To me, the very least of all the holy ones, this grace was given, to preach to the Gentiles . . . and bring to light what is the

[25] Ratzinger, *Theology of History in St. Bonaventure*, 63.

[26] Ratzinger, *Theology of History in St. Bonaventure*, 63.

[27] Ratzinger, *Theology of History in St. Bonaventure*, 59–60.

[28] Ratzinger, *Theology of History in St. Bonaventure*, 60.

plan of the mystery hidden from ages past in God who created all things." This kind of wisdom is revealed to the simple and humble people (*simplex et idiota*) and is veiled to the eyes of the impure and learned. It echoes the wisdom of the little ones in the Gospel (Matt 11:25): "I give praise to you, Father, Lord of heaven and earth, for although you have hidden these things from the wise and the learned you have revealed them to the childlike."[29] This concept of spiritual understanding as expressed here is the essence of *sapientia multiformis*.

The third face is *sapientia omniformis*, which discovers the reflection and hand of God in all created things. It recognizes the vestiges of the Holy Trinity in creation. Creation has some traces of the Trinity, and therefore, creation reveals God to some degree. It is said in the Scriptures that "Ever since the creation of the world, his invisible attributes of eternal power and divinity have been able to be understood and perceived in what he has made" (Rom 1: 20). Creation is like a book that needs interpretation in order to be understood. According to Bonaventure, Solomon symbolized this sort of wisdom. The philosophers have the same kind of wisdom, but they remain within the order of creation and do not progress toward God, who is the author of creation. Omniform wisdom remains within the created order but never transcends it. Wisdom should lead created things to the Creator, God himself.[30] Advancement occurs from one level of knowledge to another.

The final stage of wisdom is *sapientia nulliformis*. One who possesses this sort of wisdom approaches the mystery in silence. Ratzinger described that, with formless wisdom, "the mystic approaches in silence to the very threshold of the mystery of the eternal God in the night of the intellect whose light is extinguished at such heights."[31] Bonaventure believed that wisdom of this kind was shared by Paul with Timothy but is not generally accessible. Bonaventure maintained this on the basis of the passage: "the wisdom of the Lord is hidden to the rulers who are passing away" (see 1 Cor 2:6–10). It is obvious in the *Hexaëmeron* that, for Bonaventure, the highest form of wisdom is attainable only through personal holiness and humility. The first three stages of wisdom are not minimized, because they are all part of the process of attaining to the highest wisdom, that of formless wisdom. It bears repeating that the context of these *Collationes* is significant: one must remember that Bonaventure was giving spiritual

[29] Ratzinger, *Theology of History in St. Bonaventure*, 60–61.

[30] Ratzinger, *Theology of History in St. Bonaventure*, 60–61.

[31] Ratzinger, *Theology of History in St. Bonaventure*, 61.

instruction to his confrères after having profoundly experienced the spiritual world of Francis.[32] Hence, one can easily notice the priority Bonaventure places on spirituality and the regular practice of contemplation in the Franciscan Order as indispensable heuristic means to attaining the authentic interpretation of the mysteries of God in Scripture.

The Limitations of Bonaventure as regards Revelation

Ratzinger observed the differences in understanding the concept of revelation between Bonaventure and modern theology: "Bonaventure did not know the question concerning the nature of revelation in the same sense in which it is treated by our current fundamental theology in the tract, *De-revelatione*."[33] Significantly for Ratzinger, "Bonaventure does not treat 'revelation' but 'revelations.'"[34] Bonaventure considered individual revelations in history to be those written in the Scriptures, such as God revealing his name to Moses. But he did not treat the nature of revelation, which is behind all individual revelations. Ratzinger argued that individual revelations can be repeated but the public revelation of Christ, which is behind all other individual revelations, cannot be repeated. In Ratzinger's analysis, Bonaventure failed to note the different processes of revelations that could be repeated time and again by God to the individual. Bonaventure did not reflect much on the unique revelation of God, the revelation in and through Christ. Bonaventure focused more on the human desire for and approach to God instead of God's approach to human beings. In chapter 2, Ratzinger takes another significant step toward the concept of revelation in Christ, going beyond Bonaventure's notion of revelation.[35]

Ratzinger opined that the concepts that are used by Bonaventure in understanding revelation—such as *inspiratio*, *manifestatio*, and *apertio*—are not comparable with the concepts used in modern theology. He argued that the understanding of the concepts of revelation has developed since the time of Bonaventure. Ratzinger highlights the importance of Christ in revelation over and above any other individual revelations in the history of salvation.[36]

---

[32] Ratzinger, *Theology of History in St. Bonaventure*, 62.

[33] Ratzinger, *Theology of History in St. Bonaventure*, 57.

[34] Ratzinger, *Theology of History in St. Bonaventure*, 57.

[35] Ratzinger, *Theology of History in St. Bonaventure*, 57–58.

[36] Ratzinger, *Theology of History in St. Bonaventure*, 57–58.

Revelation and Inspiration

Bonaventure used the concepts *revelatio* and *inspiratio* interchangeably, as both are actuated by the Holy Spirit. For Bonaventure, the three stages of visions inspired by the Holy Spirit follow: first, *visio corporalis*, which is the physical process of sight; second, *visio spiritualis*, which is a vision that enables the person to have inner strength for imagination and understanding; third, *visio intellectualis*, which is a vision that enables one to see the hidden truth with the illumination of the Holy Spirit. In conformity with Bonaventure, Ratzinger affirms that one can speak of revelation only in terms of *visio intellectualis*. This kind of vision was granted only to a few people like Paul and the evangelists. The deeper meaning of the Scriptures is not attained according to individual whims, but according to the writings of the Church Fathers and approved theologians, who passed it on and explained it with great intensity. Some fundamental lines of Scripture are handed on to the faithful, and the faithful in turn make an effort to accept them in faith. Sacred Scripture may remain merely a random collection of books if not understood spiritually with the eyes of faith. One should read Scripture along with the Fathers of the Church in order to deepen one's understanding of Scripture.[37]

Theology plays an important role in the understanding of Scriptures. Scripture in its fullest sense *is* theology. Ratzinger states: "Bonaventure refers to the theologian as the *revelator absconditorum* and to theology as the corresponding *revelatio absconditorum*."[38] Hence, according to Bonaventure, the task of the theologian is to understand the inner meaning of the Scriptures and present it to the faithful.

Ratzinger believes that only through the Church's mediatory role can Scripture ever again be elevated to revelation. An individual cannot claim it either by study or by personal effort. This is where Ratzinger gives importance to the Magisterium of the Church and Tradition in understanding the Scriptures and interpreting them. Such understanding allows the later Lutheran notion of *sola scriptura* no place. Significantly, nowhere does Scripture identify itself as the only (positive) revelation of God's truths. The believer's task is not only to recognize the meaning of the words in Scripture but also to understand them according to the teachings

[37] Ratzinger, *Theology of History in St. Bonaventure*, 64.

[38] Ratzinger, *Theology of History in St. Bonaventure*, 67. See Fourth Lateran Council statements in Heinrich Denzinger, *Enchiridion Symbolorum: Compendium of Creeds, Definitions, and Declarations on Matters of Faith and Morals* [hereafter, DH], ed. Peter Hünermann, 43rd ed., English edition ed. Robert Fastiggi and Anne Englund Nash (San Francisco: Ignatius, 2012), 806.

of the Magisterium of the Church, for which one needs *faith*. Only within circumscribed faith can one receive Christian revelation.

Any sort of communication involves three components: messenger, message, and receiver. In the same way, revelation includes God as messenger, his will as a message, and the faithful as a receiver of the message. It is akin to personal gift. If a gift is not received by someone, it is not called a gift in its complete sense. In the same way, there must be an object as "subject" to receive what is revealed by God. This "subject" is part of revelation; otherwise, revelation does not occur, because "no veil has been removed."[39] Ratzinger stresses the necessity of Tradition to understand Scripture, as truths are passed on through Tradition. In this manner, one receives revelation. Hence, the Church, led by the Holy Spirit, continues to reveal the hidden meaning of Scripture, and every believer—in accordance with Tradition—receives it and assents to it in faith, thereby growing beyond compare and beyond human expectation.

Different Layers of Understanding the Scriptures

The understanding of Scripture as revelation is not clear in Bonaventure's thought. Ratzinger noticed that Bonaventure's answer to the question of what constituted the spiritual understanding of Scripture was "wavering between two poles; one which is academic and scientific and the other which is more prophetic."[40] Bonaventure does not take a stand, but oscillates between the academic and prophetic approaches. The soul's movement towards God in prayerful speculation will lead one to receive revelation. In the *Hexaëmeron*, Ratzinger understood revelation as identification with "speculative-scientific exegesis of scripture."[41] It is neither completely scientific nor completely speculative. Bonaventure preferred to give equal importance to both the scientific and the speculative understanding of Scripture.

Bonaventure affirms that genuine speculation is connected with grace. Ultimately, it is God who reveals himself even in speculation. Bonaventure hoped to see the full explication of the content of revelation in the Franciscan and Dominican orders. He was convinced that revelation could be received in a more comprehensive way through their life and ministry of preaching and theologizing, thus bringing the spiritual understanding of

---

39 Ratzinger, *Milestones*, 108.

40 Ratzinger, *Theology of History in St. Bonaventure*, 69.

41 Ratzinger, *Theology of History in St. Bonaventure*, 69.

Scripture into greater focus. He asserted that Francis anticipated the understanding of the Word of the Lord in a manner that was simpler than the understanding of Augustine and Dionysius.[42] Citing Matthew 11:25—"I praise you, Father, Lord of heaven and of earth, that you have hidden these things from the wise and the clever, but have revealed them to the humble"—Bonaventure, as a member of the Franciscan Order, perceived that his founder understood the mysteries of the Word in a simple way and humbly practiced this in his life.[43] Bonaventure mentioned repeatedly that, in the life of Francis, the Word of the Lord is fulfilled in a concrete way through humility. Bonaventure firmly believed in the indispensable relationship between humility and revelation.[44]

The Mediation of Revelation

According to Bonaventure, revelation engages the entire cosmos along with the faith and humility of the individual.[45] The celestial order—seraphim, archangels, angels—and creation have their mediatory roles to play in the process of revelation. Jointly they play a "factual mediatorial function."[46] Bonaventure agreed with the notion of hierarchy developed by Pseudo-Dionysius the Areopagite (ca. AD 500),[47] as he seems to adopt the notion of celestial hierarchy from him. Moreover, the notion of Dionysius's celestial hierarchy incorporates the significant role of celestial beings in comprehending God's mysteries. Dionysius writes:

> It is most fitting to the mysterious passages of scripture that the sacred and hidden truth about the celestial intelligences be concealed through the inexpressible and the sacred and be inaccessible to the *hoi polloi*. Not everyone is sacred, and, as scripture says, knowledge is not for everyone.[48]

For Dionysius, the intelligent and formless beings have more access to God and his words than human beings do. He believed that celestial

[42] Ratzinger, *Theology of History in St. Bonaventure*, 71.
[43] Ratzinger, *Theology of History in St. Bonaventure*, 71.
[44] Ratzinger, *Theology of History in St. Bonaventure*, 71.
[45] Ratzinger, *Theology of History in St. Bonaventure*, 72.
[46] Ratzinger, *Theology of History in St. Bonaventure*, 72.
[47] *Pseudo-Dionysius: The Complete Works*, trans. Luibheid Colm (New York: Paulist Press, 1987), 149.
[48] *Pseudo-Dionysius: The Complete Works*, 149.

beings had immediate access to God's revelation. Dionysius's theory of hierarchy made a significant impact on the concept of revelation in Bonaventure's thought. Bonaventure adopted his notion of hierarchy to explain the mediation of celestial being in revelation.[49] The creature's knowledge of God relies upon the place that each being has in the hierarchy. Archangels have more knowledge of God than angels, and the angels, in turn, have greater knowledge of God than human beings.

Bonaventure believed in the mediatory involvement of angels in revelation.[50] Although Ratzinger accepts that angels have some involvement in the mediation of revelation, he disagrees with Bonaventure regarding the extent to which they are involved: he proposes that celestial beings have a role *occasionaliter*, since he wants to emphasize revelation as the sovereign action of God:

> The only source of revelation is the divine ray of light. The light which illumines us immediately is the divine light. In the process of revelation, the angels act only *occasionaliter* like a man who opens the window and lets in the light though he himself is neither the source nor the cause of the light. In this way revelation remains, on the one hand, entirely the work of God; on the other hand, it is withdrawn from all individualistic isolation and is placed in the context of the divine activity which embraces the world. In this context, every creature, as a part of the "hierarchy," is engaged in a holy work which takes its origin from God and leads back to God by way of fellow creatures.[51]

Angels are not the cause or source of revelation. It is entirely the work of God the Creator. Creatures, because they receive life from God, participate in a subordinate way in the process of revelation. René Latourelle, S.J., in his magisterial book *Theology of Revelation*, highlights the teachings of the Church as formulated at the First Vatican Council. That council distinguished two types of divine manifestation: first, the natural manifestation of God through creatures; second, the manifestation of God through human reason. Bonaventure's notion of the involvement of all creation in revelation is in line with the teaching of Vatican I, as Latourelle writes:

---

[49] Ratzinger, *Theology of History in St. Bonaventure*, 89.

[50] Ratzinger, *Theology of History in St. Bonaventure*, 74.

[51] Ratzinger, *Theology of History in St. Bonaventure*, 75.

> Our Mother Church the Holy Church believes and teaches that God, beginning and end of all things, can be known with certainty in the natural light of human reason by means of creatures; in fact, what cannot be seen of Him can, since the creation of the world, be contemplated through his works . . . through the objective medium of creation and human reason as a certain revelation or manifestation of God, but a natural way.[52]

From this, we may deduce that the mediatory role of the created order in natural revelation is positive. Nevertheless, Ratzinger gives more importance to God in revealing himself in a free act. In the process of revelation, human beings have *prima facie* a passive role in revelation, as a subject that receives rather than functioning in mediatory roles—but they also need to appropriate it by living accordingly and testifying to it, thereby becoming "subjects" of revelation.

Scripture and Revelation—Bound to Historical Development

Ratzinger attempted to present the historical character of Scripture and revelation in Bonaventure's thought. He noticed an unfailing reliance on progress in the understanding of the Scriptures. The common denominator for Scripture and revelation is continuity and progress.[53] The following paragraphs illustrate progress and continuity in understanding Scripture through history.

The concept of history was viewed in the Middle Ages as "a flow of individual events; that which is common or general."[54] The theologians of the Middle Ages tried to find the common element in all the individual events. Hence, there was no systematic science of history. Ratzinger cites Augustine's quote: "Anything historical should be believed but it cannot be understood."[55] The African Church Father's statement suggests there is no secular grasp over the past. However, in this age of advancement in scientific research, one may not agree with Augustine. The modern age investigates every element of the past. It seeks scientific proofs of the past. Ratzinger argued that in Christianity the "unhistorical mode of thought"[56] is less applicable.

---

52 René Latourelle, S.J., *Theology of Revelation* (Staten Island, NY: Alba House, 1966), 332.

53 Ratzinger, *Theology of History in St. Bonaventure*, 75.

54 Ratzinger, *Theology of History in St. Bonaventure*, 75.

55 Ratzinger, *Theology of History in St. Bonaventure*, 76.

56 Ratzinger, *Theology of History in St. Bonaventure*, 76.

Everything in the Old Testament is historical. Even more, Israel's history was written in the light of faith in Yahweh. Christianity is also a historically evolved religion. The notion of historical progress is presented in the *Hexaëmeron* because of the flow of the individual events and their often hidden relations to one another.[57] Thus, Ratzinger noticed the influence of the Scholastics in the development of the understanding of Scripture and revelation.

Bonaventure emphasized the spiritual interpretation of the Scriptures. Scripture is merely a lifeless book until it is understood spiritually. It is not possible for an individual to understand Scripture spiritually without God's revelation and without looking back at the writings of saints. God inspires some individuals for this task, and chief among them, for Bonaventure, were saints and Church Fathers like Augustine and Jerome, whose writings should be read alongside Scripture to understand it. Thus, for Ratzinger, revelation is "a unique, delimited, and objectified reality which has been given its written fixation in the exegetical works of the Fathers."[58]

Bonaventure preferred Hugh of St. Victor's († 1142) concept of Sacred Scripture. For Hugh, "Scripture and the Fathers flow together into one great *Scriptura Sacra*."[59] Hugh places Scripture and the writings of the Fathers (*traditio*) on the same ground, as they *both* point to revelation. One observes the intimate connection between the Fathers of the Church and the Scriptures. In Ratzinger's words: "They stand on an equal footing with any part of the Sacred Book, which as yet is not understood to be a unified book."[60] The Fathers of the Church promulgated the Tradition through which revelation is understood. Both Scripture and patristic texts point to Christ. Ratzinger developed this thought further as *peritus* during the Second Vatican Council.

In Bonaventure's work, as is typical of the writings of other Scholastic thinkers, there is no unified understanding of the concept of revelation. Ratzinger notes the differences between our understanding of the concept of revelation and the theories of thirteenth-century theologians. Thirteenth-century theologians referred to Scripture as revelation.[61] Medieval theologians saw the problem of the biblical canon when the Scrip-

---

57 Ratzinger, *Theology of History in St. Bonaventure*, 76.

58 Ratzinger, *Theology of History in St. Bonaventure*, 78.

59 Ratzinger, *Theology of History in St. Bonaventure*, 78.

60 Ratzinger, *Theology of History in St. Bonaventure*, 79.

61 Ratzinger, *Milestones*, 109.

tures and the writings of the Fathers were so closely connected as to be regarded on almost equal grounds. Though they revered the Fathers of the Church, they did not add their writings to the Scriptures. Later, this thought would give birth to the concept of "Tradition." In understanding the concept of Tradition, the Fathers are considered "the bearers of a new spiritual 'revelation' without which Scriptures simply would not be effective as revelation."[62]

New insights into scriptural exegesis were occasioned by the life of St. Francis. His impact on the medieval Church was profound. Because Francis sought to practice the teachings of Jesus in a simple and literal way, his radical example even affected the valence of the patristic exegetical tradition. His rule of life was the Sermon on the Mount, and it was evident to all that his sanctity was the result of a deep understanding and practice of the Gospel. The literal meaning of Scripture and the new form of life paved the way for a more deliberate appreciation of the concept of Tradition. Thus, the event of Francis gave rise to a controversy concerning the proper understanding of Scripture and Tradition.[63] Until the appearance of Francis on the stage of history, the writings of the Fathers were considered to be of utmost significance and to be part of Tradition to some degree. With the event of Francis, a new understanding of Tradition came into existence. Tradition consisted not only of the writings of the Fathers, but also included other elements, such as liturgy and sacraments.[64]

Ratzinger draws significant points in relation to the Bible and history: Scripture developed in a historical way. Scripture is not merely the record of past events but also a "prediction of the future." Scripture's fullest meaning is not yet totally accessible because it encompasses the past, present, and future—in true Augustinian fashion. The understanding of the truths contained in Scripture continues to progress in every age and coincides with the dynamism of the process of revelation. Knowledge of the history of salvation is essential to the understanding of Scripture.[65] However, Ratzinger prioritizes revelation over Scripture: "Revelation precedes Scripture and becomes deposited in Scripture but is not simply identical with it. . . . Revelation is something greater than what is merely written down. And this again means that there can be no such thing as pure *sola*

[62] Ratzinger, *Theology of History in St. Bonaventure*, 80.

[63] Ratzinger, *Theology of History in St. Bonaventure*, 82.

[64] Ratzinger, *Theology of History in St. Bonaventure*, 79–80.

[65] Ratzinger, *Theology of History in St. Bonaventure*, 83–84.

scriptura."[66] This insight will have a key influence in the documents of the Second Vatican Council, especially *Dei Verbum*.

Creation and Revelation

After discussing its manners of mediation, one can notice how both creation and the Scriptures become vehicles for revelation. Bonaventure understood creation in the light of *sapientia omniformis*. For him, Scripture and creation are similar in many ways:

> There is a striking parallel between the revelation of Scripture and that of creation. In both cases, the revelation is hidden behind the letters that veil it; in both cases, the unveiling of the revelation is the task of the Spirit who transcends the level of the literal in a living, existential movement which penetrates into the realm of the intellectual-spiritual. In both cases, there is also the danger of becoming imprisoned by the letters.[67]

The similarities between creation and revelation in Scripture are quite striking. One of the significant elements common to revelation and creation is incomprehensibility. Neither revelation nor creation is fully comprehended by the human mind. The more one tries to understand them, the more elusively complex revelation and creation appear.

Ratzinger alludes to Bonaventure's *Itinerarium mentis in Deum*. There, revelation and creation are intimately connected. We come to know the greatness of the Lord through the created realities. Ratzinger quotes Bonaventure: "He who does not allow himself to be illumined by the glory of created things is blind; he who does not awaken to their call is deaf; he who does not praise God for all his works is mute."[68] Created things on this earth reveal their Creator. Creation illumines one to understand God's deeds and Scripture unveils the mysteries of God.

Bonaventure strongly affirmed the hope of a final revelation, the ultimate explication of the mysteries of God, which would occur through a grand, eschatological event. He pointed to the progressive movement of revelation, starting with the biblical patriarchs and continuing until the final days. This is a historical development in understanding revelation:

---

[66] Ratzinger, *Milestones*, 109.

[67] Ratzinger, *Theology of History in St. Bonaventure*, 85.

[68] Ratzinger, *Theology of History in St. Bonaventure*, 86.

"The historical ascent of the Church from the Patriarchs at the beginning to the People of God of the final days is simultaneously a growth of the revelation of God."[69] Revelation is dynamic, living, and progressive in nature. In the final age, revelation becomes clearer to the faithful. Ratzinger states:

> The mysticism . . . granted to the Apostles as to the "perfect" depicts the stage of revelation of the final Church which is to be a Church of the perfect. . . . The final age will involve neither the abolition of the revelation of Christ nor a transcendence of the New Testament. Rather, it involves the entrance into that form of knowledge which the Apostles had; and thus it will be the true fulfillment of the New Testament revelation which has been understood only imperfectly up till now.[70]

The travails in understanding revelation continue until the Second Coming of Christ, when full knowledge of God will be imparted. Only in the final age can one understand revelation fully.

Summary

In summary, for Bonaventure, the spiritual interpretation of Scripture is revelation. He believed that only with divine (including sacramental) assistance could one interpret Scripture in a spiritual sense. The understanding of Scripture is always tied to a progressive movement that continues until the Second Coming of Jesus Christ. Progress in understanding revelation involves the whole cosmos, including angels and created things on earth. Therefore, it is reasonable to conclude that the notion of revelation has been developed *in* the history of the Church inspired *by* the Holy Spirit.

Bonaventure treated individual revelations in his *Hexaëmeron*. However, he failed to treat the public revelation of Christ, the *Logos*, that is behind all the individual revelations. In this *ductus*, Ratzinger prioritizes Christ in understanding revelation. In this way, Ratzinger goes beyond Bonaventure's understanding of revelation. The extensive, critical study of Bonaventure's *Hexaëmeron* helped Ratzinger contribute crucially to the conciliar discussions.[71]

---

[69] Ratzinger, *Theology of History in St. Bonaventure*, 92.

[70] Ratzinger, *Theology of History in St. Bonaventure*, 92–93.

[71] Ratzinger, *Milestones*, 109.

Ratzinger and the Second Vatican Council

Ratzinger's Collaboration with Cardinal Frings

Attending the Council, Cardinal Josef Frings (1887–1978) received *schemata* that were presented to the Council Fathers.[72] He forwarded these texts to Ratzinger for suggestions and critical review. Regarding the draft on divine revelation, Ratzinger found something serious to reject. He believed that the Council Fathers gave more importance to Scholastic theology than to the Bible and the Church Fathers. He states that "they reflected more the thought of scholars than that of shepherds"[73] but admits that the Council Fathers laid a strong foundation for the Council.

Cardinal Frings took Ratzinger with him to Rome, along with two other theological advisors: Hubert Jedin (1900–1980) and Joseph Teusch (1902–1976). Ratzinger's thoughts were readily accepted by Cardinal Frings. Many paid attention to the words of Cardinal Frings, for he memorized his speeches—composed by the young *peritus* Ratzinger—and delivered them in clear Latin.[74] By the end of the first session, Frings worked to have Ratzinger recognized as a permanent *peritus*. Ratzinger was highly esteemed and must be counted among the ten most important *periti* at the Council. He recalled how this opportunity facilitated his acquaintance with many renowned theologians at the Council, such as Henri de Lubac, Jean Daniélou, and Gérard Philips. Ratzinger considered the days spent at the Council as grace-filled moments in his life because he had a chance to speak personally to many theologians from every continent.[75] The intellectual collaboration between Cardinal Frings and Ratzinger before and during the Council was significant for the final shape texts would take.[76]

The Turbulent Debate on Revelation

The Second Vatican Council's general congregation met on November 14, 1962, in St. Peter's Basilica. The first schema was *De fontibus revelationis*.[77]

---

[72] Ratzinger speaks extensively of his experience in *Milestones*, 120–31. See also Joseph Ratzinger, *Theological Highlights of Vatican II*, trans. The Missionary Society of St. Paul the Apostle in the State of New York (New York: Paulist Press, 1966).

[73] Ratzinger, *Milestones*, 120–21.

[74] Emery de Gaál, "The Theologian Joseph Ratzinger at Vatican II," *Lateranum* 78, no. 3 (2012): 515–48, at 517.

[75] Ratzinger, *Milestones*, 121.

[76] De Gaál, "Joseph Ratzinger at Vatican II," 518.

[77] De Gaál, "Joseph Ratzinger at Vatican II," 524.

There was an immediate objection to this draft from many of the Council Fathers. Sixty-two percent of the bishops deemed the preparatory schema unsuitable to develop a constitution on revelation. They felt it reflected too much a neo-Scholastic approach and dealt too defensively with past controversies.[78]

The schema displayed an imbalance between Tradition and Scripture. It reflected a naïve historical view of the Gospels and the way Tradition works in history. Frings expressed strong opposition to the schema and presented his views as prepared by Ratzinger in September of 1962. The underlying issue was a tension between different schools of theology that was sometimes misinterpreted as a struggle between a modernist and antimodernist stance. The preparatory schema, the work of the Vatican curia, was perceived as being antimodernist:

> Should one continue the antimodernist attitude, the politics of closure, of condemnation, of defensiveness, until one ends in complete fearful refusal, or shall the church, once the necessary distinctions are made, turn to a new page, and step into a new, positive encounter with her sources, with her brothers, with the world of today?[79]

For Ratzinger, Vatican II was convoked, among other reasons, to deepen the Catholic understanding of revelation as already expressed by the Councils of Trent and Vatican I and to propose its nature as more dynamic than heretofore appreciated. For him, revelation cannot be reduced only to the means of its transmission, or minimized to human or written words. Christ, the *Logos*, is the complete revelation. Ratzinger preferred to highlight this Christocentric nature of revelation. Hence, he called for a dynamic understanding of revelation. Ratzinger's study of Bonaventure's *Hexaëmeron* clarified many things in this debate. Scripture in relation to revelation points to Christ, the fullness of revelation. The first schema presented by Rome overemphasized the process of the transmission of revelation and deemphasized revelation itself, who is Christ the *Logos*. Ratzinger proposed that Scripture and Tradition should be identified as the *fontes cognoscendi*, as God cannot be reduced to human words.[80]

---

[78] De Gaál, "Joseph Ratzinger at Vatican II," 524.

[79] Lieven Boeve, "Revelation, Scripture, and Tradition: Lessons from Vatican II's Constitution *Dei Verbum* for Contemporary Theology," *International Journal of Systematic Theology* 13 (October 2011): 419.

[80] De Gaál, "Joseph Ratzinger at Vatican II," 525.

Cardinal Frings presented this revised schema prepared by Ratzinger in the presence of many bishops and theologians. After further revision, the revised schema was accepted as the final, official view.[81]

Ratzinger recalled in his book *Milestones* that Josef Rupert Geiselmann's (1890–1970) unbalanced position helped him in refining the schema. Ratzinger pointed out that, according to Geiselmann, the Council of Trent stated that revelation was contained "*partially* in Scripture and *partially* in Tradition." Later the authoritative statement took out "partim . . . partim" and stated revelation is contained in "Scripture *and* Tradition." Both Scripture and Tradition speak of revelation. Based on the above analysis, Geiselmann came to conclude that:

> Trent had wanted to teach that there can be no distribution of the contents of faith into Scripture, on the one hand, and Tradition, on the other, but rather that both Scripture and Tradition, each on its own, contain the whole of revelation, hence that each is complete in itself.[82]

Ratzinger pointed out the error in the theory of Scripture by Geiselmann, who understood Scripture as a "self-sufficient" source for revelation.[83] Ratzinger posed the fundamental question: how can revelation in its comprehensive sense be contained in human words?[84]

As the debate continued to understand the relationship between Scripture and revelation, it discussed the "material completeness" of the Bible in matters of faith. Ratzinger wrote:

> This catchword (material completeness), which was immediately on everybody's lips and was regarded as a great new realization, just as quickly became detached from its point of departure in the interpretation of the Tridentine decree. It was now asserted that the inevitable consequence of this realization was that the Church could not teach anything that was not expressly contained in Scripture, since scripture was complete in matters of faith.[85]

---

81 Ratzinger, *Milestones*, 128–29.

82 Ratzinger, *Milestones*, 125.

83 De Gaál, "Joseph Ratzinger at Vatican II," 526.

84 Ratzinger, *Milestones*, 126.

85 Ratzinger, *Milestones*, 125.

Ergo, the issue of the "material content of the Scripture and Tradition remains an open problem."[86] The Second Vatican Council's concern was to stress the organic unity of Scripture and Tradition and to reiterate the teaching of the Council of Trent, which sought the unity of Scripture and Tradition.[87] Scripture is not so self-evident as to answer all the questions that arise from faith. For this reason, the Council saw the importance of Tradition. Hence, Ratzinger believed that scholars who approach Scripture solely on the basis of the historical-critical method will have no common agreement on the findings of history. Faith has to play a significant role in the areas of uncertain historical hypotheses. However, the question of *how* revelation can be contained in human words and written words was a pressing concern in the mind of Ratzinger.[88]

He noted that the sources of revelation, according to post-Tridentine Scholasticism, are Scripture and Tradition, which would be related to the Magisterium. More recently, the historical-critical method of scriptural interpretation had influenced Catholic theology. "By its very nature," Ratzinger writes, "this historical-critical method has no patience with any restrictions imposed by an authoritative Magisterium; it can recognize no authority but that of the historical argument."[89] Sometimes the historical-critical method goes beyond the scope established by the Magisterium. This method does not easily accept the oral Tradition, which continues parallel to Scripture and, in fact, gave rise to it. Instead, it comes forward to present another, corrective "historical knowledge" besides the Bible, a theory that undervalues the concept of Tradition. There is a constant battle between the findings of the historical-critical method of interpretation and Tradition.[90]

After learning of the opposition and different views on the second schema, Pope John XXIII perceived the need to review the text in light of ecumenism and other pastoral concerns. The schema on *Divine Revelation*

---

[86] René Latourelle, S.J., *Theology of Revelation* (Staten Island, NY: Alba House, 1966), 454.

[87] Trent's Decree on the Reception of the Sacred Books and Tradition teaches that "this truth and rule are contained in the written books and unwritten traditions that have come down to us, having been received by the apostles by the dictation of the holy Spirit, and have been transmitted, as it were, from hand to hand" (DH 1501). It is very clear from the above statement that the Church held and believed in the unity of Scripture and Tradition.

[88] Ratzinger, *Milestones*, 124–25.

[89] Ratzinger, *Milestones*, 124.

[90] Ratzinger, *Milestones*, 124.

was revised by a special commission. Karl Rahner and Ratzinger worked together in this commission to prepare the revised schema of the Dogmatic Constitution on Divine Revelation. Ratzinger admitted that the revised proposal was more Rahner's work than his own. This proposal again faced reaction from the Fathers of the Council. Ratzinger noted that, though Rahner and he agreed in certain matters, their approaches differed because of their respective theological backgrounds.[91] Rahner's schema was not accepted outright. *The Constitution on Divine Revelation* was completed only after further, complex debates. The crux of Ratzinger's thoughts on revelation was as follows:

> Revelation, which is to say, God's approach to man, is always greater than what can be contained in human words, greater even than the words of Scripture. . . . Scripture is the essential witness of revelation, but revelation is something alive, something greater and more: proper to it is the fact that it *arrives* and is *perceived*—otherwise it could not have become revelation. . . . Revelation has instruments; but it is not separable from the living God, and it always requires a living person to whom it is communicated. Its goal is always to gather and unite men, and this is why the Church is a necessary aspect of revelation. . . . The historical-critical method cannot be the last word concerning revelation; rather, the living organism of the faith of all ages is then an intrinsic part of revelation. . . . Tradition is precisely that part of revelation that goes above and beyond Scripture and cannot be comprehended within a code of formulas.[92]

Ratzinger gives great importance to the concept of revelation as fulfilled in Christ, the *Logos*, over Scripture and Tradition as revelation. Scripture and Tradition mediate revelation. Though Scripture and Tradition mediate and express revelation, they are written and passed on in hu-

---

[91] Ratzinger explains how Rahner differed from his thought: "As we worked together, it became obvious to me that, despite our agreement in many desires and conclusions, Rahner and I lived on two different theological planets. . . . His theology was totally conditioned by the tradition of Suarezian scholasticism. . . . His was a speculative and philosophical theology in which Scripture and the Fathers in the end did not play an important role and in which the historical dimension was really of little significance. For my part, my whole intellectual formation had been shaped by Scripture and the Fathers and profoundly historical thinking" (Ratzinger, *Milestones*, 128–29).

[92] Ratzinger, *Milestones*, 127.

man words. For this reason, Ratzinger gives greater importance to revelation than to Scripture and Tradition. One should understand Ratzinger's point with utmost delicacy. He does not downplay Scripture or Tradition, but he is focused more on revelation as fulfilled in Christ. Thus, Ratzinger's Christocentric method is operative in the preceding arguments.

In the second session, the special commission presented its revised version of the text after a couple of amendments on March 7, 1964. The same commission divided the original first chapter into two: *Revelation Itself* (chapter I) and *Handing on Divine Revelation* (chapter II). After serious scrutiny and examination by the commission from June 1–6 of 1964, the first chapter was accepted without much difficulty. However, the second chapter failed to balance Tradition and Scripture. The Council Fathers noticed that the second chapter gave greater importance to Tradition in terms of containing truth than to Scripture. They expected to grant equal importance to Scripture and Tradition. Hence, the commission amended the second chapter according to the advice of the Fathers.[93]

The revised schema was discussed during the third session of the council from September 30 to October 6 of 1964. In this session, the commission maintained a delicate balance between Scripture and Tradition, and this was accepted by the members of the Council. Considering everything, the text was acceptable to the Council Fathers on account of its Christocentric approach to Scripture. After discussing the disputed questions particularly in chapters I and II, the commission submitted the most recent draft to the Council Fathers on the last day of the third session. Ratzinger was the main contributing *peritus* in the final formulation of *Dei Verbum* in 1964, when sections 21–26 were added, which are now to be found in chapter IV.[94]

In the beginning, the title for this document, as it was previously noted, was *De fontibus revelationis*, but after many discussions, Ratzinger suggested two titles for this document on revelation: either *De revelatione* or *De Verbo Dei*. At the end it was decided to name it *Dei Verbum*, which is very close to his second proposal.[95] This indicates Ratzinger's remarkable contribution to the Dogmatic Constitution on Divine Revelation. Blessed Pope Paul VI solemnly promulgated *Dei Verbum* on November 18, 1965.

---

93 Latourelle, *Theology of Revelation*, 454.

94 Latourelle, *Theology of Revelation*, 454.

95 De Gaál, "Joseph Ratzinger at Vatican II," 526.

Revelation and Scripture

The difference between the sacred books of other religions, such as the Bhagavad Gita or the Koran, and the Holy Bible is that the former works are considered "timeless dictations" but the Bible is "God's historical dialogue."[96] Scripture witnesses to the revelation, but it does not contain the whole of revelation. The wholeness of revelation is found in Christ, the *Logos*. One cannot limit revelation to Scripture. God, in his ineffable love for humanity, continues to reveal himself in different ways. Ratzinger noted, "The biblical word bears witness to the revelation but does not contain it in such a way that the revelation is completely absorbed in it and could now be put in your pocket like an object."[97] Scripture points to the knowledge of revelation. It cannot contain the entire revelation of God. Scripture is one of the significant mediums of revelation. Revelation is eminently dynamic in nature.

The words in the Scripture contain a surplus of meaning that goes beyond a mere historical setting. Scripture is "more than a text pieced together from what the individual authors may have intended to say, each in his own historical setting."[98] This stems from the fact that Scripture witnesses to the Word of God, to which Tradition also bears witness.

The understanding of revelation, Tradition, and Scripture is determined by the twofold shape of the Old and New Testaments. Only in light of the Christ event is the Old Testament understood in its integrity. The New Testament sets the "Christ-event":

> The formula that "Jesus" is the "Christ" signifies quite simply that the Christ-message of the Old Testament has come to fulfillment in the historical Jesus; that you can understand who Jesus is on the basis of the Old Testament and see what the Old Testament means in light of the Christ-event.[99]

The Old Testament is read in light of the Christ event, and the New Testament should be read within the framework of the prophecies of the Old Testament, which foresaw the coming of the Messiah.

According to Ratzinger, the Christ-event is reflected in the letters of Paul. He contrasts the Old and New Covenants as *gramma* and *pneu-*

---

[96] De Gaál, "Joseph Ratzinger at Vatican II," 528.

[97] Joseph Ratzinger, *God's Word: Scripture—Tradition—Office*, trans. Hendry Taylor, ed. Peter Hünermann and Thomas Söding (San Francisco: Ignatius Press, 2008), 122–23.

[98] Ratzinger, *God's Word*, 123.

[99] Ratzinger, *God's Word*, 54.

ma—word and Spirit. Paul reasserts the prophecy of Jeremiah 31:33–34: Scripture is no longer needed because the law is written in the heart; no one needs teaching from the outside anymore because God himself teaches men. The coming of Christ is seen as an answer to the hope of the Old Testament. Accordingly, Ratzinger argues: "In the New Testament conception, the Old Testament appears as 'Scripture' in the proper sense, which has attained its true significance through the Christ-event by being drawn into the living sphere of the reality of Christ."[100] Christ is the gravitational center of both the Old and New Testaments.

Scripture is surpassed by revelation in two ways: *from above*, by the words and deeds of God expressed in Jesus Christ, and *from below*, by what revelation makes present itself in the faith of the Church beyond the borders of Scripture. One can read Scripture without receiving it into one's heart. However, such a person cannot be acquainted with the dynamics of revelation.[101] Thus, without faith, Scripture means nothing to the person who reads it. Revelation, which is *from above*, reaches all in mysterious ways by words and deeds. Scripture touches only people who read and believe it. On the other hand, revelation also affects non-Christians. Revelation, which is present both in the Church and in the world, goes beyond the borders of mere text to renew and transform both.

The Problématique of the Concept of Tradition

Western Christendom split apart in its understanding of the concept of Tradition during the Reformation period. The dispute between the Reformers and Catholics centered on the meaning and significance of "Tradition." Catholics described Tradition as the transmission of revelation at the side of Scripture.[102] However, in the Middle Ages, Tradition was viewed as customs, worship, fasting, rituals, and unity in following Christ in the universal Church. This deficient understanding of Tradition negatively colored the term because of the abuses committed in the name of Tradition.

As a reformer, Luther saw these practices leading away from Scripture and, thus, deceiving people. The reformer from Wittenberg, who appreciated the simplicity of the Gospel, found the manifold religious customs useless and harmful. He saw human regulations occupying a place above

[100] Ratzinger, *God's Word*, 55.

[101] Boeve, "Revelation, Scripture, and Tradition," 422.

[102] Ratzinger, *God's Word*, 41.

God's Word. Ratzinger states some of the significant points in this regard from the *Confessio Augustana* (1530):

> Where did the bishops get the right and power to impose such requirements on Christendom to ensnare men's consciences? . . . If, then, bishops have the power to burden the churches with countless requirements and thus ensnare consciences, why does the divine Scripture so frequently forbid the making and keeping of human regulation?[103]

The Reformers misunderstood the concept of Tradition as an abuse of positive ecclesiastical rules and regulations. According to the Reformers, one does not merit anything by one's efforts in conforming to these. Only by faith does one receive grace; one does not merit it by the laws that were instituted by human beings.

When Luther discovered the concept of justification by faith alone, without taking Tradition into account, he felt God's Word was freed from the clutches of Church authorities. Luther thought that human regulations were placed above God's Word and that the Church gave importance to the law that was abolished by the New Testament. Here, Tradition is understood as a merely human regulation in opposition to the Gospel. According to the Reformers, one obtains grace from God *sola fide*, not by one's merits or by following the precepts of the Church.[104]

Ratzinger summarized the dispute between Protestants and Catholics as follows: the Catholic understanding of Church includes three important elements: *fides* (corresponding to the *pure decree)*, *communio* (corresponding to the *sacramenta*), and *auctoritas* (corresponding to the clerical orders).[105] The Church is the criterion of the Word, rather than the Word being the criterion of the Church: the Word cannot stand independently as a separate entity without the Church. These standards were the main differences between Protestants and Catholics.

The Council of Trent (1545–1563) held that the Word cannot be a separate entity, so to speak, "floating above" the Church. The Word is passed on through the Church and remains as it is beyond the reach of human authority. But the Protestant question remains the same: "Does the Word of God remain in the control of the Magisterium?" Ratzinger argues

[103] Ratzinger, *God's Word*, 43.
[104] Ratzinger, *God's Word*, 43.
[105] Ratzinger, *God's Word*, 44.

that the Lord, who established the Church as his Body, could also preserve his Word. He believes that the Church is at the service of the Word.[106]

In order to find the way back, Geiselmann, who taught dogmatic theology at Tübingen, proposed a new thesis. Geiselmann attempted to interpret the Council of Trent in a novel way regarding the nature of the Church and the sufficiency of the Scriptures. Trent taught that the Gospel was contained "*in libris scriptis et sine scripto traditionibus.*"[107] Ratzinger argued that Scripture does not contain the whole *veritas evangelii*; therefore, there was no place for the principle of *sola scriptura*, since part of the truth was also passed on by Tradition.

Geiselmann misinterpreted the position of Trent and claimed that truth was contained "partim in libris scriptis partim in sine scripto traditionibus": truth is contained partly in Scripture and partly in Tradition.[108] This articulates two sources of truth, Scripture and Tradition. The Council of Trent renounced the use of *partim* and added *et* between Scripture and Tradition. In the end, Trent proposed that "Scripture and Tradition contain truth." Geiselmann concluded that the Council Fathers of Trent turned away from the division of truth into separate sources. According to Geiselmann, even the Catholic theologian may argue for the "material sufficiency of Scripture and can also, as a Catholic, hold the opinion that Holy Scripture transmits revelation to us sufficiently."[109] But for Ratzinger, this statement dilutes the true meaning of revelation.

Ratzinger, seeing the historical problem within this thesis proposed by Geiselmann, questioned the meaning of the self-sufficiency of Scripture. He observed that this would not adhere to Catholic dogma and was a self-illusion. For him, the dogmas of Mary's Immaculate Conception (1854) and the Assumption of Mary (1950) would be deceptive and could not be sustained if one were to subscribe to Geiselmann's conclusions. Ratzinger believed that this long-standing problem between Protestants and Catholics concerning Scripture could be resolved when we embark on the question of a correlation between revelation and Tradition.[110]

According to Ratzinger, revelation cannot be reduced to Scripture alone. Revelation is the divine act and speech communicated to human

---

106 Ratzinger, *God's Word*, 45.

107 Norman P. Tanner, S.J., *Decree of the Ecumenical Councils*, vol. 2, *Trent to Vatican II* (London: Sheed & Ward, 1990), 663.

108 Ratzinger, *God's Word*, 48.

109 Ratzinger, *God's Word*, 48.

110 Emery de Gaál, *The Theology of Pope Benedict XVI* (New York: Palgrave Macmillan, 2010), 102.

beings about God and his will. Ratzinger notes that one needs to reach beyond the positive sources of Scripture and Tradition and into their inner source:

> Revelation is the living Word of God, from which scripture and tradition both spring and without which neither can be grasped in the importance they have for faith. The question of scripture and tradition remains insoluble so long as it is not expanded to a question of revelation and tradition.[111]

Revelation, who is Christ the incarnate *Logos*, is the one spring from which both Scripture and Tradition issue forth. This is the Christocentric shift that Ratzinger so eloquently advocates and argues from. One can notice that Ratzinger adopted the Christocentric approach from Bonaventure. In his theology of revelation, Ratzinger emphasized revelation rather than merely focusing on Scripture and Tradition. One can sum up that Christ, who lives in eternity, is higher than the sum of Scripture and Tradition.

The Irreducible Nexus between Revelation and Tradition

Ratzinger works out fundamental theses regarding the relation between revelation and Tradition and interprets the concept of Tradition along with the documents of Trent. In his concluding remarks, he states:

> We are faced with a concept according to which revelation does indeed have its "once-for-all" character, insofar as it took place in historical facts, but also has its constant "today," insofar as what once happened remains forever living and effective in the faith of the Church, and Christian faith never refers merely to what is past; rather, it refers equally to what is present and what is to come.[112]

For Ratzinger, revelation is not an end product, but rather an ongoing process to understand the self-disclosure of God. Tradition, like Scripture, is recorded, and both point to the revealer, who is Christ. Tradition comprises:

---

[111] Ratzinger, *God's Word*, 50.

[112] Ratzinger, *God's Word*, 86–87.

1. The inscription of revelation (the Gospel) not only in the Bible, but in hearts;
2. The speaking of the Holy Spirit throughout the whole age of the Church;
3. The conciliar activity of the Church; and
4. The liturgical tradition and the whole of the Tradition of the Church's life.[113]

Jesus promised his disciples that the Holy Spirit would guide them to the truth: "When the Spirit of truth comes, he will guide you into all the truth; for he will not speak on his own authority, but whatever he hears he will speak, and he will declare to you the things that are to come" (John 16:13). The Church, the Body of Christ led by the Holy Spirit, continues to understand the revelation who is Christ. Understanding revelation as guided by the Holy Spirit is the "Tradition" of the Church. Tradition can be regarded as a "living reality that encompasses both the learning process and the learning outcome of the whole church,"[114] fueled by its listening and worship. Hence, Tradition is not merely a matter of the Magisterium, but of the entire Church.

Christ—the Fullness of Revelation

The reality of Christ, who is revelation, has a dual presence, both in faith and in the Church. Both proclaim and interpret Our Lord. As proclamation of the Gospel by its very nature is interpretation, Tradition by its nature is an interpretation of Scripture:

a. It is the interpretation of the Old Testament on the basis of the Christ-event.
b. It is the interpretation of the Christ-event itself on the basis of *pneuma*, and that means, at the same time, on the basis of the present ecclesiastical situation. Christ is not dead, but living; he is not merely the Christ of yesterday, but just as much the Christ of today and of tomorrow. It is precisely in his Church, however, that he is living and present.
c. There is an Old Testament theology of the Old Testament in which the historian ascertains, already developed even there,

[113] Ratzinger, *God's Word*, 87.

[114] Boeve, "Revelation, Scripture, and Tradition," 423.

a number of overlapping layers in which old texts are reread and reinterpreted in the light of new events.

d. There is a New Testament theology of the Old Testament, which does not coincide with the Old Testament's own inner theology, though it is certainly linked to it in the unity of the *analogia fidei*.
e. There is a New Testament theology of the New Testament that corresponds to the Old Testament theology of the Old Testament, as it is the theology that the historian can derive from the New Testament.
f. There is an ecclesial theology of the New Testament that we call dogmatics. It relates to the New Testament theology of the New Testament in the same way that the New Testament theology of the Old Testament relates to the Old Testament theology of the Old Testament.[115]

The Old Testament should be read in the light of the New Testament. The essential nature of revelation is to reveal the triune God and his will. Hence God encounters humanity personally by taking human form. The object of revelation is the "union of man with God in a life of communion."[116]

The reality of revelation is Christ himself: "He who has seen me has seen the Father" (John 14:9). Receiving revelation means entering into relationship with Christ, who is the full revelation of God. The presence of Christ is the presence of revelation. As attested by the Scriptures, Christ's presence can be understood in two ways:: first, as it appears, as identical with faith (Eph 3:17), in which an individual meets Christ personally and in him enters Christ's saving power; second, in Pauline terms as the *Body of Christ*, which is the community of believers, the Church, through which he calls us to share his mighty presence.[117] Believing means entering into a relationship with Christ, to which Scripture bears witness.

Revelation is an act of God, and the Church, instituted by Jesus Christ as an agent, receives the mysteries of our faith. Ratzinger puts it thus:

> The reception of revelation, in which the Christ-reality becomes ours, is called in biblical language "faith." . . . For the New Testa-

[115] Ratzinger, *God's Word*, 59–61.

[116] Roger Schutz and Max Thurian, *Revelation: A Protestant View* (New York: Newman Press, 1968), 13.

[117] Ratzinger, *God's Word*, 57.

> ment, faith is equivalent to the indwelling of Christ. If we firmly hold that for scripture the presence of revelation is equivalent to the presence of Christ, a further step follows. We find the presence of Christ designated in two further ways. It appears, on the one hand, identical with the faith (Eph 3:17), in which the individual encounters Christ and in him enters the sphere of influence of his saving power. But it is also hidden under the Pauline term of "Body of Christ" which implies that the community of the faithful, the Church, represents Christ's continued abiding in this world in order to gather men into, and make them share, his mighty presence.[118]

Ratzinger observes that in the reception of revelation, the reality of the Christ-event becomes our own through faith. If we accept him, we accept his revelation. As the faithful are parts of the Mystical Body of Christ, Christ lives among them, continuously revealing God the Father through the continuous guidance of the Holy Spirit.

The Dogmatic Constitution on Divine Revelation, *Dei Verbum*, is one of the most important documents of Vatican II. It should be read in light of previous pronouncements and teachings of the Church. The Council of Trent tried to clarify the questions raised by the Protestant Reformation. In its fourth session, in April of 1546, the Council defined its attitude vis-à-vis the apostolic Tradition and the Holy Scriptures:

> In Spiritu Sancto legitime congregata, . . . hoc sibi perpetuo ante oculos proponens, ut sublatis erroribus puritas ipsa Evangelii in Ecclesia conservetur, quod promissum ante per Prophetas in Scripturis sanctis Dominus noster Iesus Christus Dei Filius proprio ore primum promulgavit, deinde per suos Apostolos tamquam fontem omnis et salutaris veritatis et morum disciplinae omni creaturae praedicari iussit (cf. Mark 16:15); perspiciensque, hanc veritatem et disciplinam contineri in libris scriptis et sine scripto traditionibus, quae ab ipsius Christi ore ab Apostolis acceptae, aut ab ipsis Apostolis Spiritu Sancto dictante quasi per manus traditae ad nos usque pervenerunt.[119]

---

[118] Karl Rahner and Joseph Ratzinger, *Revelation and Tradition* (New York: Herder and Herder, 1966), 40–41.

[119] The English translation from DH reads: "As the source of all saving truth and norms of conduct, the Council clearly perceives that this truth and rule are contained in the written books and unwritten traditions that have come down to us, having been received by

On April 24, 1870, at the end of the third session, Vatican I promulgated the constitution *Dei Filius*, which directly dealt with revelation and faith. The second chapter of the constitution explains revelation. First, it repeats the statements of the Council of Trent:

> Haec porro supernaturalis revelatio, secundum universalis Ecclesiae fidem a sancta Tridentina Synodo declaratam continetur in libris scriptis et sine scripto traditionibus, quae ipsius Christi ore ab Apostolis acceptae, aut ab ipsis Apostolis Spiritu Sancto dictante quasi per manus traditae, ad nos usque pervenerunt.[120]

Both Trent and Vatican I were faithful to Tradition, which is one of the tools used to transmit revelation. Modern research reveals that the Council of Trent did not intend to divide revelation into two distinct, partial, and independent sources, Scripture and Tradition, but tried to express the unity of both with their common source, the Gospel.[121] Vatican II goes beyond these two councils to address various teachings of the Church. It did not limit itself to a dialogue with all Christians, but expressed the authentic doctrine on divine revelation and how it is passed on to us, which gave depth and clarity to various questions.[122]

The three significant aims of the Constitution on Divine Revelation were to clarify the relationship between Tradition and the supposed self-sufficiency of Scripture, to formulate the concept of inspiration, and to respond to the pre-conciliar biblical movement. The three aims were addressed with delicacy at the Second Vatican Council. While keeping the teaching of Trent, Vatican II turned toward Christ and developed a Christocentric understanding of revelation. The Council did not restrict itself to Trent and Vatican I, but engaged in a critical hermeneutic of the teachings of these Councils in light of new theological and ecumenical

---

the apostles from the mouth of Christ himself or from the apostles by the dictation of the Holy Spirit, and have been transmitted, as it were, from hand to hand" (1501).

[120] The English translation from DH reads: "This supernatural revelation, according to the universal belief of the Church, declared by the sacred Council of Trent, is contained in the written books and unwritten traditions that have come down to us, having been received by the apostles from the mouth of Christ himself or from the apostles themselves by the dictation of the Holy Spirit, and have been transmitted as it were from hand to hand" (DH 3006).

[121] George H. Tavard, *Dogmatic Constitution on Divine Revelation of Vatican Council II* (Glen Rock, NJ: Paulist Press, 1966), 10.

[122] Schutz and Thurian, *Revelation: A Protestant View*, 12.

developments. The Council intended to avoid language that was static and notional, and instead adopted a language of dynamisms. In *Dei Verbum*, revelation is considered as the "living Word." The Council stresses faithful listening to the Word and proclamation with assurance. The text points at the evangelical themes of "word," "life," and "communion."[123]

The Fruitful Tension between Natural and Supernatural Revelation

The Council notes two forms of revelation: natural and supernatural. Natural revelation is from the created things in the world. Because they are created by God, they reveal their Creator. Paul writes: "For what can be known about God is plain to them, because God has shown it to them" (Rom 1:19). The universe points to the Creator; God is the fullness of being.[124]

Supernatural revelation is different from the natural one. The gratuitous action of God makes it different. Revelation in this form opens up for a communion, a sharing of goods between God and creation. Natural revelation speaks about the numinous, but supernatural revelation is God himself. God does not enter into a direct, personal dialogue with human beings in natural revelation. Only in supernatural revelation does a human being encounter God.

In supernatural revelation, God intervenes personally at a given point in time and space. He enters into a *dialogue* of friendship with man, making known to him the mystery of his innermost life and plans for salvation. God invites humankind to a personal communion of life. Through faith, man is directly called by God, and he freely responds to the personal call of God and enters into a covenant with him.[125]

The first chapter of *Dei Verbum* concerns "Revelation itself." In the second article it states:

> Placuit Deo in sua bonitate et sapientia Seipsum revelare et notum facere sacramentum voluntatis suae (cf. Eph 1:9), quo homines per Christum, Verbum carnem factum, in Spiritu Sancto accessum habent ad Patrem et divinae naturae consortes efficiuntur (cf. Eph 2:18; 2 Pt 1:4). Hac itaque revelatione Deus invisibilis

[123] Schutz and Thurian, *Revelation: A Protestant View*, 11.

[124] Latourelle, *Theology of Revelation*, 337.

[125] Latourelle, *Theology of Revelation*, 339.

> (cf. Col 1:15; 1 Tim 1:17) ex abundantia caritatis suae homines tamquam amicos alloquitur (cf. Exod 33:11; John 15:14) et cum eis conversatur (cf. Bar 3:38), ut eos ad societatem Secum invitet in eamque suscipiat.[126]

This article explains that the purpose of revelation by Christ is to make known to humanity the will of God. God communicates his will to humanity so that the whole human race may take part in his divine life. In his high priestly prayer in John's Gospel, Christ prays to the Father, saying:

> I revealed your name to those whom you gave me out of the world. They belong to you, and you gave them to me, and they kept your word. I pray not only for them, but also for those who will believe in me through their word, so that they may all be one, as you, Father, are in me and I in you, that they also be in us, that the world may believe that you sent me. (John 17:6, 20; author's translation)

The purpose of God's revelation to humanity is for humanity to share in his divinity. Revelation is not primarily a content, information (*revelata*), but is itself the salvific event of God's self-revelation as Charity in Jesus Christ and the Spirit.[127] Revelation is the encounter in person between God and humanity within a concrete history, which is part of salvation history and culminates in the Incarnation of the *Logos* in Jesus Christ. The Apostles and their successors handed on the revelation of Christ within the Church. Through Scripture and Tradition, the Church constantly deepens its understanding of revelation until the Second Coming of Christ.

Jesus Christ is the fullness of revelation—thus, Ratzinger states the primacy of Christ in revelation as the mediator and content of revelation. Through him, one comes to full and complete knowledge of God—to the degree granted by him. *Dei Verbum* affirms that Jesus Christ is *the* mediator and fullness of revelation: "The plan of revelation is realized by deeds and words. . . . By this revelation, then the deepest truth about God and the salvation of man shines out for our sake in Christ who is both mediator

[126] *Dei Verbum* 2. The English translation from DH reads: "In his goodness and wisdom, God chose to reveal himself and to make known to us the hidden proposal of His Will by which through Christ, the Word made flesh, man might in the Holy Spirit have access to the Father and come to share in the Divine nature" (4202).

[127] Boeve, "Revelation, Scripture, and Tradition," 421.

and the fullness of all revelation" (DV 2). To see Jesus is to see his Father (John 14:9). Jesus perfected revelation:

> Through His words and deeds, His signs and wonders, but especially through His death and glorious resurrection from the dead and final sending of the Spirit of Truth . . . we now await no further new public revelation before the glorious manifestation of our Lord Jesus Christ. (DV 4)

This explains the primacy of Christ in revelation. "In times past, God spoke in partial and various ways to our ancestors through the prophets; in these last days, he spoke to us through a son, whom he made heir of all things and through whom he created the universe" (Heb 1:1; author's translation). The faithful came to know God as Trinity through Jesus Christ. He spoke to humankind personally. Jesus is *the* mediator between God and humanity and the fullness of revelation. Through the Church, one continues to understand revelation. The centrality and finality of Christ is made clear in a letter of Paul:

> [Christ] is the image of the invisible god, the first born of all creation, for in Him were created all things in heaven and on earth. . . . He is before all things, and in Him all things hold together. He is the head of the body, the church. He is the beginning, the firstborn from the dead, that in all things He himself might be preeminent. (Col 1: 15–18; author's translation)

This Christological hymn proclaims Christ as preeminent in all things. This preeminence manifests the nature and scope of revelation. Christ is *the* mediator between God and human beings who takes primacy over all prophets, kings, and judges of the Old Testament, who pointed to him as the revealer of the Father.

The second chapter of *Dei Verbum* addresses the "Transmission of Divine Revelation." *Dei Verbum*'s prologue opens with a citation from 1 John 1:3: "What we have seen and heard we announce to you, so that you may have fellowship with us and our common fellowship be with the Father and his Son Jesus Christ." The Church proclaims the historical revelation of God in Christ and calls everyone to salvation. The Church highlights the Christocentric approach to explain revelation. Christ's revelation and his teachings are handed down over centuries according to the commandment of the Lord before his Ascension: "Go into the whole world and proclaim the gospel to every creature" (Mark 16:15; author's translation). Scripture and Tradition are linked to the original transmission of the Gospel by the Apostles, who passed on to the faithful by their preaching and example all that they had received from Christ: his words, his ways, his life, and his works.[128]

The concept of revelation has important consequences for understanding the meaning of Tradition. By her teaching and liturgy, the whole Church witnesses to it. Hence, Tradition cannot be reduced to the transmission of static doctrinal contents or limited to decisions made by Church authorities. In this context, Ratzinger points out the importance of the believers who contemplate and ponder the Word. In his commentary on *Dei Verbum*, he states:

> The dynamics of this new view on tradition stem from the acknowledgement of the tension between "what is expressed" and "what remains unexpressed" in revelation, the all-encompassing character of tradition (referring to the teaching, life and worship of the ecclesial community), and the recognition that tradition develops over time, not only through its proclamation by the magisterium, but also through contemplation and study by believers, who "ponder these things in their hearts" (Luke 2:19, 51) through the intimate understanding of spiritual things, which they experience.[129]

In Ratzinger's view, Tradition is not reducible to a positivist caricature of the Magisterium, since both are guided by the Holy Spirit. At the same time, the spiritual contribution of the laity cannot be belittled and should be taken into account. Both the divine and the human elements are engaged in the process of the transmission of revelation.

The question of revelation, proclaimed in Christ, and its presence in history split Western Christendom in the age of the Reformation. Ratzinger observed that the problem at that time was that Luther intended to equate *traditio* with *abusus*. The Council Fathers of Trent, on the other hand, had to face both the question of Tradition and the Reformation. According to Ratzinger's analysis, Trent was faithful to Tradition, affirming that Scripture cannot stand independently, apart from the Church: "Trent continued to maintain that the Word is not a reality standing in-

[128] Boeve, "Revelation, Scripture, and Tradition," 422.

[129] Boeve, "Revelation, Scripture, and Tradition," 423.

dependently above the Church, but that it is delivered by the Lord to the Church."[130] The Catholic Church transmits divine revelation through both Scripture and Tradition.

Summary

In conclusion, the collaboration with Cardinal Frings gave an opportunity for Ratzinger to take part in the Second Vatican Council as one of its preeminent council theologians. His active participation and his theological insights made him one of the important theologians of the Council. His significant contributions to the Dogmatic Constitution on Divine Revelation, along with those of Karl Rahner and other theologians, were recognized by the Council Fathers.

Ratzinger's study of Bonaventure's theology helped him considerably in understanding the concept of revelation in drafting *Dei Verbum*.[131] His theology of revelation is Christocentric. In his understanding of the concept of revelation, Ratzinger emphasizes the importance of revelation over Scripture and Tradition. It is made clear that Scripture and Tradition mediate revelation. They do not contain the fullness of revelation. Revelation goes beyond Scripture and Tradition as it exists outside of both. Revelation is not restricted to Scripture and Tradition. Ratzinger makes a strong effort to adhere to the teachings of the previous councils and understands revelation anew with a Christocentric approach.

The Primacy of Christ in Revelation

The Desire for Knowing God

The desire for God is innate in the human heart, as man shares in the *image* of God. This drives our relentless quest for the knowledge of God and our strong desire to commune with God. Augustine expresses this desire in his *Confessions*: "You stir us so that praising you may bring us joy, because you have made us and drawn us to yourself, and our heart is unquiet until it rests in you."[132] Human history has witnessed many who aspired to know God through ardent devotion, prayer, sacrifices, and rituals.

---

[130] Rahner and Ratzinger, *Revelation and Tradition*, 29–30.

[131] De Gaál, "Joseph Ratzinger at Vatican II," 526.

[132] *The Confessions of Saint Augustine*, trans. Maria Boulding, O.S.B., with introduction and notes, ed. John E. Rotelle, O.S.A. (New York: New City Press, 2012), 14.

The *Catechism of the Catholic Church* offers two ways of approaching the knowledge of God from creation: first, the physical world and, second, the human person.[133] In the physical world, creation reveals the invisible nature of God from its order, becoming, contingency, and beauty. As Paul writes: "For what can be known about God is plain to them, because God has shown it to them. Ever since the creation of the world his invisible nature, namely, his eternal power and deity, has been clearly perceived in the things that have been made" (Rom 1:19–20). The human person, by opening his or her heart to truth and moral goodness, and with an infinite urge for the ultimate Truth, attains knowledge of God to some degree:

> Man's faculties make him capable of coming to a knowledge of the existence of a personal God. But for man to be able to enter into real intimacy with him, God willed both to reveal himself to man and to give him the grace of being able to welcome this revelation in faith. The proofs of God's existence, however, can predispose one to faith and help one to see that faith is not opposed to reason. (CCC 35)

As the human person has an innate desire for the knowledge of God, so also God, who created human beings in his image, *willed to reveal* himself to humanity. God, with his grace, enabled human persons to open their hearts to divine self-revelation. By virtue of his faculties, a human person is capable of knowing God to some degree, however, this knowledge is limited.

The Church and the Knowledge of God

The Church is another important source from which one attains knowledge of God. Human reason attains a certain knowledge of God. However, a number of obstacles prevent the human person from attaining complete knowledge. This is mainly due to the consequences of original sin. Thus, human beings depend on God's revelation and respond in faith by opening their hearts. Hence, only through God's revelation can personal acquaintance with God be attained: "God communicates himself to man gradually. He prepares him to welcome by stages the supernatural revelation that

[133] *Catechism of the Catholic Church*, 2nd ed. (Washington, DC: United States Conference of Catholic Bishops, 2000), 31–34 (hereafter cited in text as CCC).

is to culminate in the person and mission of the incarnate Word, Jesus Christ."[134]

God communicates himself through various means by different people throughout the history of salvation. God's plan of revelation had different stages in the history of salvation.[135] The Father, through Jesus Christ, his Son, completes supernatural revelation via Incarnation and mission: "In many and various ways God spoke of old to our fathers by the prophets; but in these last days he has spoken to us by a Son, whom he appointed the heir to all things, through whom also he created the world" (Heb 1:1–2).

God revealed himself in human history. He willed to reveal himself and gave human beings the privilege to know him and to be united with him. "It pleased God, in his goodness and wisdom to reveal himself and make known the mystery of his will. His will was that all men and women should have access to the Father, through the Word made flesh, in the Holy Spirit, and thus become sharers in the divine nature" (CCC 51). God's eternal plan was to make human beings sharers in his divine nature. Jesus Christ, the Son of the Father, made this possible by taking human flesh and dying on the Cross to unite humankind to God.

Contemporary theology connects revelation with the Incarnation. Present-day theologians assert that through Jesus Christ God is fully revealed. Theologians such as Henri de Lubac, Karl Rahner, and Romano Guardini reiterate that God revealed himself completely through Christ. In his human form, the Son of God revealed the Father. His gestures, signs, attitude, conduct, and words reveal to us the identity of God the Father.[136] *Gaudium et spes* stresses the incarnate Word, the second Adam revealed by the Father:

> Only in the mystery of the incarnate Word does the mystery of man take on light. For Adam, the first man, was a figure of Him who was to come, namely Christ the Lord. Christ, the final Adam,

---

[134] CCC 40–41: "We can name God only by taking creatures as our starting point, and in accordance with our limited human ways of knowing and thinking. [41] All creatures bear a certain resemblance to God, most especially man, created in the image and likeness of God. The manifold perfections of creatures—their truth, their goodness, their beauty—all reflect the infinite perfection of God."

[135] CCC 54–65. God made known to the first parents with created realities. The revelation was not broken with the original sin. He continuously made covenants with individuals and Israel. He made covenants with Noah, Abraham, and Israel, his people, and in the fullness of time, he sent his Son as mediator to reveal Himself completely.

[136] Latourelle, *Theology of Revelation*, 359.

> by the revelation of the mystery of the Father and His love, fully reveals man to man himself and makes his supreme calling clear.[137]

Only in light of the Incarnation can one understand the fullness of revelation in Jesus Christ. Jesus Christ fulfilled the will of the Father on this earth. In God's plan, only in Jesus Christ did God want to fulfill his revelation. The Church, which was instituted by Christ, accepts and responds to the revelation in faith. In this way, the Church goes beyond human reason in knowing God and his plan of salvation.

Ratzinger's theology of revelation emphasizes Christ, the revelation of the Father. By encountering Christ in the Scriptures, in the sacraments, and in worship, one comes to knowledge of God. Ratzinger's theology invites one to seek a more profound understanding of the concept of revelation in Christ.

The writings of Benedict XVI reflect a synergistic approach of faith and reason. His theology includes the whole history of human questioning that is relevant even today. He attempts to answer these questions by employing the answers given in the course of history and strives to interpret God's self-revelation in Jesus Christ. In all his writings, the focus is on Christ. This Christocentric approach invites the reader to encounter Christ.[138]

The Concept of Revelation in Ratzinger's Post-Conciliar Writings

In his book *Introduction to Christianity*, Ratzinger reflects on the Apostles' Creed and challenges contemporary atheism. He retrieves the treasures of the Christian faith. Discussing the doctrine of the Blessed Trinity, he justifies the use of negative theology to understand the triune God. He highlights the danger of reducing God to limited human understanding. He notes: "Any doctrine of the Trinity, therefore, cannot aim at being a perfect comprehension of God."[139] The mystery of the Blessed Trinity is not comprehended fully by contingent beings. Human language, reasoning, and comprehension of the mysteries of God are limited.

In understanding the doctrine of God, Ratzinger echoes the theology

---

[137] Second Vatican Council, Pastoral Constitution on the Church in the Modern World *Gaudium et Spes* (December 7, 1965), available from http://www.vatican.va.

[138] D. Vincent Twomey, S.V.D., *Pope Benedict XVI: The Conscience of Our Age: A Theological Portrait* (San Francisco: Ignatius Press, 2007), 39–40.

[139] Joseph Ratzinger, *Introduction to Christianity*, trans. J. R. Foster (San Francisco: Ignatius Press, 2004), 171.

of Augustine, who also employed the concept of "relativity" to understand the Trinitarian God. The relationship among the persons of the triune God is "not something extra, added to the person, as it is with us; it only exists at all as relatedness."[140] For Ratzinger, the concept of "Son" is the concept of relation. The Father is not called "father" unless he has begotten a child. When Jesus is called "Son," he is "relative" to the Father. According to the evangelist John, "Son" is a being from another. Jesus Christ is a being "from" and "toward" the Father. As an ambassador strips off his identity and represents the one who sent him, so also Jesus, as the mediator, represents and reveals the Father. Everything Christ did during his ministry on earth manifests the actions of God. Thus, Jesus is the "true ambassador" who reveals the Father.[141]

The application of the concept of *Logos* to Christ imparts significant meaning in the Gospel of John. Ratzinger states: "*Logos* does not mean simply the idea of the eternal rationality of being, as it did essentially in Greek thought. . . . It no longer denotes simply the permeation of all being by meaning; it characterizes this man: he who is here is 'Word.'"[142] The ancient Greeks understood the term "*logos*" as "meaning or *ratio*,"[143] but John focuses on the meaning of *Logos* as "word" (*verbum*). There is a relation between the one who pronounces the *word* and the *word* that is being pronounced by the speaker. Once again, this indicates *relation* between the Father and the Son, Christ the *Logos*. The filial relationship between the Father and the Son was evident whenever Jesus prayed during his salvific mission on earth. According to Ratzinger, the *Logos* is not understood in an abstract sense, but as made visible to the world in Jesus, who is the Word of the Father.

Ratzinger notices the difficulties in understanding the second part of the Creed: "I believe in Jesus Christ, his only Son, Our Lord." He points to the difficulty in understanding Christ in the man Jesus. For Ratzinger, one who tries to examine Christology with the historical-critical method alone faces the danger of reducing theology to history.[144] The historical-critical method can demonstrate positively very much, but it cannot reach the height of faith. Amidst various modern theologies, Ratzinger

[140] Ratzinger, *Introduction to Christianity*, 183.

[141] Ratzinger, *Introduction to Christianity*, 182–88.

[142] Ratzinger, *Introduction to Christianity*, 189.

[143] Ratzinger, *Introduction to Christianity*, 189.

[144] Ratzinger, *Introduction to Christianity*, 193. The same problem of understanding Christ Jesus is discussed in his book *Behold the Pierced One*, trans. Graham Harrison (San Francisco: Ignatius Press, 1986), 13.

tries to bring together the historical Jesus and the Christ of faith, thus giving legitimacy to the historical-critical method without absolutizing it. He strongly believes that Christ and Jesus cannot be separated:

> I believe that it can even become a very useful pointer to something, namely, to the fact that the one (Jesus) cannot exist without the other (Christ), that, on the contrary, one is bound to be continually pushed from one to the other because in reality Jesus only subsists as the Christ and the Christ only subsists in the shape of Jesus.[145]

Thus, for Ratzinger, the historical Jesus cannot be separated from the Christ of faith and the Christ of faith cannot be separated from the historical Jesus. One subsists in the other. If one separates Jesus and Christ in understanding Christology, one falls back into the Arian heresy. Ratzinger points out that *Christ* (Messiah, the anointed) is a title of Jesus and eventually became part of the name of Jesus. In his view, it is not possible to distinguish the person from his office. The office *is* the person, and vice versa, the person *is* the office. There cannot be any separation between "I" and the works, between "I" and what "I" does. In an ordinary sense, one understands the person by his or her actions. Hence, one cannot separate the works of Jesus from his office as Christ.[146] Thus, one understands that Jesus's office as the one anointed (Messiah) cannot be separated from him. The integrity of the person of Jesus vouches for the harmonious collaboration of the human and divine natures.

The Primacy of Christ in Revelation according to the Gospels

As discussed above, one cannot divide Christ and Jesus. Jesus, as the anointed one, reveals God as Trinity. The purpose of God sending his Son into the world to save humanity was fulfilled when his *Word* became visible. God uttered himself in Jesus once and for all. Revelation came to an end as it fulfilled this goal. Ratzinger reiterates: "The fact that in Christ the goal of revelation and, thereby, the goal of humanity is attained, because in him divine existence and human existence touch and unite, means at the same time that the goal attained is not a rigid boundary but an open

[145] Ratzinger, *Introduction to Christianity*, 201.

[146] Ratzinger, *Introduction to Christianity*, 203.

space."[147] Because Christ was truly human and truly divine, he was fully united with God and fully united to humanity. In this way, the fullness of revelation was made possible in Jesus Christ. There is nothing hidden in God that was not revealed in his Son Jesus Christ.

When God revealed himself, he appeared as charity and meek gentleness in the Incarnation of Christ. However, for Ratzinger, one of the significant ways that God revealed himself in Jesus was through the Cross. The Cross revealed both God and man to humankind.[148] Ratzinger argues that Jesus's death on the Cross is a revelation of God, citing Plato's (albeit interpolated) image of the crucified "just man." The position of a truly just man in this world is when a righteous man takes the place of an unrighteous one to make others righteous. Though this was said long before the birth of Jesus, it was fulfilled in Jesus, the "Just One." Jesus identified himself with the unrighteous and sinners. Jesus's death on the Cross revealed both God and man. He identified and sympathized with man. Jesus revealed the abundant love of the Father to sinful humanity. Hence, the Cross is truly *the* center of revelation. It revealed how sinful humankind is and how merciful God is. As dust is seen clearly in light, so human sinfulness is seen at the Cross. Thus, Ratzinger claims that the *Cross* revealed both God and man.[149]

The Son of God reveals the depth of his love for humanity on the Cross. The Cross becomes the center of revelation among many other ways: God is revealed also in the Incarnation, in the miracles, in forgiving sinners, in the parables, and in living among the poor. Thus, it is not only on the Cross that Jesus Christ revealed God, but throughout his entire earthly mission.

The filial relationship between Jesus and the Father through prayer is evident in the Gospels. Jesus prays before all important events in his life: before calling the Twelve, before the Transfiguration, in the Mount of Olives, and on the Cross. Jesus calls God "my Father," but he invites his disciples to pray with him the "Our Father." Only Jesus can address God as "my Father" because of his Sonship and relation with the Father. Human beings are entitled to call God Father because he created us in his image and united us to his Son through Baptism. But no one can build a bridge between the Father and humanity except Jesus Christ. This bridge is made

[147] Ratzinger, *Introduction to Christianity*, 263.
[148] Ratzinger, *Introduction to Christianity*, 292.
[149] Ratzinger, *Introduction to Christianity*, 293.

possible only through Jesus, the mediator, who fully reveals the Father.[150]

As a human being, Jesus had an intimate relationship with the Father despite being one with humanity. He lived his religious life like any other Jew of his time. Ratzinger alludes to the dialogue with Moses and Elijah on the mountain (Mark 9:4) in order to present Jesus's unique place in revelation. Ratzinger believes that Jesus went beyond the Old Testament prophets in his relationship with the Father. In doing so, Jesus displayed a profound knowledge of the Father.[151] Because he was both human and divine, his knowledge and relationship with the Father superseded that of others.

In his book *On the Way to Jesus Christ*—subtitled, significantly, *The Face of Christ in Sacred Scriptures*—Benedict presents the "face of Jesus" and Jesus's identity as revealer of the Father on the basis of the Gospel according to John. When Jesus foretells his passion and death to his disciples, Thomas asks: "Lord, we do not know where you are going; how can we know the way?" (John 14:5). Jesus answers him saying: "I am the way, and the truth, and the life; no one comes to the Father, but by me" (John 14:6). This raises another question from Philip, who says, "Lord, show us the Father, and we shall be satisfied" (John 14:8). Jesus reveals his identity again saying, "He who has seen me has seen the Father" (John 14: 9). This dialogue with his disciples is the strongest evidence that Jesus Christ is the revelation of the Father. However, Jesus's answer surprises Philip: whoever has seen Jesus has seen the Father. This reveals the intimate relationship between the Father and Son. It is echoed by Paul when he writes, "For it is the God who said, 'Let light shine out of darkness,' who has shone in our hearts to give the light of the knowledge of the glory of God in the face of Christ" (2 Cor 4:6). The light of Jesus Christ shed on humankind brings it to the knowledge of God.[152]

Another explanation that Benedict presents to show the primacy of Christ in revelation is a comparison of Jesus with the prophets of the Old Testament. God reveals himself through the prophets in the Old Testament; for instance, "the Lord used to speak to Moses face to face, as a man speaks to his friend" (Exod 33:11). Moses again requests of God: "show me your glory!" and the Lord says: "you cannot see my face; for man shall not see me and live" (Exod 33:18, 20). In contrast to Moses, who only desires

---

[150] Ratzinger, *Introduction to Christianity*, 293.

[151] Ratzinger, *Behold the Pierced One*, 29.

[152] Joseph Ratzinger, *On the Way to Jesus Christ*, trans. Michael J. Miller (San Francisco: Ignatius Press, 2005), 13–16.

to see the face of God, Christ actually sees the face of God, and in his own face, the glory of God is made visible. More than a prophet and a friend, Jesus is the "Son." Jesus said that his disciples were no longer called slaves but friends, and all believers have access to the knowledge of God through Jesus Christ. The knowledge of God is made accessible by encountering Christ. Thus, most concretely, Jesus Christ is the face of God who reveals the glory of God.[153]

The Primacy of Christ in Revelation according to the Letters of Paul

In Pauline Christology, Christ is the "image of the invisible God" (Col 1:15). Paul, in his Christological hymn, highlights the relationship of God and Christ: "He is the image of the invisible God, the first-born of all creation. . . . He is before all things, and in him all things hold together. . . . he is the beginning, the first-born from the dead, that in everything he might be pre-eminent" (Col 1:15, 17, 18). For Benedict, the Letter to the Philippians emphasizes the way in which God is revealed in the self-abasement and exaltation of Christ and the Letter to the Colossians highlights the mystery of God revealed in Christ.[154]

Benedict explored the legacy of Paul in his Wednesday audiences in the "Pauline Year."[155] Benedict reflected on Jesus as the head (*kephalé*) of the Church in the theology of Paul: "He is the *head* of the body, the church" (Col 1:18; emphasis added). As the head, Jesus is the governor, the leader, and the guide who leads the Christian community. He also *innervates and vivifies* the members in the one body.[156] Living the truth in love, the faithful should grow in every way into him who is the *head*, the Christ, from whom the whole body is joined and is held together by every

[153] Ratzinger, *On the Way to Jesus Christ*, 26. See also Joseph Ratzinger, *Jesus of Nazareth*, vol. 1, *From the Baptism in the Jordan to the Transfiguration*, trans. Adrian Walker (San Francisco: Ignatius, 2008), 265.

[154] Frank J. Matera, *God's Saving Grace: A Pauline Theology* (Grand Rapids, MI: Eerdmans, 2012), 242.

[155] Pope Benedict XVI, *Saint Paul* (San Francisco: Ignatius Press, 2009), 7. The year from June 29, 2008 (beginning with First Vespers on June 28), to the same feast in 2009 was dedicated to the great Apostle Paul. According to Pope Benedict: "The Apostle Paul, an outstanding and almost inimitable yet stimulating figure, stands before us as an example of total dedication to the Lord and to his Church, as well as of great openness to humanity and its cultures" (General Audience on Saint Paul [July 2, 2008], available from http://www.vatican.va0.

[156] Pope Benedict XVI, *St. Paul*, 111–12.

supporting ligament (Eph 4:15–16). Citing the above Pauline texts, Benedict XVI affirms:

> He is the governor, the leader, the person in charge who guides the Christian community as its leader and Lord. . . . He innervates and vivifies all the members of the body that he controls. . . . He is not only one who commands but also one who is organically connected with us, from whom comes the power to act in an upright way.[157]

As the head of the Church, Jesus Christ leads and directs the Church. As the head is a significant part of the human body that directs the other organs to function, so Christ directs, guides, and nourishes. He is supreme over the Church and its Tradition.

The Church is "subjected" to Christ: she must be both guided and vivified by him. "And his gifts were that some should be apostles, some prophets, some evangelists, some pastors and teachers" (Eph 4:11). Thus, Jesus Christ guides, empowers, and leads the Church in the right direction. When the Church passes on its teaching or proclaims dogma, Christ guides the Church. Benedict observes that the work of governance is not traced back to the Spirit, but to Christ (1 Cor 12).[158] After the Ascension, everything that was carried out in the Church was attributed to the Spirit. But here we notice that it has been attributed to Jesus Christ as the governor of the Church.

Christ is not only the head of the Church, but he is also superior to the heavenly beings. The cosmos is subject to him and converges in him as its head. Citing Ephesians 1:10—"to unite all things in him, things in heaven and things on earth"—Benedict goes on to say, "Christ has no possible rival to fear since he is superior to every form of power that might presume to humble man."[159] Christ revealed God the Father so profoundly that his footprints are the very footprints of God. Christ himself is God's impression. Hence, Benedict affirms the primacy of revelation *in* Christ. For him, centrality and finality is Christ over everything else. He is supreme over all things visible and invisible.

---

[157] Benedict, *St. Paul*, 112.

[158] Benedict, *St. Paul*, 112.

[159] Benedict, *St. Paul*, 113.

Revelation in Benedict XVI's Jesus of Nazareth *Trilogy*

Benedict XVI presents Jesus to the world in the three-volume work *Jesus of Nazareth*.[160] In the first volume, Benedict demonstrates the commonalities and differences between Moses and Jesus. "And from his fulness have we all received, grace upon grace. For the law was given through Moses; grace and truth came through Jesus Christ. No one has ever seen God; the only Son, who is in the bosom of the Father, he has made him known" (John 1:16–18). Citing this passage, Benedict claims that Jesus made God the Father known to humanity as revealer of the Father. The Law was given through Moses, but Jesus Christ brought grace upon grace to the world and has shown the love and mercy of God.[161]

God had already revealed his name to Moses and built a relationship with humankind. He communicated his will to Moses. Moses acted as the mediator between God and Israel in the Old Testament. In his high priestly prayer, Jesus emphasized that he revealed the name of the Father (see John 17:6, 26). Jesus brought to completion what began with Moses. Benedict observes that Jesus goes beyond any prophet in revealing God.[162] The face of Jesus was revealed whenever he spoke and acted in the name of the Father. Jesus was never alone. There was reciprocity between the Father and the Son. Benedict reflects on this perfect unity of the Father and the Son in his first volume of *Jesus of Nazareth*, speaking about the face of Jesus:

> Jesus' own "I" is always opened into "being with" the Father; he is never alone, but is forever receiving himself from and giving himself back to the Father: "My teaching is not mine"; his "I" is opened up into the Trinity. Those who come to know him "see" the Father; they enter into this communion of his with the Father.[163]

Jesus's teaching is not his own, but from the Father. His words are the words of the Father and his works are the works of the Father. Jesus is the Word of the Father. Hence, Jesus revealed the Father in all the aspects of

---

[160] These volumes of *Jesus of Nazareth* are his personal search "for the face of the Lord," states Benedict (1:xxiii). The first volume, *From the Baptism in the Jordan to the Transfiguration*, deals with the public ministry of Jesus. The second volume, *Holy Week: From the Entrance into Jerusalem to the Resurrection*, discusses the Passion narratives of Jesus. The third volume, *Infancy Narratives*, discusses the birth of Jesus Christ.

[161] Ratzinger, *Jesus of Nazareth*, 1:236.

[162] Ratzinger, *Jesus of Nazareth*, 1:267.

[163] Ratzinger, *Jesus of Nazareth*, 1:283.

his life on earth. Benedict calls attention to the evangelist John, who does not present a genealogy at the beginning of his gospel, but presents Jesus as the *Logos* in his prologue. Pope Benedict investigates the question of Jesus's provenance in the Gospel of John in the third volume of *Jesus of Nazareth*, subtitled *Infancy Narratives*. He states: "Jesus' origin, his provenance, is the true 'beginning'—the primordial source form which all things come, the 'light' that makes the world into the cosmos. He comes from God. He is God."[164] The three volumes of *Jesus of Nazareth* show remarkable continuity and coherence in his theology from his earliest writings onward.

Also in these three volumes, Benedict supports his argument for "the face of Jesus" as the revealer of God the Father. Thereby, he maintains a Christocentric approach to affirm that Christ goes beyond all prophets in revealing God. His Christocentric *point d'appui* is irreproachably consistent with Scripture and the Tradition of the Church.

Further Elucidations on God's Personal Self-Disclosure in Christ

During his pontificate, Benedict penned a number of exhortations and encyclicals. Some of these writings demonstrate his Christocentric theology and the person of Jesus as the definitive revelation. Oftentimes in his encyclicals, Benedict invites the faithful to *encounter Christ* through Scripture and the sacraments. The theme of encountering Christ pervades all his writings. A selection of these papal writings illuminates the concept of revelation and the Christocentric approach that he already unfolded profoundly at Vatican II.

Revelation in Papal Writings

Deus Caritas Est

Benedict wrote his first encyclical, *Deus caritas est*, on God's love for humanity. "In a world where the name of God is sometimes associated with vengeance or even a duty of hatred and violence," Benedict seeks to speak of the limitless love that God bestows on humanity.[165] The first section of the

[164] Joseph Ratzinger, *Jesus of Nazareth*, vol. 3, *The Infancy Narratives*, trans. Philip J. Whitmore (New York: Image, 2012), 11.

[165] Pope Benedict XVI, Encyclical Letter on Christian Love *Deus Caritas Est* (December 25, 2005), 1, available from http://www.vatican.va (hereafter cited in text as DCE).

encyclical focuses on God's love and the reality, or potential, of human love. Here, Benedict demonstrates God's love as the highest form of love, *agape*. In the second part, he discusses the commandment to love one another.

In the introduction, Benedict elucidates what it means to be a Christian in terms of encountering Christ the Son of God. He states: "Being Christian is not the result of an ethical choice or a lofty idea, but the encounter with an event, a person, which gives life a new horizon and a decisive direction" (DCE 1). A Christian should encounter Christ, who is the revealer of God's love in his words and actions. Unless one is rooted in Christ, he or she will not be able to present Christ as love to the world.

Jesus Christ is the incarnate love of God. Benedict reflects on the New Testament, particularly focusing on the figure of Christ, who gives himself to us. In Jesus Christ, God searches for his lost sheep. Benedict believes that divine activity took on a dramatic form when Jesus lived among the outcasts, the poor, and sinners. In Jesus Christ, God showed his love to humanity. God is revealed in Christ Jesus most explicitly on the Cross in a most radical form—to raise us up to himself. Benedict goes on to say that in Christ we see the invisible God:

> True, no one has ever seen God as he is. And yet God is not totally invisible to us; he does not remain completely inaccessible. . . . He has become visible in as much as he "has sent his only Son into the world, so that we might live through him" (1 *Jn*. 4:9). God has made himself visible: in Jesus we are able to see the Father (cf. *Jn*. 14:9). (DCE 17)

God made himself visible in Christ Jesus; the faithful see God in Jesus Christ. Through Jesus Christ, the faithful experience the love of the Father. An encounter with Jesus is an encounter with God. In encountering Christ, one encounters God in his human nature.

Spe Salvi

In his second encyclical, *Spe salvi*, Benedict presents a masterful survey of the abandonment of Christian hope in favor of faith in progress and technology that ultimately led to atheism, communism, and more suffering for humanity. He contends that man's true hope is not found in ideologies, but in God, who has loved man to the end.

According to Benedict, only in encountering the person of Christ can one have hope amidst innumerable problems in the modern world. In order to hope in Jesus Christ in hopeless situations, Benedict draws the attention of the reader to the Letter to the Ephesians and explains that: "The Ephesians, before their encounter with Christ, were without hope because they were 'without God in the world.' To come to know God—the true God—means to receive hope."[166] Only in encountering Christ can one possess and receive hope. Only in knowing him can one come to the knowledge of the redemption Christ brought to humankind. If one is cognizant of Jesus's redemptive work through his death on the Cross, one acknowledges and accepts him as one's hope. This kind of hope not only enables one to endure the sufferings of this world but also transforms one and allows one to become truly oneself. It is in and through Jesus that one hopes in God. Christ elevates man's hope in God. The Ephesians had no hope before encountering Christ, for they did not find God in the world. When they came to the knowledge of God through the Gospel of Christ, they came to the knowledge of the true God whom Jesus revealed.

Benedict calls the attention of the faithful to the First Letter of Paul to the Thessalonians: "you may not grieve as others do who have no hope" (1 Thess 4:13). Likewise, Benedict exhorts the faithful to have hope in God, which should be a distinguishing mark of the Christian life. Man has a future, but he does not know the details of what awaits him in the future. Nevertheless, a person knows that God holds his future, and he knows that it will not end with emptiness.[167] Reflecting on the "image of God" in Christ, Benedict notes: "God has given himself an 'image': in Christ who was made man. In him who was crucified, the denial of false images of God is taken to an extreme. God now reveals his true face in the figure of the sufferer who shares man's God-forsaken condition by taking it upon himself" (SS 43). God's true face is found in the suffering Jesus who laid down his life for humanity. The innocent suffering of Christ on the Cross offers the assurance of hope: God, in his mysterious ways, offers us justice that we can conceive of only in faith.

Benedict's encyclical *Spe salvi* exhorts the people of the modern world to find hope by encountering Christ on the Cross. Here again, one notices Benedict's Christ-centered theology and his continuity of thought.

---

166 Pope Benedict XVI, Encyclical Letter on Christian Hope *Spe Salvi* (November 30, 2007), 3, available from http://www.vatican.va (hereafter cited in text as SS).

167 SS 2: "The Christian message was not only 'informative' but 'performative.' That means: the Gospel is not merely a communication of things that can be known—it is one that makes things happen and is life-changing. The dark door of time, of the future, has been thrown open. The one who has hope lives differently; the one who hopes has been granted the gift of a new life."

Caritas in Veritate

Benedict's third encyclical, entitled *Caritas in veritate*, starts with a discussion of Christ, who witnessed to the truth: "Charity in truth, to which Jesus Christ bore witness by his earthly life and especially by his death and Resurrection, is the principal driving force behind the authentic development of every person and of all humanity."[168] The strength of the encyclical lies in its use of theology to direct Catholics and other Christians away from thinking in a secular way about the questions of politics and economics.

Benedict examines the social teachings of the Church already voiced by popes in the past, such as *Rerum novarum* (1891), by Leo XIII, and *Populorum progressio* (1967), *Humanae vitae* (1968), and the apostolic exhortation *Evangelii nuntiandi* (1975), all by Paul VI. With his Chalcedonian approach to interpreting the truth and charity, Benedict once again orients his logical arguments toward Christ the revealer of the Father and humanity itself:

> In promoting development, the Christian faith does not rely on privilege or positions of power, nor even on the merits of Christians . . . but only on Christ, to whom every authentic vocation to integral human development must be directed. *The Gospel is fundamental for development*, because in the Gospel, Christ, "in the very revelation of the mystery of the Father and of his love, fully reveals humanity to itself." (CIV 18)

Benedict focuses on the integral development of the human person, not just the material development of society. Knowing more, having more, and doing more should be integrated with the truth. Human development should not be confined to one nation or culture. Development is not comprehensive if it excludes any group of people, any culture, or any nation. Human development should aim at the good of every person and of the whole person (CIV 18).

Benedict invites the Church to give importance and value to every individual equally. Human development does not rely on the power and position possessed in this world, but relies on Jesus Christ. Benedict points out that God gives a "resounding yes" to the pleading of human beings

---

168 Pope Benedict XVI, Encyclical Letter on Integral Human Development in Charity and Truth *Caritas in Veritate* (June 29, 2009), 1, available from http://www.vatican.va (hereafter cited in text as CIV).

who cry for help. He calls on us to open our hearts and to pursue an integral development of humanity. The Christian vocation to this development achieves its perfection only in Christ (CIV 18).

Verbum Domini

Verbum Domini is a response to the Twelfth Ordinary General Assembly of the Synod of Bishops, which met in 2008. Its theme was "The Word of God in the Life and the Mission of the Church."[169] One of the significant goals of the assembly was to review the implementation of the directives on Scripture as found in the Second Vatican Council, especially its dogmatic constitution *Dei Verbum*. Another goal was to address the new challenges of the day.

In this post-synodal apostolic exhortation, *Verbum Domini*, Benedict points out some fundamental approaches to rediscovering the Word of God in the life of the Church (VD 1). The document has three parts, entitled *Verbum Dei*, *Verbum in Ecclesia*, and *Verbum in Mundo*.

Initially, Benedict reflects on the journey of the universal Church from *Dei Verbum* to the Synod on the Word of God. For Benedict, the Word of God is the "heart of the Christian life." The Church is built and grows on the Word of God. Saints and faithful have found strength in the Word of God. Benedict invites the Christian communities to study, meditate, celebrate, and be strengthened by the Word of God (VD 3). The Word of God leads and transforms the lives of the people. Benedict exhorts the universal Church to encounter Christ in Scripture. This Word is Jesus Christ. Benedict reiterates that Jesus Christ is "the fullness of revelation":

> Jesus Christ is to be acknowledged as "mediator and fullness of all revelation." To each generation the Church unceasingly proclaims that Christ "completed and perfected revelation. Everything to do with his presence and his self-manifestation was involved in achieving this: his words and works, signs and miracles, but above all his death and resurrection from the dead, and finally his sending of the Spirit of truth." (VD 3)

---

[169] Pope Benedict XVI, Post-Synodal Exhortation on the Word of God in the Life and Mission of the Church *Verbum Domini* (September 30, 2010), available from http://www.vatican.va (hereafter cited in text as VD).

In the above statement, Benedict again affirms Jesus as the *fullness of all revelation*. Jesus Christ reveals God the Father to this world by his words and deeds and by his Paschal Mystery, which is the ultimate expression of God's love for humanity. When God spoke in history, the same Word *was* present. "God was never without *Logos*" (VD 6). The heart of divine revelation is the Incarnation. God made known his mysteries to humankind when he took human form in Jesus Christ, and this Word of God is handed on in the Church's living Tradition.

Benedict notes that the fullness of revelation in Christ is witnessed by Scripture and living Tradition. Jesus revealed the Father fully, and thus there will be no further public revelation. The same assertion is maintained in the *Catechism of the Catholic Church*.[170]

The *Catechism of the Catholic Church* affirms that there is no new public revelation until the Second Coming of Our Lord. The Church and the Magisterium continue to understand the mystery of revelation guided by the Holy Spirit. Thus, one discovers a profound continuity in Benedict's theology of revelation. His Christocentric approach invites the universal Church to encounter Christ ever anew—including in Scripture.

Porta Fidei

Porta fidei was an apostolic letter in which Benedict announced the "Year of Faith" (October 11, 2012, to November 24, 2013). The Year of Faith corresponded with the fiftieth anniversary of the opening of the Second Vatican Council and the twentieth anniversary of the publication of the *Catechism of the Catholic Church*. The purpose of the year was to arouse among the faithful the desire to profess the faith with conviction. Benedict invited the faithful to "rediscover the journey of faith so as to shed ever clearer light on the joy and renewed enthusiasm of the encounter with Christ."[171]

In this letter, Benedict again exhorts the faithful to convert to Christ, the Savior of the world. He points out that the Christian mystery is Christ's fullness of revelation:

---

[170] "The Christian economy, therefore, since it is the new and definitive Covenant, will never pass away; and no new public revelation is to be expected before the glorious manifestation of our Lord Jesus Christ. Yet, even if revelation is already complete, it has not been made completely explicit; it remains for Christian faith gradually to grasp its full significance over the course of the centuries" (CCC 66).

[171] Pope Benedict XVI, Apostolic Letter for the Indiction of the Year of Faith *Porta Fidei* (October 11, 2011), 2, available from http://www.vatican.va (hereafter cited in text as PF).

> The Year of Faith . . . is a summons to an authentic and renewed conversion to the Lord, the one Saviour of the world. In the mystery of his death and resurrection, God has revealed in its fullness the Love that saves and calls us to conversion of life through the forgiveness of sins. (PF 6)

God revealed himself in Jesus Christ, the Savior of the world and the revealer of God's will. Benedict invites the faithful to focus their gaze on Christ—the "pioneer and perfecter of faith" (PF 13; cf. Heb 12:2 and PF 6). By taking on human form in the world and sharing our weakness, Jesus Christ transforms the whole of humanity. Benedict goes on to reflect on different aspects of faith in Christian life by citing the faith of Mary, the Apostles, the disciples, and the martyrs in history.

Conclusion

The "encounter with Christ" is a recurring *leitmotif* in Benedict's entire opus. His unbroken, consistent line of thought in understanding the concept of revelation as being ultimately the person of Jesus Christ is much in evidence. Jesus Christ is *the* mediator and *the* revealer of the Father in the fullest sense—a thought that finds its origin in Scripture and Tradition: "In all things he himself might be preeminent" (Col 1:18; author's translation). Christ's primacy over the Old Testament prophets, in the revelation of God, is a fundamental belief of every Christian. Benedict learned from the theology of Bonaventure: revelation is dynamic, personal, and progressive in its nature. Bonaventure's study decisively informed Ratzinger's contribution to *Dei Verbum*. Benedict employs a Christocentric approach to understanding the concept of revelation that he adopted from Bonaventure, who preached the centrality and finality of salvation history in Christ: "Christ is the head of the body, the Church. He is the beginning, the firstborn from the dead, that in all things he himself might be preeminent" (Col 1:18; author's translation).

Benedict XVI has a theological tone akin to Augustine, the Victorines, Bonaventure, Newman, and Guardini. As a young theologian, he studied the theology of Augustine. Thus, he became familiar with the Fathers of the Church. He approached the Middle Ages by dedicating his second major work to Bonaventure's theology. He wrote *The Theology of History in St. Bonaventure* for his post-doctoral dissertation. In this study, Ratzinger attempted to understand the concept of revelation from Bonaventure's *Collations on the Six Days of Creation*, which are Bonaventure's formal series of sermons preached to his fellow Franciscan friars.

Ratzinger appreciated that for Bonaventure in the *Hexaëmeron*, revelation is the spiritual understanding of the Scripture and that this understanding comes from "manifold divine wisdom" granted by divine grace to those who are humble and holy.[172] Manifold wisdom includes the allegorical, the anagogical, and the tropological interpretation of Scripture. The spiritual understanding of Scripture is dynamic and continues until the Second Coming of the Lord. Ratzinger also noted the shift that other thirteenth-century theologians made in understanding Scripture. They considered Scripture as revelation, while Bonaventure considered the personal apprehension and appropriation of Scripture as revelation. Ratzinger further developed this thought with a Christocentric approach at the Second Vatican Council and contributed decisively to the final form of *Dei Verbum*.

Ratzinger decisively clarified that Scripture and Tradition witness to and mediate revelation. They do not contain the fullness of revelation. Scripture and Tradition are mediated in human, historical ways. Revelation is dynamic in its nature. Christ is present in Scripture, in the Church, and in the world. His revelation is not confined just to Scripture and Tradition, but supersedes both, as they are cast in human words and manners. Hence, Benedict gives much importance to Christ the *Logos*, who is the fullness of revelation.

His post-conciliar writings demonstrate his unbroken line of thought on the concept of revelation: in *Introduction to Christianity*, the three volumes of *Jesus of Nazareth*, and his papal writings.

In *Introduction to Christianity*, Ratzinger reflects on the Creed and retrieves the treasures of the Christian faith. He argues that Jesus's death on the Cross is *the* center of revelation. The uniqueness of Jesus's revelation is that he *is* the Son of God and the eternal *Logos*. Christ's revelation supersedes all other revelations in the history of salvation. Benedict's love for Christ and the Church motivated him to present Jesus Christ to the world through his three volumes of *Jesus of Nazareth*. In all three volumes, Benedict argued that Jesus is the face of the Father.

Benedict's encyclicals and other papal writings invite the reader to have a personal relationship with Christ. "Encountering Christ" is the phrase that pervades all of his texts. In this light, Benedict's Christocentric approach offers a fresh and deeper understanding of the concept of revelation. Benedict prioritizes Christ the *Logos* over Scripture and Tradition.

[172] Ratzinger, *Theology of History in St. Bonaventure*, 59.

One might venture to conclude that Ratzinger's / Pope Benedict XVI's lasting legacy is to state vigorously that revelation in Christ is the definitive, personal self-disclosure of the triune God—and thereby, also as the identity of the human being. It is as addressees of God's revelation that human beings experience themselves as persons in the full sense. Due to the signal, epochal alienation from natural revelation (intimating the existence of something divine) by virtue of the advances of technology and the positive sciences, a return to a pre-critical (Kantian) naïveté is not possible. Only by believing in a God revealing himself as a "Thou"—as prophetically taught by *Dei Verbum* and Ratzinger/Benedict XVI—can humankind retain and enrich her personhood.

CHAPTER 8

Theology as Lived Christian Discipleship

Joseph Ratzinger's Contribution to a Vatican II Understanding of the Loci Theologici[1]

> Daring the folly of truth with a merry heart without cheapening truth, appears to me the task at hand.[2]
>
> —Joseph Ratzinger 1975

AMID A PROLIFERATION of images and an inflation of words in fragmented postmodernity, the Christian imagination has lost much of its vividness and, *a fortiori*, its credibility for large segments of society. Ratzinger speaks of a *historia calamitatum*, with theology on an ignominious retreat in the face of popular ideologies and currents such as relativism, secularism, evolutionism, consumerism, and eclectic pluralism, and seemingly incapable of preserving her own identity and mission.[3]

---

1 This essay was originally published in *Lateranum* LXXIX, no. 2 (2013): 435–467. Used by permission.

2 "Die Narrheit des Wahren heiteren Herzens ohne Abstriche zu wagen, scheint mir die Aufgabe für heute und morgen"; see Joseph Ratzinger, "Der Weltdienst der Kirche: Auswirkungen von 'Gaudium et Spes,'" *Communio* 4 (1975): 439–53, at 453.

3 In the discussion with K. Hummel, "Was Theologen nicht mehr sagen sollten, Überlegungen eines Naturwissenschaftlers," *Theologische Quartalschrift* 149 (1969): 336–49, at 343.

A reflection on the nature, mission, sources, and scope of theology is an ongoing theme among contemporary theologians.[4] Recently, Melchior Cano's treatise *De locis theologicis*, published posthumously in 1563, enjoys increased attention, being seen by posterity as guided by the dogmatic concern to provide the bases for a theological proof.[5] Thus, it is perceived as primarily focused on supplying a contribution to the controversial inter-denominational disputes in the second half of the sixteenth century and onward. This utilization by posterity notwithstanding, Cano may equally

---

[4] See: P. Coda, *Teo-logia: La Parola di Dio nelle Parole dell'Uomo* (Rome: Lateran University Press, 2002); E. Farley, *Theologia: The Fragmentation and Unity of Theological Education*, 2nd ed. (Philadelphia, PA: Fortress, 1983); P. Hünermann, "Neue 'Loci Theologici': ein Beitrag zur methodischen Erneuerung der Theologie," *Cristianesimo nella Storia* 24 (2003): 1–21. B. Körner, *Melchior Cano: De locis theologicis: Ein Beitrag zur theologischen Erkenntnislehre* (Graz, AT: Ulrich Moser, 1994); *La Frammentazione del Sapere teologico*, ed. G. Lorizio and S. Muratore (San Paolo, IT: Cinisello Balsamo, 1998); E. Salman, "Liturgie und Kunst als 'loci theologici,' zur 'Poetischen Theologie' von Alex Stock," *Ecclesia Orans* 19 (2002): 419–33; A. Scola, "Chiesa e metodo teologico in M. Cano," in *Avvenimento e traditione: Questioni di ecclesiologia* (Milan, IT: Jaca, 1987), 57–92; M. Seckler, "Die ekklesiologische Bedeutung des Systems der loci theologici: Erkenntnistheoretische Katholizität und strukturale Weisheit," in *Weisheit Gottes—Weisheit der Welt* [Festschrift for Joseph Ratzinger], ed. W. Baier et al. (St. Ottilien: EOS, 1987), 37–65; Seckler, "Die Communio-Ekklesiologie, die theologische Methode und die Loci-theologici-Lehre Melchior Canos," *Pontificia Academia Teologica Romana* 5 (2006): 17–43; T. Söding, "Die Seele der Theologie," *Communio* 35 (2006): 545–57. Of value to this day is Matthias J. Scheeben, *Handbuch der katholischen Dogmatik*, vol. 1, *Theologische Erkenntnislehre*, Gesammelte Schriften 3, ed. M. Grabmann (Freiburg im Breisgau: Herder, 1959 [first published 1873]). In a 1959 book review of this third imprint of Scheeben's grand nineteenth-century summary of Catholic theology, Professor Ratzinger wrote, concerning its first volume: "Es gibt keine neuere deutschsprachige Dogmatik, deren theologische Erkenntnislehre an äußerem Umfang und innerem Gewicht derjenigen Scheebens an die Seite gestellt werden könnte. . . . Daß diesem ersten Band der Scheeben-Dogmatik erst noch die Zeit seiner eigentlichen Fruchtbarkeit bevorsteht" ("Review of M. J. Scheeben, *Handbuch der katholischen Dogmatik*," *Klerusblatt* 39 [1959]: 421). He claims here that there is no German-language book on dogmatics that presents a broader or deeper presentation of theological epistemology than Scheeben's study and expresses confidence that its day is yet to come.

[5] In ch. 3 of bk. 1, Cano lists ten authorities: (1) Sacred Scripture, (2) the Tradition of Christ and his apostles, (3) the Catholic Church, (4) the councils, (5) the apostolic Church of Rome, (6) the old saints, (7) Scholastic theologians, including canonists, (8) natural reason, (9) philosophers following nature, including secular, imperial canonists, and finally (10) natural history (Melchior Cano, *De Locis Theologicis*, in *Theologia Cursus Completus*, 28 vols., ed. J. P. Minge [Paris: Migne, 1840–1845], 1:62–63; originally published Salamanca, ES: Roderich Vadilaeus, 1563; Migne ed. repr. from *Mechiori Cani Episcope Canariensis ex Ordine Praedicatorum Opera*, ed. H. Serry [Padua, IT: Johannes Manfré, 1762]).

have been motivated by the intention of providing, *intra muros*, a theological epistemology. After the International Theological Commission's publication of *Theology Today: Perspectives, Principles and Criteria*[6] in 2012, it is of particular interest to ponder how the former Supreme Pontiff might select and order the *loci theologici*. This is all the more intriguing and promising because the theologian Ratzinger is one of the most productive living theologians and has contributed much to a theological epistemology while never expressly writing something devoted exclusively to Cano's book.

Yet more than only being impeded in relating the unchanged *fides quae* of Catholic faith *ad extram*—that is, to an increasingly secularized world—the Catholic way of theologizing has changed significantly in the last fifty years—manifest in a particular and, in fact, quite normative manner in the Second Vatican Council's Dogmatic Constitution on Divine Revelation. To no small degree, it was the young theologian and *peritus* Ratzinger who ushered in a new and dynamic understanding of Scripture, Tradition, and the Magisterium when co-drafting *Dei Verbum*. He advocated apprehending revelation no longer as a static, instruction-theoretical occurrence—as neo-Scholastic theology had subscribed to—but as a spiritual, historical, personal, and dialogical event ingenerating discipleship. Scripture and Tradition are no longer the sources of revelation, but the means for transmitting revelation. Revelation is a person: the second Person of the Blessed Trinity, Jesus Christ, the definitive self-communication of the triune God. Unlike Hermes bringing a message to humankind from celestial realms, Jesus is not merely a divine messenger, but *is* the message. Ergo, for the authors of the conciliar texts, the later and much-discussed, -misunderstood, and -maligned term *aggiornamento* by no means implies accommodating Christian faith to the ways of the world. Nor does it mean a solipsistic redefinition or repositioning of the Church in modernity, as some representatives of the mass media then had assumed. Rather, the Italian term means making Christ unambiguously present and accessible for our own age and time.[7] In their opening words, the dogmatic constitutions

6 International Theological Commission, *Theology Today: Perspectives, Principles and Criteria*, accessed December 6, 2017, http://www.vatican.va/roman_curia/congregations/cfaith/cti_documents/rc_cti_doc_20111129_teologia-oggi_en.html.

7 Symptomatic for the misunderstanding defining the immediate postconciliar era is the statement by then-eminent theologian Karl Rahner, S.J., and his former student Herbert Vorgrimler: "The Council was a council of the Church about the Church [Das Konzil war ein Konzil der Kirche über die Kirche]" (Karl Rahner and Herbert Vorgrimler, *Kleines Konzilskompendium* [Freiburg im Breisgau: Herder, 1966], 24). To no small degree, this

Dei Verbum and *Lumen gentium* define the conciliar program of *aggiornamento*. It is centered on making God's very own Word, Jesus Christ, afresh, present, and comprehensible to a world that undergoes changes heretofore unparalleled in their suddenness and radicalness. Does this epochal, revolutionary Christocentric vision call for a recalibration of the *loci theologici*?[8] What might be the theologian Ratzinger's contribution to a discussion on the *loci theologici*?

Truth and Freedom

The newly appointed prefect of the Congregation for the Doctrine of the Faith delivered a lecture celebrating the twenty-fifth anniversary of the foundation of the much noted *Katholische Akademie in Bayern* in Munich, Germany, in 1982. There he spells out the inseparable connection between truth and freedom. He is acutely mindful that freedom cannot exist against truth and that, likewise, there can never be something like truth against freedom. Exclusively in relationship to one another do both prosper.

The great father of liturgical renewal, Romano Guardini (1885–1968), is quoted often by Ratzinger, saying: "Truth has such a clear and calm power. My aim in pastoral work [*Seelsorge*; 'caring for souls'] is this: to help by the power of the truth."[9]

A disciple of Augustine, Ratzinger is opposed to academic discourse as *l'art pour l'art*. It cannot engage in a solipsistic exercise, lest it miss the mark it intends. It must be bound to something grander than itself. For Augustine, the author of *Contra academicos*, academicians need to free themselves from a purely cerebral understanding of philosophy and live from contemplation. All philosophy ultimately intends reaching a numinous,

---

determined the reception of that council for many decades. Regarding the term *aggiornamento*, see: M. Quisinky, "Aggiornamento—aber wie?: die Konzilstheologen Henri de Lubac, SJ und Yves Congar, OP zwischen 'nouvelle théologie' und Konzilsrezeption," *Freiburger Zeitschrift für Philosophie und Theologie* 58 (2011): 5–33; D. del Gaudio, "Per una scienza dell'anima: La teologia sfidata," *Rassegna di teologia* 48 (2007): 921–24.

8 *Gaudium et spes* 22: "Christ the Lord, Christ the New Adam, in the very revelation of the mystery of the Father and of his love fully reveals man to himself and brings to light his most high calling." Consistent with this Christocentric shift, *Lumen gentium*, the Dogmatic Constitution on the Church, begins: "Lumen Gentium cum sit Christus" ("Christ is the light of the peoples").

9 Joseph Ratzinger, *The Nature and Mission of Theology*, trans. Adrian Walker (San Francisco: Ignatius Press, 1995), 92n20. See also Romano Guardini, *Wahrheit des Denkens und Wahrheit des Tuns: Notizen und Texte*, 3rd ed. (Paderborn: Schöningh, 1980), 80.

spiritual goal. At long last, and not without the aid of supernatural grace, this African Church Father realized that philosophizing means becoming Christian. Not reaching any level of contemplation of being makes one vulnerable to the temptation of being "maîtres et possesseurs de la nature," Ratzinger concludes. Invariably, such unmetaphysical thinking leads to the present-day debacle: human beings subjugating the environment (unbridled capitalism) and society (totalitarianism). He argues that genuine academic pursuit is free from any utilitarian interest. Possessing an authentic philosophical disposition means freedom from reification. Otherwise, one falls for a one-sided hermeneutics of praxis—as do all ideologies.[10] Provocatively, Ratzinger asks whether the Italian jurist and philosopher Giambattista Vico (1668–1744) is correct in saying that only what man produces (and only what is producible) counts as valid, or if, rather, truth exists prior to utilitarian interests.[11] He cites John 8:32 in response: "the truth will make you free." Only if the truth sought for possesses an inherent value apart from any immediate, quantifiable success is the philosopher free. As a consequence, Ratzinger advocates universities enjoying the right to exist independently from ulterior political or economic interests—and probably laments the current large-scale reductions of departments and the number of courses in the area of the humanities in the universities of Western Europe and, to a lesser degree, in North America. This singular and unparalleled phenomenon is a glaring symptom and confirmation of Ratzinger's thesis that unmetaphysical philosophy leads invariably to a horizontal, dull, and wholly uninspiring worldview that defines success in exclusively economic, scientific, and/or technical terms. Such a dramatic, dehumanizing development accentuates what Ratzinger warns of as the inescapable consequence of the sundering of truth and freedom: the question and riddle of human life is no longer thematized. But every generation and every person must pose this question anew. This defines the *humanum* in the human person and in society. In this context, he quotes the German nuclear physicist and Lutheran peace activist Carl Friedrich von Weizsäcker (1912–2007): "In the long term only a society oriented towards truth can flourish, not one oriented towards happiness."[12]

---

10 See Josef Pieper, *Was heißt akademisch?: zwei Versuche über die Universität heute*, 2nd ed. (Munich: Kösel, 1964).

11 Joseph Ratzinger, "Interpretation—Kontemplation—Aktion," *Communio* 12 (1983): 167–79, at 172: "Gilt Giambattista Vicos Definition, Wahrheit sei allein das Gemachte (und damit das Machbare) oder gilt der christliche Entscheid, daß Wahrheit dem Machen vorausliegt?"

12 Ratzinger, "Interpretation—Kontemplation—Aktion," 173.

This permits both the world to become true to us—in the sense that life's vivacity can speak immediately to us—and us to be true to ourselves, as truth purifies us from a naïve, autarkic self-understanding. Such insight in turn enables adoration and cult to come about for everyone. He reminds his listeners that, in its heyday, Plato's Academy (founded 387 BC) did not consider itself an intellectual club, but an independent, cultic association (*Kultverbund*) oriented toward sacrifice. Safeguarding "the freedom of truth" and "the truth of freedom" entails recognizing and adoring the numinous—which is ever beyond our manipulation.[13] Thereby, humankind also eludes the cold grip of *techne*.

Israel and the Old Testament

In the early 1970s, the theologian Ratzinger became an advisor to a loosely organized group of German Catholics called Katholische Integrierte Gemeinde. One of the reasons for the formation of this new international Catholic community of lay people, religious, and priests was the question of how the heinous crimes perpetrated against Jews could come about prior to and during World War II. This group further asked, "How could God have two brides, the *synagogue* (Israel) and the *ecclesia* (the Christian Church)?"[14] In the process, they alerted Catholics to the need to be mindful of Christian faith and theology as grounded in the faith of Israel and the Old Covenant and stressed the essential unity of the two Testaments. Pope Benedict XVI continues to maintain a close relationship with this group, which now operates an academy in Villa Cavaletti, near Frascati, and endows a chair at the Lateran University dedicated to a major *topos* of Vatican II: the theology of the people of God.

In a brief study written for this group, Ratzinger postulates the priority of the one Judeo-Christian covenant in the face of a plurality of religions. Amid a technically integrated world, he articulates the revolutionary vision of Jews and Christians reconciled and laboring together for peace in the world.[15] In 1994, at a Jewish-Christian conference in Jerusalem, Ratzinger closed his lecture with these words:

---

13 Ratzinger, "Interpretation—Kontemplation—Aktion," 174.

14 Emery de Gaál, *The Theology of Pope Benedict XVI: The Christocentric Shift* (New York: Palgrave Macmillan, 2010), 53.

15 See Joseph Ratzinger, *Die Vielfalt der Religionen und der eine Bund*, 4th ed. (Bad Tölz: Verlag Urfeld, 2005).

> Already as a child it was incomprehensible to me how some intended to deduce from Jesus' death a condemnation of Jews, as a profoundly consoling thought had deeply entered my soul: Jesus' blood arouses no claims for retribution, but calls to reconciliation. . . . Jews and Christians should accept one another in deep, interior reconciliation, not by ignoring one's own faith or let alone denying it, but rather from the depth of that faith itself. In their reciprocal reconciliation they should become a power of reconciliation to the world. By way of their witness to the one God, who cannot otherwise be worshipped but in the unity of love of God and of one's neighbor, they should open for this God a gate to the world, so that his will be done and it may be on earth "as it is in heaven": "so that His Kingdom might come."[16]

By Abraham, "all the families of the earth shall bless themselves" (Gen 12:3). It is the commission of the people of the Old Covenant to announce their God to all nations. Christians are the heirs to this faith. In Christian liturgy, one hears "the voices of Moses and the prophets," and "Israel's book of psalms is also the big prayer book of the Church." Ratzinger ties the woman adorned with twelve stars in Revelation 12 back to Israel and Mary giving birth to the one destined to rule the nations "with an iron scepter" (Psalm 2:9; author's translation). With Paul, Christians esteem Israel (Rom 9:4–5), as its "gifts and the call of God are irrevocable" (Rom 11:29). In sum, Israel's faith is the *conditio sine qua non* for Christian theology.[17]

When reflecting on the crisis of catechesis at a conference held at Fourvière, France, in 1983, Ratzinger emphasized that Scripture is not merely a record meant to satisfy the curiosity of the historian, but is of far greater relevance to theology, to understanding God's plan of salvation. Never does it relativize Israel's narrative as a mere Christian *adiaphoron*. It verbalizes far more than historical facts. At every stage, the whole canon assists in discerning God's action in Israel's history. The complete Bible facilitates an encounter with the living God in which also Jesus Christ and the Holy Spirit manifest themselves. Amid the vicissitudes of history, the

---

[16] *30 Jahre Wegbegleitung: Joseph Ratzinger, Papst Benedikt XVI und die Katholische Integrierte Gemeinde*, ed. T. Wallbrecher, L. Weimer, and A. Stötzel (Bad Tölz: Verlag Urfeld, 2006), 90.

[17] Ratzinger, 1994 Jerusalem Lecture, in Wallbrecher, Weimer, and Stötzel, *30 Jahre Wegbegleitung*, 99–101.

complete canon retains its integral identity and becomes an instrument of a divine–human encounter.[18]

In spite of their small numbers and dispersion from their homeland, the Jews remained one people loyal to the Old Covenant for over two thousand years. This fact in and of itself, says Ratzinger, must stir up Christians to appreciate Israel more. This fact suggests something most unusual operative in the case of the Israelites. The people of the Old Covenant always preserved their faith and identity. In their singular steadfastness, the people of the Old Covenant reveal something of "God's mystery." And it is "Christianity [that] . . . sprang out of the story of Israel and is inseparably bound up with it."[19]

Christians are convinced that the Old Testament's content is oriented toward Jesus Christ. This dignifies Israel in a unique way. The texts of the Old Testament, composed at various stages in Israel's long history, possess from their earliest beginnings an entelechy toward the Lord and are understood in their deepest meaning through the mystery of the Incarnation. Christianity is not a radically different or new religion, but organically unfolds and realizes the religion of Israel. In his ethnicity and religion, Jesus is a Jew. Reading the Old Testament, one recognizes that the Christian faith is not artificially superimposed upon first-century Palestine.

On the contrary, with Jesus Christ, the Old Testament is no longer "an unfinished fragment," but part of a grand *symphonia*, as the Church Fathers teach: the symphony of prophets and apostles.[20] Having stated this, Ratzinger demonstrates his acute awareness that Israel continues to have a particular calling to this very day. Israel's mission to the world includes its status as standing at the gate of Christianity without entering it. Thus it occupies a particular place in God's saving plans for humankind. By its very nature, all Christian theologizing incorporates this as one of its *loci*—lest it denies the continuum of its own historically evolving identity.

JESUS CHRIST AND THE BLESSED TRINITY

A line from Matthew's Gospel constitutes the heart of Ratzinger's theology: "He who finds his life will lose it, and he who loses his life for my

[18] Joseph Ratzinger, *Die Krise der Katechese und Ihre Überwindung: Rede in Frankreich* (Einsiedeln: Johannes, 1983), 28–30.

[19] Joseph Ratzinger, *God and the World: A Conversation with Peter Seewald*, trans. Henry Taylor (San Francisco: Ignatius Press, 2002), 148.

[20] Ratzinger, *The Nature and Mission of Theology*, 83. See also Ratzinger, *God and the World*, 149–50.

sake will find it" (Matt 10:39). This is the basis for the conversion of the great German theologian and precursor of liturgical renewal Romano Guardini. It situates the theological *locus* of Ratzinger on a grand arch spanning from the Transfiguration of Our Lord on Mount Tabor (Mark 9:2–10), through the conversion of Paul on the road to Damascus (Acts 9:1–19), through Augustine of Hippo, Anselm of Canterbury, the Victorines, Bonaventure, Blaise Pascal, and John Henry Newman, all the way to Guardini in the twentieth century. Some call it the illuminatist tradition. In each case, this line of theological thought expresses well that divine initiative brings about sudden conversion and that therein exists the indispensable spiritual basis for theology. Consequently, the words of Paul—"I have been crucified with Christ; it is no longer I who live, but Christ who lives in me; and the life I now live in the flesh I live by faith in the Son of God, who loved me and gave himself for me" (Gal 2:20)—are foundational for Ratzinger's understanding of theology.

There is a spiritual, existential, and sacramental ground for theologizing: Jesus Christ.[21] A change of subject occurs. The "I" of the individual human person ceases to be autonomous and voluntarily enters the greater "I" of the Church, and is thereby configured into Jesus Christ. Faith means partaking in Jesus Christ's vision of God.[22] In silent prayer, Christ is in unity with his divine Father. Theology means to think by assent. Volition means, for both Aquinas and Ratzinger, affirmation of something beyond our own human making. Human volition and heart are "touched by God." When receiving an honorary doctoral degree at Wrocław University in Poland, he elaborated: If the ground of the human soul is touched by God's Word, the whole of the human person assents to the whole of Christian faith. However, the desire to give account of Christian hope drives the theologian to capture this assent as "a pilgrimage of cognition."[23] Bonaventure concedes that there is some kind of violence to reason that cannot be brought into harmony with faith. Nevertheless, he affirms that there is also an inquiry inspired by another motive: "Faith can wish to understand because it is moved by love for the One upon whom it has bestowed its consent."[24] The salient feature of faith is its nature as gift, which grants a new beginning to human thought in the form of Christian theology. Faith

[21] Ratzinger, *The Nature and Mission of Theology*, 45–72.

[22] Joseph Ratzinger, *Behold the Pierced One*, trans. Graham Harrison (San Francisco: Ignatius Press, 1986), 37–38.

[23] Joseph Ratzinger, *Weggemeinschaft des Glaubens: Kirche als Communio* (Augsburg: St. Ulrich, 2002), 15–25.

[24] Ratzinger, *The Nature and Mission of Theology*, 27.

addresses reason, but it obliges theology to grow out of its encounter with the living Lord. It requires a conversion that is a departure from heretofore known patterns, which may often be a form of hopeless self-imprisonment, and an entry into the radicalness of Jesus Christ.[25]

"The knowledge of God is a way; it means discipleship. It is not revealed to the uncommitted, permanently neutral observer but, rather, is disclosed in the measure in which one sets out on the way."[26] Such knowledge requires deep conversion so that it remains a constant encounter. True reasoning requires "a purification of heart." It is bound to the *Logos* and includes death and resurrection. Christian thinking arose from the need for catechesis on the Paschal Mystery. Current theologizing will renew itself by being cognizant of this origin.

The new being in Christ has a sacramental structure, "for you are one in Christ Jesus" (Gal 3:28). Ratzinger emphasizes that the text in German does not read "ihr seid eins" ("you are one thing"), but "ihr seid einer" ("you are one person"). Christians become a fused subject with Christ.[27] This is not, however, in the Plotinian sense of fusion into one undifferentiated divine reality. They retain their personalities precisely as Christified individuals. However, while sin is the riddle of separation turning individuals against one another, baptism is the mystery of unity and peace. He reminds one that, for Gregory of Nyssa, it is just as inappropriate to speak of three gods as it is to speak of Christians in the plural.[28]

The prologue to John's Gospel insists forcefully that in Jesus Christ nothing short of a congruence of "truth" (*aletheia*) and *Logos* occur: "And the Word became flesh and dwelt among us, full of grace and truth" (John 1:14). *Logos* does not mean simply divine revelation, and "truth" does not signify merely "trustworthiness." To interpret Scripture as not conjoining these two terms in the person of the Redeemer amounts to a denial of the symbiosis that Hellas and the Bible had entered already prior to the Incarnation. Among other locations, this is intimated in a statement from 1 Peter 3:15: "Always be prepared to make a defense to any one who calls you to account for the hope that is in you." Combining Bonaventure's interpretation

---

[25] Ratzinger, *The Nature and Mission of Theology*, 50–51.

[26] Joseph Ratzinger, *Dogma and Preaching*, trans. Michael J. Miller and Matthew J. O'Connell (San Francisco: Ignatius Press, 2011), 87.

[27] Joseph Ratzinger, *Wesen und Auftrag der Theologie: Versuche zu ihrer Ortsbestimmung im Disput der Gegenwart* (Einsiedeln: Johannes 1993), 44 [English: *The Nature and Mission of Theology*, 52].

[28] Joseph Ratzinger, *Die Einheit der Nationen: Eine Vision der Kirchenväter* (Salzburg/Munich: Pustet, 1971), 32–33.

of "the *locus classicus* for the justification of systematic theology in general" with Augustine's understanding of Christian faith, Ratzinger observes:

> The Greek text is by far more expressive than any translation. Believers are enjoined to give an *apo-logia* regarding the *logos* of our hope to whoever asks for it. The *logos* must be so intimately their own that it can become *apo-logia*; through the mediation of Christians, the Word [*Wort*] becomes response [*Antwort*] to man's questions. . . . Christian faith can say of itself, I have found love. Yet love for Christ and of one's neighbor for Christ's sake can enjoy stability and consistency only if its deepest motivation is love for the truth.[29]

Of overriding importance for the success of theology, and for the credibility of all individual scholars, is apprehending this academic discipline as a lived response to the divine Person who is "the way, and the truth, and the life" (John 14:6). On the part of the theologian, this requires a constant rapport with Jesus Christ. It thrives wherever the joy of Christian interiority is lived.

Faith and Reason

The theologian Ratzinger, as Pope Benedict XVI, has repeatedly underlined the intrinsic relationship between faith and reason: in his doctoral dissertation on Augustine, in his *Habilitationsschrift* on Bonaventure, and again during his inaugural lecture at the University of Bonn. More recently, he discussed this germane topic in a 1999 lecture on the encyclical *Fides et ratio* at the Sorbonne University in Paris, during his conversation with philosopher Jürgen Habermas in 2004, in his much noted *Regensburg Address* in 2006, and at the Paris *Collège des Bernardins* in 2008.[30] Ancient philosophy refers to a unifying rational divine reality. The pre-Socratic philosophers had assumed a numinous "One" that unites the multifarious and perishable things in the contingent world. The Roman scholar Mar-

---

29 Ratzinger, *The Nature and Mission of Theology*, 26–27.

30 See Jürgen Habermas and Joseph Ratzinger, *The Dialectics of Secularization: On Reason and Religion* (San Francisco: Ignatius Press, 2006); Pope Benedict XVI / Joseph Ratzinger, Regensburg Address on Faith, Reason, and the University: "Memories and Reflections" (September 12, 2006), available from http://www.vatican.va; and "Address at the Collège des Bernardins" (September 12, 2008), available from http://www.vatican.va.

cus Terentius Varro (116–27 BC) had contrasted *theologia naturalis* with *theologia mythica vel civilis*. Natural theology he identifies as true philosophy. Without apprehending it as a personal entity, Heraclitus encapsulates divine reason as *Logos*. This *Logos* addresses human reason. Ratzinger uses these thoughts to illustrate that in Christian faith "enlightenment has become part of religion" in a positive sense of the term. It demythologizes "poetry and politics" and rests on genuine insight.[31]

He holds that godless reason lacks a compass. It is debated whether Ratzinger believes, in agreement with Augustine, that only faith in God allows man to be rational.[32] However, as prefect, he did warn equally against "pathologies of unbelieving reason" and "pathologies of unbelieving religion." The latter might mean controlling God or reifying belief to further ulterior interests. The correlation between faith and reason is so essential that, ultimately, only a religion that binds the human person to God is capable of vouching for a reason that is universally valid. Such an understanding invariably identifies both fideism and rationalism as equally untenable. In the line of argumentation established by Varro, Ratzinger holds that Christian revelation is joined to Greek philosophy's "enlightenment." Further, as truth is pre-given, he warns against reducing reason to whatever momentary discourse can establish a consensus—as his interlocutor, the German philosopher Jürgen Habermas (1929–), also advocates. There is a metaphysical ground of truth that precedes any social, communicative discernment. Thought and speech are grounded in a reality defying any sociological reduction. Christian faith orients all of life and every human being to something greater than simply stating "what is the case" horizontally, à la Ludwig Wittgenstein (1889–1951).

Jesus Christ places all of reality under the purpose of charity as expressed on the Cross. Only if God is rational can human beings own a hope not defined facilely by the positive sciences. As a consequence, Habermas readily admits that there is no alternative to the Judeo-Christian ethos, lest society becomes inhumane.[33] The Christian is the true philosopher, as he has knowledge of the nature of death, argues Ratzinger. The one who vanquished death in his Resurrection, Jesus Christ, becomes the true philosopher par excellence to late antiquity. Subsequent Christian apolo-

---

31 Joseph Ratzinger, *Truth and Tolerance: Christian Belief and World Religion*, trans. Henry Taylor (San Francisco: Ignatius Press, 2003), 170.

32 K. M. Menke, "Quaerere Deum: Joseph Ratzingers Plädoyer für die Unabdingbarkeit der Wahrheitsfrage," *Theologie und Glaube* 100 (2010): 133–48, at 136.

33 Jürgen Habermas, "Über Gott und die Welt: Eduardo Medieta im Gespräch mit Jürgen Habermas," *Befristete Zeit* 3 (1999): 190–209, at 191.

gists such as Justin Martyr pointed out that in Christ the search for life's meaning arrives at its fulfillment, and absurdity is no longer an option.[34] A rejection of the role of philosophy in theology, à la Martin Luther, is not viable, as human language is inextricably drenched in philosophical terms. Furthermore, interpreting faith as paradox—as Karl Barth famously attempts—offers only a cul-de-sac, as such faith offers no answers to the pressing philosophical questions every human being entertains.[35] Since theology involves discipleship and ministry, it maintains a dialogue between faith and reason cognizant of "a mutual relationship" between the two, since "neither can wholly dispense with the other."[36]

Quite forcefully, Ratzinger warns theologians against being lured into turning their discipline into religious studies or a history of religion for the short-term benefit of remaining plausible and acceptable to the contemporary scientific-technical age. If theology abdicates its commitment to a rationality grounded in God, it loses its relevance in the choir of academic disciplines. In this context, Ratzinger recalls a story from C. S. Lewis's *The Screwtape Letters*. There, a student-demon of deception complains to his teacher-demon that people read books full of truth and wisdom, thereby threatening his attempts to lure them into a world of falsehood. The teacher-demon calms such fears by telling the student-demon that educated readers nowadays see everything as merely historically conditioned, and therefore as relative. Likewise, in *The Abolition of Man*, Lewis argues that the failure to uphold the absolute, binding nature of truth makes philosophy and theology complicit in the larger cultural project of reducing human beings to animals.[37]

In his much discussed talk at the Collège des Bernardins in Paris in 2008, Ratzinger goes further. As every academic discipline is ordered toward self-transcendence when embarking on a *quaerere veritatem*, it requires ultimately a *quaerere Deum*. In principle, human cognition must be open to the possibility of God becoming epiphanic in human thought and action. This necessary movement of any human cognition is complemented and answered from the side of Christian revelation. For Christian theology, critical rationality does not approach faith externally, but rather as complementary and necessary as it strives for universality—which invari-

34 Ratzinger, *The Nature and Mission of Theology*, 13–15.

35 Ratzinger, *The Nature and Mission of Theology*, 20–21.

36 Ratzinger, *The Nature and Mission of Theology*, 24.

37 Joseph Ratzinger, "Die Einheit des Glaubens und die Vielfalt der Kulturen: Reflektionen im Anschluß an die Enzyklika 'Fides et Ratio,'" *Theologie und Glaube* 89 (1999): 141–52, at 142–43.

ably entails intelligibility.[38] The common basis is the rationality inherent to both created reality and supernatural faith. For Christians, this coincidence occurs in Jesus Christ as the *Logos*: the coincidence par excellence of faith and reason.

Scripture and Tradition

In his Bonaventure studies, Ratzinger discovered that Scripture is far from synonymous with revelation. To the Doctor Seraphicus, revelation is an event wherein God allows access to himself in the historic Incarnation of his Son Jesus Christ.[39] This process is perfected in the life-giving space of the Church professing the apostolic faith.[40] In contrast to Josef Rupert Geiselmann (1890–1970) and Reformation theology's insistence on the principle of *sola scriptura*, Ratzinger's research into the theology of Bonaventure and the Council of Trent allows him to apprehend a more comprehensive understanding of revelation. He argued, along with Cardinal Josef Frings, his advisee at Vatican II, that identifying Scripture and Tradition as the "sources" of revelation is not in keeping with the understanding of revelation as expressed by the Church from her beginnings and well into the early part of modernity. Accordingly, following Ratzinger's discovery in the writings of Bonaventure, the dogmatic constitution *Dei Verbum* centers revelation in Christ. Previously, fundamental theology had referred to Jesus Christ under the heading *De Christo legato*, thus reducing Our Lord to a messenger. With Guardini, Ratzinger recognizes in Jesus Christ both messenger *and* message, revealer and revelation at the same time. Thereby, the Council Fathers, Ratzinger, and other *periti* frustrate, *ab initio*, any attempt to render Christ palatable to a pluralistic redefinition.

Under the fresh impression of Vatican II, in 1965, Ratzinger authored an entry titled "Tradition III: Systematisch" for a theological encyclopedia.[41] There he argues that Christian tradition liberates us from both hu-

---

38 Ratzinger, "Die Einheit des Glaubens und die Vielfalt der Kulturen," 147–48.

39 Prior to Ratzinger, one finds such thought already in the main French representatives of *ressourcement* theology. See Jean Daniélous, S.J., "La théologie et ses sources," *Recherches de science religieuse* 33 (1946): 385–401; and Henri de Lubac, "La problème du développement du dogme," *Recherches de science religieuse* 35 (1948): 130–60. See also Martin Hengel, *The Four Gospels and the One Gospel of Jesus Christ: An Investigation of the Collection and Origin of the Canonical Gospels* (Harrisburg, PA: Trinity, 2000).

40 Joseph Ratzinger, *Milestones: Memoirs, 1927–1977*, trans. Erasmo Leiva-Merikakis (San Francisco: Ignatius Press, 1998), 103–14.

41 Joseph Ratzinger, "Tradition III: Systematisch," *Lexikon für Theologie und Kirche*, 2nd ed., vol. 10 (Freiburg im Breisgau: Herder, 1965), 294–99.

man customs evolving in history and Gnostic speculations. Christian tradition preserves the *Jesusüberlieferung*, the singular Jesus Christ narrative/tradition, as something alive and enlivening: "the Lord is the Spirit" (2 Cor 3:17). This attests to the salutary transformation of human existence into Christ, and Ratzinger cites Tertullian's remark that Christ called himself the "Truth," not "custom."[42]

Such an organic understanding of Scripture and Tradition was prepared in the nineteenth century by the Tübingen School of Theology, Blessed John Henry Newman, and Maurice Blondel. Christ left no written document. Moreover, Tradition is more than a catalogue of insights into revelation handed down orally. It is a comprehensive process of accepting, living, interpreting, and handing down revelation parallel to and through Scripture. Likewise, Scripture is more than simply a book. It is the product of a Church living already in a Tradition accepting and attesting to revelation. Therefore, it would be shortsighted to present Christianity as "a religion of the book."[43] Analogously, the Bible is not the result of a divine dictation, but thrives in the ambience called "Tradition."[44] Such correlation of the two occurs in the Church. Ratzinger had presented this understanding already in 1958 in a relatively brief essay.[45] With this *instrumentarium*, the Church is able, in one stroke, both to affirm the historicity and personal nature of revelation and, at the same time, to fend off a Deistic understanding of God.

The reservations the Pontifical Bible Commission had previously expressed concerning the historical-critical method are not only overcome, but this method, when properly used, is now deemed indispensable. As *Dei Verbum* 12 emphasizes, Tradition is no external, alien authority, but is the living context in which the Scriptures must be interpreted. The correlation between Scripture and Tradition enables something significant to come to light: the biblical text is open, and reading it is an ongoing process.[46] The Christ-event inaugurates a definitive *relecture* of the Old

---

42 Tertullian, *De virginibus velandis* 1.1.

43 *Catechism of the Catholic Church* (Washington, DC: United States Conference of Catholic Bishops, 2000), 108.

44 Brevard S. Childs coined the phrase "canonical approach" in *Biblical Theology of the Old and New Testaments: Theological Reflections on the Christian Bible* (Minneapolis, MN: Fortress, 1993).

45 Joseph Ratzinger, "Offenbarung—Schrift—Überlieferung: Ein Text des Hl. Bonaventura und seine Bedeutung für die gegenwärtige Theologie," *Trierer Theologische Zeitschrift* 67 (1958): 13–27.

46 See R. Voderholzer, "Offenbarung, Schrift und Kirche," *Communio* 39 (2010): 287–303, at 297.

Testament from Christ and toward Christ. The time-honored practice of *lectio divina* is relevant for every Christian, as well as every theologian. For Ratzinger, good theology is cognizant of the inseparable unity of Scripture and Tradition, as interpreted by the Church. The three are but different aspects of the one reality of divine self-communication.[47] The implication is that only within the defined matrix of Scripture, Tradition, and Church is theology, as an academic discipline, viable.

CHURCH AND LITURGY

Obedience to the greater ambience of the Church must come from the theologian's heart. It is trust in the greater knowledge of the Church spanning the globe and the millennia. And here it must be emphasized that the Church is far more than a sociological entity. Commenting on the twelfth chapter of Paul's First Letter to the Corinthians, Ratzinger says: "The Church is in no wise a separate subject endowed with its own subsistence. The new subject is much rather 'Christ' himself, and the Church is nothing but the space of this new unitary subject, which is, therefore, much more than mere sociological interaction." Then, citing 1 Corinthians 10:17—"Because there is one bread, we who are many are one body"—he explains that *soma* in Greek translates as "one subject" and that this Pauline term includes the dimensions of bodiliness and historicity.[48]

At the center of the mystery of the Church is the transformation of bread and wine into the Body and Blood of the Lord in the Eucharist (transubstantiation).[49] Thus, existence is, at its root, personal. Divine persons and finite persons are perceived as relational. Ratzinger points out that while in the Eucharistic Prayer the first person plural ("we") is used, this becomes first person singular ("I") during the communion. "Conversion does not lead to a private relationship with Jesus."[50] The acid test of one's conversion occurs in the Church: "He who finds his life will lose it, and he who loses his life for my sake will find it" (Matt 10:39). The incarnate Word remains in the flesh in the Church. Quoting Guardini, Ratzinger observes:

---

[47] R. Voderholzer, "Dogmatik im Geiste des Konzils," *Trierer theologische Zeitschrift* 115 (2006): 149–66, at 162.

[48] Ratzinger, *The Nature and Mission of Theology*, 53–54.

[49] When referring to liturgy, Ratzinger usually means the Eucharist. See also H.-J. Schutz, *Die apostolische Herkunft der Evangelien: Zum Ursprung der Evangelienform in der urgemeindlichen Paschafeier*, 3rd ed. (Freiburg im Breisgau: Herder, 1997).

[50] Ratzinger, *The Nature and Mission of Theology*, 59.

> Christ's Church never ceases to challenge the individual to give his own life, so that he might receive it again in a new and authentic form." Obedience to the Church is the concreteness of our obedience to [Jesus Christ]. The Church is that new and greater subject in which past and present, subject and object come into contact. The Church is our contemporaneity with Christ: there is no other.[51]

This circumstance establishes the close nexus between liturgy and the Church.[52] It furnishes an ecclesial hermeneutics not based on an institution, hierarchy, or juridical entity, but on a living organism. It is not invented by human beings, but grounded in the Eucharist, a divine gift. This notion is prefigured in the Eucharistic ecclesiologies of Guardini and Henri de Lubac (1896–1991) and was developed in critical dialogue with the Russian exile theologian Nikolai Afanas'ev (1893–1966). The innermost being of the Church is Jesus Christ.[53] The Church is a living subject with a concrete identity.[54] Ratzinger is happy to point to the opening words of the Second Vatican Council's Dogmatic Constitution on the Church: "Lumen Gentium cum sit Christus"—Christ is the light of humanity. The Church reflects the Lord's effulgence. The Jews had held fast to the notion of the unity of the Passover and the temple as the source of unity for the covenantal people of God. Now, Jesus, accused of destroying the temple, becomes the new temple (Matt 12:6; 27:40). In a lecture held in 1958 in Salzburg, the promising young theologian stated that Jesus Christ "is the only place of God's presence among people, and whoever wishes to come to God must come through Him."[55] Secondary concepts such as primacy, episcopacy, and priesthood can be properly apprehended only from the overarching reality of the Church's liturgical-sacramental life. On this point, his understanding is informed by Odo Casel, Gottlieb Söhngen,

---

51 Ratzinger, *The Nature and Mission of Theology*, 60.

52 See *Der Logos-gemäße Gottesdienst: Theologie der Liturgie bei Joseph Ratzinger*, ed. R. Voderholzer, Ratzinger-Studien 1 (Regensburg: Pustet, 2009).

53 Romano Guardini, *Die Kirche des Herrn: Meditationen über Wesen und Auftrag der Kirche* (Freiburg im Breisgau: Herder, 1969), 41.

54 In his inaugural lecture in Bonn, Guardini developed the notion of the Church as the true subject of theology; see Romano Guardini, "Anselm von Canterbury und das Wesen der Theologie," in *Auf dem Wege: Versuche* (Mainz: Matthias Grünewald, 1923).

55 Joseph Ratzinger, "Kirche und Liturgie," in *Mitteilungen des Institut-Papst-Benedikt XVI*, ed. Rudolf Voderholzer, Christian Schaller, and Franz-Xaver Heibl (Regensburg: Schnell & Steiner, 2008), 13–27.

and de Lubac.[56] He cites Augustine's dictum: the Church is *Christus totus, caput et corpus.*[57] Cult, or liturgy, and Church live from one another:

> Wherever there is . . . liturgy, there also is the whole Church. Also where the priest prays his breviary in solitude, or where an ever so small congregation gathers to celebrate the Eucharist, it is in truth the whole Church, co-praying, co-sacrificing and co-loving in hidden manner.[58]

One can cavalierly disregard the liberal notion, à la Hugues Felicité Lammenais (1782–1854), of Jesus being of interest while the Church is a failed undertaking, as this *bon mot* is oblivious to the exegetical evidence and consequently fails understanding both who Jesus Christ is and what the sacramental essence of the Church is. As Paul informs us, the Church is the mystical body of Christ: "so we, though many, are one body in Christ" (Rom 12:5). By virtue of communion, the Church partakes in the Eucharistic Lord and is defined from this relationship. This insight is captured in the *communio* ecclesiology, a core teaching of Vatican II, as advocated by Ratzinger and others. The Eucharist unites people and peoples among one another by uniting them to Jesus Christ. Quoting from a Mozarabic prayer, *Lumen Gentium* 26 states: ". . . so that, by means of the flesh and blood of the Lord the whole brotherhood of the Body may be welded together." The attendant realities are the local churches forming one Eucharistic community in the one Lord (*Ad Gentes* 19–22). As the Eucharist is common to all, an isolation of any particular church from another or from the universal Church is theologically not possible, lest one do an injustice to what both the Eucharist and the particular churches are in their essences. In a similar vein, one cannot do justice to the local churches without doing justice to the universal Church, and vice-versa. At a 1985 conference in Foggia, Italy, Ratzinger succinctly concluded: "I can have the Lord only in unity, which He is, in unity with others,

---

[56] See: Henri de Lubac, *Catholicism and the Common Destiny of Man*, trans. Lancelot C. Sheppard and Sr. Elizabeth Englund, O.C.D. (San Francisco: Ignatius Press, 1988); de Lubac, *Corpus Mysticum: the Eucharist and the Church in the Middle Ages, Historical Survey*, trans. Gemma Simmonds, C. J., Richard Price, and Christopher Stevens, ed. Laurence Paul Hemming and Frank Parsons (Notre Dame, IN: University of Notre Dame, 2007).

[57] Augustine, *In Ioannem* 1.2: "Verbum caro factum est, et habitavit in nobis; illi caro adiungitur ecclesia, est Christus totus, caput et corpus."

[58] Ratzinger, "Kirche und Liturgie," 20.

who *also* are His body and should will to become this ever anew in the Eucharist."[59]

The Church Fathers and History

Ratzinger calls to mind that the Christ mystery is, for the Church Fathers, one of unity and unification.[60] As Paul assures us, "[Christ] is our peace" (Eph 2:14) who tears down separating walls, alienation, and enmity.[61] Jesus Christ restores the original unity. Already for early Christian theology, this means that the figure of Christ is of central historic import for human society and the individual. This is gained afresh in every age by beholding Our Lord with the eyes of the early Church. Christ enables a unity that permeates all books of Scripture and all forms of human existence. By dehistorizing Tradition, one diminishes the role of the Church Fathers and, consequently, reduces Christian faith to a momentary event with little connection to a particular past. Yet more importantly, the Church Fathers are teachers of an essentially undivided Christendom and, therefore, can contribute to a common basis in ecumenical dialogue. The Church Fathers recognized in time and space something sacramental and eschatological and used this view as their interpretament for history. By deliberately incorporating the Patristic heritage into theologizing, theologians consciously affirm history as salvation history. Ratzinger carries over an image of Patristic theology to bear out the relationship between Christ and his Church. In the Church, the Fathers see the moon generating no light on its own, but passing on Christ's sun.[62]

Much like word and response, so too Scripture and the Church Fathers—as the primordial responses—belong together, actually providing the organic basis for and dignifying the value of all subsequent responses, rather than denying them. Therefore, to Ratzinger, more than merely of antiquarian interest, the Church Fathers are of lasting—in fact, consti-

---

59 ". . . deshalb kann ich den einen Herrn nur in der Einheit haben, die er selber ist, in der Einheit mit den anderen, die *auch* sein Leib sind und in der Eucharistie es immer neu werden sollen" (Joseph Ratzinger, "Die Ekklesiologie des Zweiten Vatikanums," *Communio* 15 [1986]: 41–52, at 46).

60 Joseph Ratzinger, *Principles of Catholic Theology: Building Stones for a Fundamental Theology*, trans. Sr. Mary Frances McCarthy, S.N.D. (San Francisco: Ignatius Press, 1987), 133–52.

61 Joseph Ratzinger, *Die Einheit der Nationen: Eine Vision der Kirchenväter* (Salzburg/Munich: Pustet, 1971), 32.

62 Joseph Ratzinger, *Weggemeinschaft des Glaubens*, 121.

tutive—relevance to Christian theology as they have (1) perceived Christian faith as *philosophia*, (2) established the basic liturgical forms, and (3) formed the canon of Scripture. Today's theological reflection, liturgies, and use of Scripture would be unimaginable without the Patristic genius. The Fathers understood theology as eminently rational, as *Logos*- and faith-filled philosophy. Jesus Christ is the rational *Logos* illuminating all of reality. This *Logos* is already in pre-Christian times the philosophically—albeit only implicitly—sought-for truth. The ever greater effulgence of divine Truth vis-à-vis contingent, but nevertheless theonomous, human rationality is captured in the Augustinian words *credo ut intelligam*, paradigmatic for all subsequent generations of theologians.[63] The Church Fathers were not interested in establishing a theoretical system, but in preaching and bearing witness to the Truth. For them, theology was spoken ministry. Ratzinger forcefully affirms the *unanimus consensus Patrum* as relevant to every age of theological investigation.[64]

Sensus Fidelium and Magisterium

The Church as a social reality is the appropriate vessel of Scripture, Tradition, the *sensus fidelium*, and the teaching office. This implies apprehending the sense of the faithful and the Magisterium as one, dynamic unit of divine, salvific self-communication. Therefore, neither can be understood as the sole means of establishing faith, nor can either be seen as extrinsic to the believing community. The faithful, as bearers of the common priesthood of all, are an expression of "expanding Christian liturgy into the world" and universe. Discipleship cannot be one that simply affirms indiscriminately the values of the secular realm, nor may it passively accept creedal statements that have been handed down. Rather, by drawing from Scripture and the teaching office, it affirms the biblical testimony of the crucifixion of the God-man as defined also by the Magisterium at the Council of Chalcedon in AD 451. Together, both the *sensus fidelium* and the Magisterium serve the "becoming present" of the Passion and Resurrection of Jesus Christ. Amid the justified enthusiasm Vatican II unleashed, Ratzinger wrote: "Whoever lives as Christian in the world and truly attempts to live as Christian not according to the 'pattern of this world' (cf. 1 Cor 7:31; Rom 12:2), will necessarily experience faith also as 'sword,' piercing his earthly existence (cf. Heb 4:12; Lk

63 See: Augustine, Sermon 43, 7ff; Epistle 120, 1.3; *In Ioannem* 27.7; 29.6; and 40.9.

64 Ratzinger, *Principles of Catholic Theology*, 136–37.

2:35)."[65] Christian witness requires content, but the creedal content experiences verbalization and existential expression in the tension between *sensus fidelium* and Magisterium. For this reason, Christian faith cannot collapse into either crude fundamentalism or simple gnosis.

The reality underlying this unity is found in the third Person of the Blessed Trinity, the Holy Spirit. The Christians, the bishops, and the Church as a whole are products of the Holy Spirit. Ratzinger reminds his readers that, in Greek tragedies, as well as subsequently in the Book of Wisdom, Philo, and the Sibyls, God was designated *episkopos*, the one keeping watch over human behavior. Philo expands this term to include Moses as *episkopos*.[66] In the First Letter of Clement, this use is continued.[67] Upon this etymological background, it becomes obvious that a council cannot be a parliament, nor are bishops delegates of a sovereign people. All represent Christ, as Ratzinger demonstrates in *Das neue Volk Gottes*, penned shortly after Vatican II. Bishops are delegated by Christ, who grants them mission and ordination. Similarly, a pope is not a speaker appointed by bishops, but the one commissioned by Christ as the head of "the Twelve" and formed to "a collegial and monarchical organ." The Twelve represent the old covenantal people of God, which existed as twelve tribes centered around one religion and cult. As all ecclesial realities are indebted to Christ for their existence, neither bishops nor the people of God are subservient to one another (Mark 3:14); no one is condemned to a passive role of mere obedience and execution. "Rather, both are organs in the living whole of the body of Christ, which as a whole is the tent of God's Word in this aeon."[68]

The individual believer and the people of God find themselves in Peter's profession: "You are the Christ, the Son of the living God" (Matt 16:16). Ratzinger shows that the subsequent verses 17–19 bear out that this profession of faith does not reflect a human achievement; rather, God himself imparts this knowledge to Peter. Nevertheless, faith requires personal attestation. In Peter's words, something like a paradigm of everyone's faith is captured. The "we-unity of Christians" ("Die Wir-Einheit der Christen") is encapsulated in Peter's words and, henceforth, in the Petrine ministry.[69] It is entry into and part of the divine, who in turn reveals him-

[65] Joseph Ratzinger, "Sentire ecclesiam," *Geist und Leben* 36 (1963): 321–26, at 325.

[66] Philo, *Quis rerum divinarum heres sit* 30.

[67] 1 Clem 59:3.

[68] Joseph Ratzinger, *Das neue Volk Gottes* (Düsseldorf: Patmos, 1969), 169–70.

[69] Joseph Ratzinger, "Der Primat des Papstes und die Einheit des Gottesvolkes" [originally, 1978], in *Joseph Ratzinger Gesammelte Schriften*, vol. 8.1, ed. Gerhard Ludwig Müller (Freiburg im Breisgau: Herder, 2010), 660–675, at 666.

self as a "we," more precisely as a divine triune reality. The ecclesial "we" cannot thrive without the ecclesial "I," and vice-versa. This correlation of the divine and human in Peter is borne out in *Lumen Gentium* 8 when it refers to the Church's nature as "one complex reality."

Scripture is much more than a record of something past—it is an ongoing and always present event wherever it is read. The Eucharist is likewise an ongoing reality. Acquiring the Lord thus is a dynamic actuality. The people of God constantly live from the Eucharist and Scripture and actuate them. Assuredly, the *sensus fidelium* brought about Scripture at one time. While bearer of Scripture, the people of God know it is not the actual author of Scripture. Accepting the biblical canon entails accepting, through this people, God as the text's true inspirer.[70]

The First Letter of Peter 2:25 presents Christ as shepherd and *episkopos*.[71] To the mind of Ratzinger, rejecting the Church's teaching office amounts, in the final analysis, to a dehistorization of Christianity and a denial of Church history as a part of God's story of saving all people(s) in all epochs. Yet, more than that, it is tantamount to the individual Christian's self-denial. It is the Church canonizing a list of Old and New Testament texts "who" is already aware that she can definitively settle (even dogmatize) matters of faith. The formula of baptizing someone into the triune God permits the early Church to experience God as Blessed Trinity. This crystallizes itself in early dogmas solemnly pronounced at various councils. From the very beginning, Ratzinger reasons, one cannot divorce the Church from any of the following realities: Bible, Tradition, teaching office, and *sensus fidelium*. No one of these may become self-referential; each needs to be constantly mindful of its indebtedness to the other elements. They are essential, interdependent constituents of the one

70 "Das Wort bloß ins Vergangene einhausen heißt, die Bibel als Bibel leugnen. Tatsächlich führt eine solche bloß historische, bloß auf das Gewesene bedachte Auslegung mit innerer Konsequenz zur Leugnung des Kanon und insofern zur Bestreitung der Bibel als Bibel. Den Kanon annehmen heißt immer schon, das Wort Gottes über seinen bloßen Augenblick hinaus zu lesen; es heißt, das Volk Gottes als den bleibenden Träger und Autorin den Autoren zu vernehmen. Da kein Volk aus Eigenem Volk Gottes ist, heißt die Annahme dieses Subjekts aber zugleich, in ihm und durch es hindurch Gott als den eigentlichen Inspirator seines Weges und seiner Schrift gewordenen Erinnerung anzuerkennen" (Joseph Ratzinger, "Perspektiven der Priesterausbildung heute," in Joseph Ratzinger and P.-W. Scheele, *Unser Auftrag: Besinnung auf den priesterlichen Dienst* [Würzburg: Echter, 1990], 11–38, at 28).

71 Joseph Ratzinger, "Der Bischof—Künder und Hüter des Glaubens," *Communio* 31 (2002): 456–67, at 456–58.

Church.[72] Theology can do justice to itself only insofar as it is rooted in the Church.[73]

The *dilemmata* experienced by Christian theologians during the Nazi regime sheds additional light on a nuanced understanding of theological freedom as a freedom possible only *in* Jesus Christ. An acquaintance of Ratzinger, the noted Lutheran theologian Heinrich Schlier (1900–1978), converted to the Catholic faith precisely for the sake of her Magisterium. Protestant theologians during the Third Reich had no instrument by which to defend their Christian faith and academic independence vis-à-vis a liberal accommodation to the reigning ideology. On the background of such painful history, the prefect concluded during a 1986 talk at St. Michael's College, Toronto, that it is "evident that the liberty of theology consists in its bond to the Church and that any other freedom is a betrayal both of itself and of the object entrusted to it."[74] Principled dissent from the teaching charism of the whole Church amounts to a betrayal not so much of an institution as of a person: Jesus Christ. However paradoxical it may sound *prima vista*, it is loyalty to the Magisterium that serves as a sure orientation for abiding in the Lord in tempestuous times.

Not only the Magisterium but also the *sensus fidelium* is a helpful signpost for theology. In the ancient world, Christian faith democratized religion over and against elitist specialists of religion, such as the gnostics, since it permitted also the less educated to become true philosophers. Jesus's words regarding the lack of comprehension on the part of the wise and the understanding of the babes is pertinent (Matt 11:25). The *simplex et idiota* (Bonaventure) become a normative criterion for theologians.

> This primacy of simple faith, moreover, is also in perfect accord with a fundamental anthropological law: the great truths about human nature are grasped in a simple apprehension which is in principle available to everyone and which is never wholly retrieved in [academic] reflection.[75]

[72] Joseph Ratzinger, *Das Problem der Dogmengeschichte in der Sicht der katholischen Theologie* (Köln/Opladen: Westdeutscher, 1966), 20.

[73] See the conclusion section below, which identifies the root of this view in the nineteenth-century Tübingen School of Theology.

[74] Ratzinger, *The Nature and Mission of Theology*, 45–46.

[75] Ratzinger, *The Nature and Mission of Theology*, 63.

> The dogmas of 1854, 1870 and 1950 became possible because the *sensus fidei* had discovered them, while the Magisterium and theology followed its lead and tried slowly to catch up with it.[76]

Defending this faith obligates both the Magisterium and theologians. "The highest ranking good, for which the Church bears responsibility, is the faith of the simple."[77]

The Holy Spirit and Prayer

"Spirituality" as a term is by no means as old as religion or Christianity. Nevertheless, there is no gainsaying that people sought for spirituality in all ages.[78] Perusing Ratzinger's bibliography, one soon recognizes that his theology is eminently spiritual and his spirituality is theologically embossed. The interwovenness of philosophy, theology, and spirituality is treated analogously to the triad of faith, hope, and charity. These terms allow one to comprehend the *Logik des Ganzen* (the logic of the whole).[79] The merging and fusion of spirituality and theology in the person of the theologian is one of the outstanding characteristics of Ratzinger's theology.[80] Any theological discourse on God lacks seriousness if it is conducted by participants who lack a lived, Christ-centered spirituality. Far from accommodating the Creed in an unreflective manner to the prevalent currents, such a combination allows the theologian to insert Christian faith into his particular age courageously. Spiritual theology striving to be inspired ever again by the third Person of the Blessed Trinity preserves theology's objectivity. Such theology is aware that it is under the rationality of the divine *Logos*. It is the *Logos* who endures in time through the presence of the Holy Spirit, who vouches for the intelligibility of Christian faith, which includes theology. Spiritual theology (1) prevents theological discourse from delighting in abstract terms and (2) reminds all academic discourse that it is one of divine giftedness.

---

76 Ratzinger, *The Nature and Mission of Theology*, 105.

77 Ratzinger, *The Nature and Mission of Theology*, 68.

78 See B. Körner, "Mystik und Spiritualität—ein *locus theologicus*? Erste Hinweise an Hand der Theologie von Hans Urs von Balthasar," *Rivista Teologica di Lugano* 6 (2001): 221–38.

79 See Joseph Ratzinger, *Salz der Erde: Christentum und katholische Kirche an der Jahrtausendwende* (Stuttgart: Deutsche Verlags-Anstalt, 1996), 66.

80 Gerd Lohaus, "Theologie der Spiritualität und Spiritualität der Theologie: (Teil 1) Joseph Ratzingers Verständnis von Spiritualität," *Geist und Leben* 80 (2007): 193–208, at 197: "Das Ineinander von Theologie und Spiritualität ist einer der Grundzüge, wenn nicht der Grundzug seines theologischen Werks."

Following the Gospel of John, Ratzinger writes that only the Holy Spirit as the Spirit of both the Father and the Son can make known the formal object of theological inquiry—namely, Jesus Christ. The Spirit never imposes himself, but brings into memory, "teaches and listens and teaches how to listen." He "acts as a guide into the heart of the Word, which becomes light in the act of listening."[81]

Spirit and matter are conjoined in one reality. Cosmos, the human being, and God are related to one another in such a way that no radical hiatus between the two is possible. The multifarious reality is held together by the *Creator Spiritus*. If indeed this is the case, then Ratzinger seems to argue that one can never limit God to subjective interiority: the "I" of the believer and the universe are held together by the Holy Spirit. This is the import of a Bonaventurian understanding of revelation. It is a process of inspiration that is defined by the Doctor Seraphicus as *visio intellectualis*. One moves from the palpable to the spiritual core. For this reason, Scripture cannot be identical with revelation. It is, however, Scripture that permits grasping its real, spiritual meaning. This neither relativizes Scripture nor limits revelation to subjectivism. In organic continuity with the early Church and the Church Fathers, the spiritual meaning of the text is apprehended ever anew by every Christian and theologian.[82] As Gerd Lohaus well summarizes: for Ratzinger, Christian thinking realizes "an incarnational piety," "passionate" in the literal sense of the term, as it constantly explicates the *Mysterium Paschale*.[83]

The Holy Spirit guarantees the unity of a person's spiritual experience with a faith community's spiritual experience. It never contradicts the whole Church—as also the Church is the Holy Spirit's product. In order to summarize his understanding of how Holy Spirit, Church, belief, and theology are existentially intertwined, the theologian Ratzinger quotes Augustine in *Weggemeinschaft des Glaubens*:

> "You want to have the Spirit of Christ?" the African Church Father answers: "So be in the body of Christ! You cannot have

[81] Ratzinger, *The Nature and Mission of Theology*, 54–55.

[82] H. J. Verweyen, *Joseph Ratzinger—Benedikt XVI: Die Entwicklung seines Denkens* (Darmstadt: Wissenschaftliche Buchgesellschaft, 2007), 25–26.

[83] Lohaus, "Theologie der Spiritualität," 201. See also Joseph Ratzinger, *Skandalöser Realismus? Gott handelt in der Geschichte*, 3rd ed. (Bad Tölz: Urfeld, 2005), 7–8; and Ratzinger, *Principles of Catholic Theology*, 30: "As though we ourselves had invented God, we erect a contradiction that is ultimately fatal between tradition and reason, between tradition and truth."

> the Spirit severed, so to speak, freely hovering, but rather it is the Spirit of the body of Christ, and if you intend having the Spirit, if you want to be a pneumatic, you must first undergo the humiliation of having the 'soma' befall you."[84]

This indicates the ecclesial root of Christian spiritual existence. Materially, Christ and the Church belong intimately together. One cannot comprehend the Savior without the Holy Spirit operative in the Church, and vice-versa. Though the Church is not identical with Jesus Christ, one cannot adequately apprehend the Augustinian and Vatican II concept of "people of God" without a Eucharistic and pneumatological basis. As Ratzinger succinctly observes when explicating Galatians 3:28 ("for you are all one in Christ"): "at the beginning the Church was not made, but born."[85]

Then Church is *communio* as ontic community with the triune God, thereby enabling its individual members' openness for one another.[86] Prayer with Jesus enables genuine dialogue amongst people. In the prayer of Jesus Christ, the identity of the second Person of the Godhead shines forth. The essence of his Person is contained in his prayer. Prayer becomes for Christians what it is already for Jesus: self-transference of one's own being into that of Christ and his Body, the Church. This necessarily involves the *mysterium Crucis*. It includes a piety of the Passion and the Cross. Such piety expresses itself in adoration as perduration of Christ's suffering into the present. Adoring prayer is the outcome of a fusion or blending of existences in the Eucharist, which constantly actuates the Church.[87] Calling God "Abba" with Christ, Christians participate in the sonship of Christ. This makes deification possible via Christification. As a Christian disciple, the theologian is the one who has a heightened awareness of this process.[88] The theologian knows himself as part of a whole not of his own making, but of a divine milieu. Whenever a unity of theology and spirituality is attempted, a life that truly "succeeds" is achieved. This is the unique nature of theology:

> It turns to it, which we did not invent on our own and which precisely thereby can become the foundation of life as it precedes

[84] Ratzinger, *Weggemeinschaft des Glaubens*, 37.

[85] Joseph Ratzinger, *Vom Wiederauffinden der Mitte: Grundorientierungen: Texte aus vier Jahrzehnten* (Freiburg im Breisgau: Herder, 1997), 28–29 (this text was edited by Ratzinger's Schülerkreis).

[86] Ratzinger, *Weggemeinschaft des Glaubens*, 156.

[87] Ratzinger, *Principles of Catholic Theology*, 169–71.

[88] Ratzinger, *Vom Wiederauffinden der Mitte*, 14–15.

> and sustains us. Therefore it is greater than our own thinking. . . . I accept a template, in order to find from it and in it access to the proper life, to the proper comprehension of my self.[89]

For Ratzinger, being Christian and being a theologian means exercising the art of life. The *Chalcedonense* holds that the full God-man Jesus Christ is *the* template for what human life is: "no longer I who live, but Christ who lives in me" (Gal 2:20).

During the commemoration of the sixtieth anniversary of the landing of the Allied Forces in Normandy in 1944, the then-Cardinal Ratzinger addressed an international audience in the venerable Cathedral of Bayeux. The homily is titled "Faith in the Triune God and Peace in the World." Felicitously, the date, June 6, 2004, coincided with the Solemnity of the Most Holy Trinity. Ratzinger did not address the gathering as a Vatican diplomat or as someone who considered himself also liberated from the Nazi regime. Rather, as a theologian, he shares with his illustrious audience an essential component of Christian faith and suggests this teaching of central relevance to overcoming strife, hatred, and war in this world. In this address, he speaks with a theologian's competence and reflects on the Lord's promise to send the Spirit of Truth, highlighting the word "Paraclete" (John 16:13). This Greek word translates into English as "consoler." The homilist interprets its meaning quite literally: "The one who enters our loneliness and shares it (with us)." Thereby, loneliness ceases to exist. The Holy Spirit enters the void created by loneliness and reveals the triune God as charity. Divine charity is evidenced as "the innermost condition of our life." Whoever does not like God does not like human beings, he forcefully asserts. Not being loved is the root cause for human suffering and human sadness. The term "consoler" conveys the firm Christian belief that man is never left to his own devices. He is never alone. The theologian, Ratzinger implies, is called to live in this confidence and to spell out this salient fact of human life to all those willing to lend the Christian message a well-disposed ear.[90]

---

[89] "Daβ sie sich dem zuwendet, was wir nicht selbst erfunden haben, und was uns gerade dadurch Fundament des Lebens sein kann, daβ es uns vorausgeht und trägt, also gröβer ist als unser eigenes Denken. . . . Ich nehme eine Vorgabe an, um von ihr her und in ihr Zugang zum rechten Leben, zum rechten Verstehen meiner selbst zu finden" (Ratzinger, *Weggemeinschaft des Glaubens*, 28).

[90] Joseph Ratzinger, "Der Glaube an den dreifaltigen Gott und der Friede in der Welt: Predigt am Dreifaltigkeitsfest 6, Juni 2004, in Bayeux," in *Werte in Zeiten des Umbruchs* (Freiburg im Breisgau: Herder 2005), 148–53, at 150–51.

Mary and the Saints

Ratzinger is sensitive to the self-deceptive dangers of the *homo faber*. In the classic German drama *Faust* by Goethe, the highly educated Faust, distinguished by a multitude of doctorates, ponders on an Easter Sunday morning whether at the beginning of creation was the word or the deed. This is the modern ambuscade. In contrast, Guardini had called at the beginning of the liturgical movement for the Church to "awaken in the souls of believers." In no small part due to Ratzinger, *Lumen Gentium* concludes with a lengthy discussion on Mary. It heightens awareness of the Church as far more than merely an institution or organization. In her essence, the Church is a person. The Church is referred to by Ratzinger as "woman" and "mother." This overcomes apprehending the Church as a human contrivance.

> Only to the degree faith informs our being beyond human making, *are* we Church, Church is in us. Only in Marian being do we become Church. Also in its origin the Church was not made, but rather born. This is the Council's deepest intention: that the Church awakens in our souls. Mary shows us the way.[91]

More than an inspiring signpost, Mary *is* the Church at her beginning. It is with a trusting Marian disposition that Christians and theologians are Church. Mary fulfills to the highest degree imaginable what the Old Testament prefigures in Sarah and the mothers of Samuel and Samson, and the New Testament in Elizabeth, the mother of John the Baptist. All these narratives relate the same insight: salvation does not come from human beings: "'whoever believes in the Son has eternal life' (see Jn 3:15; 3:36; 5:24)."[92]

The Laurentine Litany praises Mary as "the throne of wisdom." It underscores that wisdom is not a product of this world, but granted to people through Mary. The throne fitting to God in this world is not something material, but only the human being at God's disposition—namely, Mary. Her "simplicity of heart" becomes God's abode and entry into our world. He cites the wonderful words of Augustine: "Prior to receiving the Lord bodily, she had born Him in her heart." She had placed her whole life un-

---

[91] Joseph Ratzinger, "Die Ekklesiologie des zweiten Vatikanums," *Communio* 15 (1986): 41–52, at 52.

[92] Joseph Ratzinger, *Introduction to Christianity*, trans. J. R. Foster (San Francisco: Ignatius Press, 2004), 352.

der the claim of God's Word.[93] In this way, Mary becomes paradigmatic for the nature of Christian faith in general and is the template for a theology on grace, "forming a whole with ecclesiology and anthropology." As the favored Daughter of Zion, she is the image of the Church and the image of every believing person. As all saints, she knows even more acutely that "all is grace"[94]—quoting George Bernanos's *The Diary of a Country Priest.*

Along with Søren Kierkegaard, Ratzinger knows that faith is "second hand." However, this is not cause for regret. In contradistinction to the Christian existentialism of the Danish philosopher, for Ratzinger, the terms *communio* and *corpus Christi* are recurring leitmotivs. It is normal for someone to trust someone else who has (had) a personal encounter with God. The saints' exemplary participation in the Church's sacramental life invites others to join.[95] The connection between theology and sainthood is not an accidental one, but one that arises from the very logic of Christian existence as Eucharistic discipleship. Contrary to what preconciliar neo-Scholastic theology or postconciliar anthropocentric thought seem(ed) to suggest, mere rationality does not suffice to generate great Christian thought.[96]

With Mary and the saints, one senses the nature and cost of discipleship. The saints become explications of Jesus Christ in this concrete life. This leads Ratzinger to conclude: "Only when we rediscover the saints will we also find the Church again."[97] Already during Vatican II, he wrote that the term *communio sanctorum* implies sharing in the seven sacraments. But the second meaning of this expression conveys the notion of sharing in the community of believers. This teaches that all are sanctified by common participation in Christ's Word and reality in order to become thereby more deeply members of the Church.[98]

> Athanasius is inconceivable without Anthony, the father of monasticism, and the latter's new experience of Christ; Augustine

---

[93] Joseph Ratzinger, "'Maria—Du Thron der Weisheit': Ansprache bei der Maiandacht in der Wallfahrtskirche München-Ramersdorf am 23, Mai 1977 anlässlich des Empfangs des neuen Erzbischofs Joseph Ratzinger in seiner Bischofsstadt," *Mitteilungen: Institut Papst Benedikt XVI* 3 (2010): 28–29.

[94] See Ratzinger, *Introduction to Christianity*, 354.

[95] Ratzinger, *Principles of Catholic Theology*, 351–52.

[96] See Ratzinger, *The Mission and Nature of Theology*, 49–50.

[97] Ratzinger, *Dogma and Preaching*, 55.

[98] Joseph Ratzinger, "Kritik an der Kirche? Dogmatische Bemerkungen: Kirche der Heiligen—Kirche der Sünder" [originally 1962], in Müller, *Joseph Ratzinger Gesammelte Schriften*, 8.1:482–94, at 489.

> is likewise unthinkable without his passionate journey to radical Christian life. Moreover, Bonaventure and the Franciscan theology of the thirteenth century would not have been possible without the imposing new representation of Christ in the figure of Saint Francis of Assisi, nor could Thomas Aquinas have existed without Dominic's breakthrough to the gospel and to evangelization. . . . Pure rationality is not itself sufficient to bring forth great Christian theology: at bottom, even such outstanding figures as Ritschl, Jülicher, and Harnack appear curiously empty theologically when we read them from the distance of later generations.[99]

All theological labors are secondary and subservient to the vision Jesus Christ occasionally grants saints. "This is the humility imposed upon theologians."[100] Faith and theology are on a pilgrim fellowship (*Weggemeinschaft*) of faith with the second Person of the Blessed Trinity and the people of God—not definable via an intellectualistic system.[101] Theology as discipleship is inspired and supported by Mary and the saints and considers them as of decisive relevance to the theological enterprise. The theologian's creativity depends directly on the depth of his conversion to sainthood.

Academics and Wisdom

Particularly in German academia, there exists a special relationship between a student and his *Doktorvater.* Any attempt to fathom the mind of Pope Benedict XVI will be illuminated by reflecting on Gottlieb Söhngen's (1892–1971) understanding of theology. His student Ratzinger delivered the eulogy during the requiem of his *Doktorvater* at St. Agnes Church in Cologne on November 19, 1971. He defines the search for knowledge by way of methodologically ordered thought as a major concern for Söhngen. Never had he been exclusively a scholar or researcher in the limiting sense of the terms, but a human being, God-seeker, and priest. Reflecting on Kant and Augustine, Söhngen, in the words of Ratzinger, was cognizant that:

---

99 Ratzinger, *The Nature and Mission of Theology*, 58.

100 Ratzinger, *Behold the Pierced One*, 41: "Indeed, it is as if we were actually looking in on the inner life of the Word-made-man."

101 Ratzinger, *Truth and Tolerance*, 146–47. See also Benedict XVI, "Address at the Collège des Bernardins."

> Theology relates all to wisdom, but on the path of academics. His goal was wisdom, the tangating of truth itself, advancing to the core of reality and becoming one with it. His concern was truth, which is at the same time the path making the human being be a human being and teaching him to live. Thus the second impetus of his life becomes comprehensible: love of beauty, poetry and especially music. For him, who believed in the origin of the world from the Creator Spirit—from the creative imagination of God—beauty was a form to become interiorly aware of wisdom. He knew that truth is never to be encapsulated completely in theory and method; he knew following the trace of truth when listening to beauty.[102]

Ratzinger relates how Söhngen ever again turned to consulting Kant—the object of his dissertation—to improve his "own earnestness of method and fearlessness of thinking," shying back from no question and from no questionable proposition. At the same time, he was acutely aware of his responsibility for human beings and the humaneness of society. In the thoughts of Thomas Aquinas, he discovered a kindred spirit, both daring and interested in objectivity, constantly trying to understand the totality of the phenomena. Thomas's struggle to understand the unity of the whole of reality and the unity of comprehension and reality became a leitmotiv of Söhngen's own scholarly endeavors. An early pioneer in ecumenical dialogue, he discovered in Karl Barth's insistence on the Word of God the limitations of philosophizing. God relativizes human speech, and human beings become listeners. The theologian cannot "lord" over revelation. Söhngen discovered the need to receive truth and learn obedience to the Gospel. He was willing to expound the Catholic position to partners in dialogue. His theology was informed early on by the rich liturgical customs of his home city Cologne. This was deepened by Söhngen's encoun-

[102] Joseph Ratzinger, "Von der Wissenschaft zur Weisheit," *Catholica* 26 (1972): 2–6, at 2–3: "Theologie bezieht alles auf Weisheit, aber auf dem Weg der Wissenschaft. Sein Ziel was Weisheit, das Berühren der Wahrheit selbst, das Vorstoßen auf den Kern der Wirklichkeit und das Einswerden mit ihr. Es ging ihm um die Wahrheit, die zugleich Weg ist, die den Menschen zum Menschen macht und ihn zu leben lehrt. So wird von da aus der zweite Antrieb seines Lebens verständlich: die Liebe zum Schönen, zur Poesie und besonders zur Musik. Für ihn, der an die Herkunft der Welt aus dem Schöpfergeist, aus der schöpferischen Phantasie Gottes glaubte, war das Schöne eine Form, der Weisheit inne zu werden. Er wußte, daß Wahrheit nie gänzlich in Theorie und Methode einzufangen ist; er wußte, daß er der Spur der Wahrheit folgte, wenn er dem Schönen lauschte."

ters with a precursor of the liturgical movement: the Benedictine abbot of Maria Laach, Odo Casel. He valued Eastern icons for their communication of eternal beauty. He incorporated the thoughts of Blessed John Henry Newman and Plato's philosophy into his theology.

Such a broad vision produces an attendant feature that Ratzinger observes. It defies facile systematization. In fact, beholding "the whole in fragment" becomes programmatic. One apprehends shards of the whole and sees reality but as refractions of an overarching unity. Söhngen refrained from the temptation of pressing outstanding issues into solutions. He who had argued against the dogmatic definition of Our Lady's Assumption into heaven, prior to 1950, stated afterwards that God's wisdom and that of "the Church always remain greater" than that of a theologian. Along with the Church Father Ignatius of Antioch, he knew that the Church exists where the bishops are. His ecclesiality was never doubted. Never may theology be subservient to the dictum "publish or perish" or enter the lowly spheres of politics. To his mind, Pentecost had entrusted divine assistance to the Apostles, their successors, and the whole Church—yet never to individual believers.

Conclusion

Is Catholic theology as lived Christian discipleship still a viable academic discipline in an age of the universal dominance of economic pragmatism, of the Bologna Process in Europe, and of studiously analyzed outcome assessments in the early twenty-first century? During his own time, Guardini faced great obstacles in his attempt to pursue theology. In his age, theology was often reduced to historical theology, with theologians quite frequently expressing no confidence in Christian faith as divine revelation. Guardini would claim to be "working for a university of the future which did not yet exist."[103]

The theologian Ratzinger has reflected on this crucial issue from varied angles during his long life. Theology is the science that reminds academia that human reason is not left to its own devices when pondering the origin and meaning of life. It relegates all ideological, political, scientific, and economic considerations to second place vis-à-vis the question humankind is to itself, the quest for truth and divine revelation. Christian faith reveals truth as a divine Thou: Jesus Christ. When safeguarding the riddle of human life, theology retains its identity and is not reduced to a

[103] Ratzinger, *The Nature and Mission of Theology*, 78.

pure *religio civilis*, suspiciously friendly to external interests but corrosive to faith. Theology cautions human reason that it "is preceded by a Word which, though logical and rational, does not originate from reason itself but has been granted it as a gift and, as such, always transcends it."[104]

There is an inclusive Catholic "both and" ("*kai . . . kai*" or "*et . . . et*" in contrast to a delimiting "*aut . . . aut*") resonating in all of Ratzinger's writings without his thoughts thereby becoming dialectical.[105] It may be debatable in what sequence the pairs of terms here presented could appear. Yet, the *cardo*, the hinge point to accessing the *loci theologici*, is the figure of Jesus Christ revealing God as triune. The present article suggests that Ratzinger echoes throughout his theological epistemology a central insight of the much-noted nineteenth-century theologian Johann Adam Möhler (1796–1838): neither the Church nor theology are fixed systems, but tension-filled realities that reciprocally penetrate and mutually enable one another. Möhler's much-celebrated line reads: "Neither can one nor can everyone intend to be all; only all can be all, and only the unity of all [can be] the whole."[106] The conscious realization of this thought renders theology organic, alive, joyful, and fecund.

If Ratzinger at all would advocate retaining the term *loci theologici*, it would be with a comprehensive understanding in mind. He would employ the term *locus* as "source" or "wellspring" for theology, but not so much in the sense of "a proof" for a theological claim. Ratzinger uses dynamic terms such as *communio* and "person" to describe faith. Cano would not have done so. Remarkably, however, both Cano and Ratzinger apprehend theology as interwoven in an interactive fabric. No one *locus* suffices, but together all attest to the whole. Every *locus* represents but a moment of the whole. The epistemological Catholicity of every element bears witness to the irreducible plurality of theology constituting Catholic truth.

In keeping with Augustine, Ratzinger argues in agreement with Cano that there is nothing like a *tabula rasa* in the human mind. Human reason is gifted by someone and oriented toward this personal reality to which it is ontologically indebted. Thus, a relationship is stated between human rationality and divine wisdom. This is in agreement with Cano's *ratio naturalis* (authority no. 8 in Cano's system; see note 4 above) and *auctoritas*

[104] Ratzinger, *The Nature and Mission of Theology*, 103–4.

[105] L. Scheffczyk, *Katholische Glaubenswelt* (Aschaffenburg: Pattloch, 1977), 4–5.

[106] A. Knöpfler, *Johann Adam Möhler: ein Gedenkblatt zu dessen hundertsten Geburtstag* (Munich: Lentner, 1896), 146: ". . . es muß aber weder Einer noch Jeder alles sein wollen; alles können nur Alle sein, und die Einheit Aller nur ein Ganzes."

philosophorum (no. 9). Consonant with this vision, however, Ratzinger seems not to favor a hierarchy of *loci theologici*, but prefers establishing firmly Jesus Christ as *the* revealer of the triune God and as the all-decisive hinge point of all *loci*. This invariably removes Jesus Christ from being one *locus* among many, as in Cano's perspective (*auctoritas Traditionem Christi et Apostolorum*, Cano's no. 2). Such a holistic perspective allows Ratzinger to give precedence to the Church Fathers vis-à-vis the *auctoritas Theologorum scholasticorum* (no. 7). At the same time, the correlation of the people of God as *sensus fidelium* and the Magisterium leads him to join the *auctoritas Traditionem . . . apostolorum* (no. 2), the *auctoritas Ecclesiae Catholicae* (no. 3), the *auctoritas conciliorum* (no. 4), and the *auctoritas Ecclesiae Romanae* (no. 5).

As Mary is "the Church at its source," she is beheld as the cause for the Church's holiness—again, unlike Cano. This salient feature is continuously borne out by the saints. Along with Bonaventure, Ratzinger sees Jesus Christ and the Blessed Trinity as the *locus theologicus* par excellence, as every theologian can flourish only within a lived relationship with God. The dynamic understanding of revelation in *Dei Verbum* leads to apprehending Jesus Christ alive in His Church. Such a spiritual understanding of theologizing has little appreciation for law as a source for theology, as Cano had (nos. 7 and 10 in his list). With Scripture no longer isolated as *auctoritas Sacrae Scripturae* (Cano's no. 1), for Ratzinger, the dynamics between Scripture and Tradition enable revelation to become present. Ratzinger ascribes to liturgy far greater weight than does Cano, who may have subsumed it under *auctoritas Ecclesiae Catholicae* (no. 3). The definitive self-communication of God through Jesus Christ in history is elongated in the sacraments, preeminently in the Eucharist. Amid postmodern particularizations, it is thus Jesus Christ who, for Ratzinger, overcomes the contemporary fragmentation of theological disciplines and reestablishes theology's inner coherence and cogency.

Thereby, Ratzinger re-spiritualizes theology not by denying scholarly rigor, but enabling it. Theology is a particular form of discipleship of Jesus Christ. Theology perceives itself as part of the ongoing, living Tradition. It is neither antiquarian nor fixed solely on the moment, nor utopian, but always fixes its gaze firmly on the risen Lord in the *eschaton* within that realm sustained by the abiding presence of the Holy Spirit, called Church.[107] The

---

[107] For a similar understanding of tradition, see Johann S. Drey, "Vom Geist und Wesen des Katholizismus," *Theologische Quartalschrift* 1 (1819): 8–23; 193–210; 369–91; and 559–74.

Eucharistic Lord provides a structured organism that is no longer apprehended as an amorphous "it" (Church as juridical or hierarchical institution), but as a life-granting whole. There is "a cohesive logic of faith."[108] The integrating figure of Jesus Christ becomes the *principium essendi et cognoscendi* by localizing theological insight within the *communio* of Christian faith and sacramental life. This squarely establishes the topological and methodological plurality of theological insight.

The *point d'appui* for Ratzinger is the obvious: theology presupposes faith in Jesus the Christ. "It draws its life from the paradoxical union of faith and science. Whoever pretends to abolish this paradox does away with theology and also ought to have the courage to admit it. Whoever, on the other hand, embraces it in principle is bound to accept its inherent tensions."[109] Without stating so *expressis verbis*, Ratzinger considers such tension as parallel to the tension residing in the God-man. The Chalcedonian formula "perfect in divinity and perfect in humanity" expresses a tension-filled faith, wherefrom issues forth invariably a theology that must be paradoxical in nature. This explains the present author's suggestion of a presentation of *loci theologici* in pairs. More importantly, only thus can theology be conceived, and thus only Christianity can pursue theology, as it alone is based on the divine *Logos*, the second Person of the Blessed Trinity. Interestingly, such polarities give rise to new life. The teaching office enables a dynamic plurality without an evaporation of Christian faith. Vice-versa, the teaching office would be lifeless without being informed by theological research. This expresses itself also in the Catholic Church's repeated struggle for freedom from the state. A concrete example is that only a thus-perceived "universal Church is capable of safeguarding the distinction of the particular churches from the state and society."[110] All participants in these polarities are indebted to their respective counterparts in order to thrive, and all entities are possible only in the one Lord—"only pluralism in relation to unity is great."[111]

Jesus Christ establishes a unity that does not do violence unto plurality and diversity, but grants each element its unique individuality by relating its being to the whole. Theology thrives on this fact. This patristic, symphonic understanding of all—Old and New Testaments, Christ and Church, people of God and apostolic succession, one universal Church

[108] Ratzinger, *Principles of Catholic Theology*, 26.

[109] Ratzinger, *The Nature and Mission of Theology*, 55–56.

[110] Ratzinger, *The Nature and Mission of Theology*, 90.

[111] Ratzinger, *The Nature and Mission of Theology*, 98.

and many particular churches, body and soul, and so on—is grounded in the one God creating and redeeming the one world. Thus, Ratzinger would probably not identify something as a *locus alienus*, as some texts do, nor relegate it to the *loci theologoci adscriptuti*, as Cano did.

> When I consider the great believing teachers from Möhler to Newman and Scheeben, from Rosmini to Guardini, or in our day de Lubac, Congar, Balthasar—how much richer and more relevant is their testimony than the witness of those who let the corporate subject Church slip through their fingers. . . . The great French theology was born, not because theologians wished to do something French, but because they expected nothing less from themselves than to find the truth and to express it as adequately as possible. For that reason it proved to be both French and universal. The same is true of the great theology of Italy, Germany and Spain. It is perennially true. Only [Christlike] freedom from ulterior motives is fruitful.[112]

[112] Ratzinger, *The Nature and Mission of Theology*, 97.

Book Review: *Joseph Ratzinger—Kirchliche Existenz und Existenzielle Theologie: Ekklesiologische Grundlinien unter dem Anspruch von Lumen Gentium*

By Maximilian Heinrich Heim[1]

With a Foreword by Joseph Cardinal Ratzinger[2]

THIS SUBSTANTIAL STUDY is a doctoral dissertation submitted to the University of Graz in Austria. It received two distinguished awards since: the prestigious Kardinal Innitzer Förderpreis in Vienna and the Johann Kaspar Zeuß-Preis from the author's hometown, Kronach, Germany. Perhaps yet more indicatively and significantly, the then-Cardinal Ratzinger supplied the foreword to this second edition. Heim had previously been prior of the Cistercian monastery in Heiligenkreuz, Austria, and now serves in the same capacity in Stiepel, Germany. Since 2003, he teaches fundamental theology at the Cistercian college in Heiligenkreuz.

After a thorough analysis, the author concludes that Benedict XVI

---

1 This book review was originally published in Theological Studies 67 (September 1, 2006): 685–87. Used with permission.

2 Maximilian Heinrich Heim, *Joseph Ratzinger—Kirchliche Existenz und Existenzielle Theologie: Ekklesiologische Grundlinien unter dem Anspruch von Lumen Gentium*, foreword by Joseph Cardinal Ratzinger, 2nd improved ed., Bamberger Theologische Studien 22 (Frankfurt am Main: Peter Lang, 2005), 521 pp. This volume will be cited in text parenthetically by page number, unlabeled. All English translations of Heim is the work of the present author.

subscribes to and contributed to a Christocentric, Eucharistic, and pneumatic ecclesiology, thereby prevailing over the inherent deficiencies of the apologetic and legalistic *societas perfecta* position of the nineteenth century. In the vein of Pauline theology, Pius XII had already established the basis for overcoming this exclusively juridical or extrinsic understanding of the Church in 1943 by identifying her as the Mystical Body of Christ. Heim takes care to show that there remains in Ratzinger's mind a "Christological difference" between Christ and the Church (312), allowing for a "dynamics of unity" (380). In 1950, Gottlieb Söhngen (1892–1971), Ratzinger's dissertation director, gave a question for a competition among doctoral students: could Augustine's definition of the Church as "the people of God" be the hermeneutic key to comprehending the patristic intuition of the Church's essence? As Heim illustrates, for both Augustine and Ratzinger (the winner), the Church is a dynamic reality assembled and ever renewed by Christ in the power of the Holy Spirit. The term "people of God" defines the Church essentially as Christocentric and pneumatic. Only by way of a Christological "prolongation" of the Old Testament term "sons of Abraham" into the New Testament, and defining it now as a sacramental reality in the New Testament, does the Church become real and historical. Thus, the Church transcends pneumatically any empirical entity. As God's covenantal pledge in time and space, the sacrament Church is not without an institutional form, but it can never be reduced to a merely juridical structure—"she is person!" (375).

In the first part, Heim presents the Council's definition of the Church as found in *Lumen Gentium* [LG], in which he discovers the term "people of God" closely linked to "mystery," "sacrament," "mission," and "communion." Among these five, "people of God" enjoys preeminence. It is precisely this term that had also been the central focus of Ratzinger's studies in the 1950s. Heim concludes that *Lumen Gentium* liberated the Church "to its proper possibility: to live under its head, Christ, from his Spirit" (142).

In the second part, Heim first traces Ratzinger's life and compares his ecclesiology with that of *Lumen gentium*. Indebted to Johann Adam Möhler and Matthias Scheeben, and influenced by Cyprian, Ratzinger perceives the Church as "the continuous incarnation," united as people "by the unity of the Father and the Son and the Holy Spirit" (LG 4). The Church is nothing less than the "transpersonal subject of faith, rooted in the Trinitarian mystery, attesting to its identity in Christ" (147). "Jesus' Last Supper"—along with his death and Resurrection—"is the actual act of the Church's foundation" (257). But "one sees this only if one lives the mystery." Based on his study of Bonaventure's understanding of history, who develops it in opposition to Joachim of Fiore, Ratzinger concludes in his *Habilitationsschrift* (1959) that the Church needs to be both Christological and pneumatic—lest one subscribe to Joachim's heresy of a pneumatic-prophetic Church. This is the motivation for Ratzinger's unequivocal rejection of some aspects of liberation theology. Heim investigates whether Ratzinger's ecclesiology underwent a profound change during the Second Vatican Council or thereafter. Already during the Council, Ratzinger had detected a misunderstanding among some: the Council as a parliament producing new approaches and wishing to accommodate to the "modern ways" (1963). In a different tenor, Ratzinger now affirms expressly the sinful nature of the Church's members (1971). Only personal, sacramental "conversion to Christ" describes genuine reform.

A dense but nuanced clarification on the hotly contested meaning of *subsistit* (LG 8) and the way Ratzinger contributed to this formula is presented. In the context of "the plurality of local churches," he emphasizes the Church's universality. The author notes a shift of concentration also regarding the episcopal-collegial structure of the Church, due to its origin in the Last Supper. Heim demonstrates that Ratzinger's understanding of collegiality is more palatable to the Eastern-rite Churches, while Karl Rahner's is more congenial to the denominations emanating from the Reformation. Heim touches on how Romano Guardini and the Protestant theologian Oscar Cullmann's notion of the "living-concrete" informed Ratzinger. In addition, he shows how Ratzinger was early on aware of ambiguities in *Lumen Gentium*, but he no longer articulated these as cardinal. In a revolutionary way, he had proposed in 1964 dissolving the Latin Patriarchy and establishing a multitude of patriarchical territories within bishops' conferences, living perichoretically as "churches communicating with one another" (435). Also, Ratzinger suggested, bishops should share in the responsibility of governing the universal Church. Later he stresses that bishops cannot delegate their responsibilities. Consistently underlying all of this is Ratzinger's understanding of the ontological priority of the universal Church à la the Tübingen School. The Church is created ever anew not by structures but by the Holy Spirit. His central ecclesiological concern is the sacramental communion of the Eucharistic Church. This is the *cantus firmus* resonating throughout Ratzinger's writings, and Heim attests that in his ecclesiology over the past fifty-five years, Ratzinger maintains a remarkable "consistency in spite of a change of perspective." Despite some differences between the "early and later Ratzinger," Heim discovers yet greater and deeper continuity (459).

Furthermore, Heim establishes convincingly a consonance between Ratzinger's theology and a pivotal conciliar term. "The people of God" describes ecclesial existence transformed by grace. The discussion of this correlation is paralleled by an insightful portrait of Ratzinger's significant role during the Second Vatican Council.

There is no gainsaying that this is the heretofore most exhaustive and comprehensive, erudite and profound—but nonetheless also balanced—study on Benedict XVI's ecclesiology. It establishes a reliable and indispensable resource in comprehending his ecclesiological loci and central concerns as priest, theologian, prefect of the Congregation for the Doctrine of the Faith, and pontiff.

Book Review: *Joseph Ratzinger—Ein Brillanter Denker? Kritische Fragen An Den Papst Und Seine Protestantischen Konkurrenten* By Thomas Rießinger[1]

This book is printed by a noted German academic publishing house. Rießinger examines Pope Benedict XVI's theology. Under the heading "Papal Purification" (3–33) he treats *Deus caritas est,* followed by "Papal Hope," analyzing *Spe salvi* (35–82). "Papal Economics" (83–140) reflects on *Caritas in veritate,* and he rounds off his treatment of Ratzinger's theology with a section titled "Papal Hermeneutics" (141–171), which discusses the second volume of *Jesus of Nazareth.* In a final chapter he critiques the central positions of contemporary Protestant thinkers Jürgen Moltmann, Wolfgang Huber, and Margot Käßmann.

The author is a retired professor of mathematics and information technology at a college in Frankfurt am Main (1992-2010). The various chapters of this book had previously been published as articles in the journal *Aufklärung und Kritik,* issued by the *Gesellschaft für kritische Philosophie.* This explains both the author's style and line of argumentation. Rießinger's language is non-technical and his worldview is decidedly deistic. He approaches theological texts not only as a layman, but more

[1] This book review was originally published in *Theological Studies* 74 (December 1, 2013): 1015–17. Used by permission.

importantly as a non-Christian, subcutaneously probing everywhere for convincing responses to the late eighteenth-century theodicy question. One finds comparatively few footnotes and a very selective bibliography, listing almost no theological texts pertinent to his object's writings. An index is missing.

Not accepting such basic Christian tenets as God being good, being triune, and effecting atonement, he finds no justification for Benedict's claim that God loves the world he has created (11). Regarding the Eucharist, he rejects wanting to be party to the self-sacrificing act of Jesus, for it is cruel and inhumane (14).

In Augustine's statement "si comprehendis, non est Deus" (DCE 38), Rießinger detects on Ratzinger's part an attempt "to immunize" Christianity against accusations from "reasonable people" (33).

Assuming an unbridgeable Kantian bifurcation between the noumenal and phenomenal realms, and echoing Richard Dawkins, he asks whence Paul and Ratzinger know the nature of hope (36). He critiques Ratzinger for assuming that God's death should be necessary to overcome human transgressions and speculates why God should not simply have forgiven humankind (46 and 61). When *Spe salvi* mentions that Augustine found strength for his life in the Incarnation, Rießinger observes that this requires ignoring the cruelty of God's plans to save humanity by "his son's murder"—"an altogether not encouraging source for strength" (63). The greatness of the divine *kenosis* remains hidden to Rießinger (150). He asks why the Old Testament God did not do away with suffering (70). Suffering's salvific dimension is denied. Neither the tragic content of human existence nor the drama of freedom and sin are countenanced. A Christian God claiming "he who believes in me . . . shall never die" (*Jesus of Nazareth*, vol.2, 83; John 11:25-26) (156) must be "schizophrenic" (157). If one does not accept the Council of Chalcedon's teaching of Jesus Christ's two natures (divine and human), God is responsible for suffering (159). In fact, on the Cross "Jesus recognized God had forsaken him" (165). Rießinger assumes that only Christians can be saved according to Catholic teaching (80).

He detects Ratzinger "arbitrarily" redefining eternity as timeless in order to avoid the "problem of God's eternal boredom" (47). Little does Rießinger know of Augustine discovering in the *Confessions* that divine eternity is beyond temporality. Lacking familiarity with the encyclical *Fides et ratio* and Ratzinger's Bayeux talk in 2004 on the pathologies to which both faith and reason may fall victim if they are not constantly related to one another, he sees faith promoting obscurantism (50–57). The

Christian identification of Christ with the *Logos* sought by the pre-Christian philosophers is unknown to Rießinger (87). Therefore he is incapable of countenancing Jesus as *the* template for genuine humanity (GS 22).

Believing that Jesus is not a descendent of David, he rejects Ratzinger calling Jesus "heir of David" in *Spe salvi* 50 (81). Here again, unfamiliarity with Christian theology is obvious. This leads him to see in Catholic social teaching only "a tool to evangelize," but not to improve material well-being (95). He does not appreciate that the Catholic understanding of the human person is essential for defending union rights and a social free-market system. Ratzinger's thoughts on human life as gift remain beyond comprehension, as Rießinger does not see the ramifications of human beings created in the image and likeness of God and therefore called to worship Him (111-117). Yet only if God is tri-personal is man a person (127) are the concepts of "subsidiarity and solidarity" viable (129) and are Catholic positions on social ethics and morality comprehensible. To Rießinger, the transcendentals of truth, goodness, and beauty are "meaningless and hollow words," incapable of contributing to the solution of the world's problems (125).

Since he is not acquainted with theological or metaphysical terms, it is understandable that he accuses Ratzinger of circular arguments: only a hermeneutics of faith can access faith (143). He bases his sweeping conclusions on exclusively four texts of a Ratzingerian *œuvre* of over 1600 titles. Using Ratzinger as the preferred opponent, Rießinger settles the score with Christianity in general.

The book highlights an important development since 1989: as ideologies have lost their fascination, deism becomes *en vogue* in postmodernity. Is there a common basis for dialogue between Christianity and Enlightenment?

—Emery de Gaál
University of St. Mary of the Lake / Mundelein

INDEX

C

D

E

N

O

P

T

U

V

W

Y